LOCAL POLITICAL LEADERSHIP

Steve Leach and David Wilson

The POLICY PRESS

First published in Great Britain in 2000 by

The Policy Press
University of Bristol
34 Tyndall's Park Road
Bristol BS8 1PY
UK

Tel   +44 (0)117 954 6800
Fax   +44 (0)117 973 7308
e-mail tpp@bristol.ac.uk
http://www.bristol.ac.uk/Publications/TPP

British Library Cataloguing in Publication Data
A catalogue record for this book is available from the British Library

ISBN 1 86134 154 7

Steve Leach is Professor of Local Government, De Montfort University and
David Wilson is Head of Department of Public Policy and Professor of
Public Administration, De Montfort University.

Cover design by Qube Design Associates, Bristol.

Front cover: Photograph supplied courtesy of the *Bristol Evening Post*: 'Liberal
Democrat Colin Eldridge, 21, celebrates his victory as councillor for Cotham
ward, with party workers, at Bristol Council House, Bristol City Council
elections 1998.'

Printed and bound in Great Britain by Hobbs the Printers Ltd, Southampton.

Contents

List of tables and figures

Tables

Figures

Preface

The nature of local political leadership in Britain is likely to be transformed over the next few years by the introduction of 'elected mayors' and 'cabinet government' into local authorities. Although there is a good deal of resistance to change, it is now widely acknowledged that change is on the way. But this will inevitably be strongly influenced by current views within local authorities about political leadership and the relationship between leadership and party groups. Though the nature of political leadership will change, the strength of existing political culture is certain to influence the way in which the new structures are developed and integrated.

In these circumstances a book on local political leadership is timely. There has been no text that provides an overview of local political leadership in Britain since the book edited by George Jones and Alan Norton in 1978. There have, however, since that date been many changes in local politics that have impinged upon local political leadership. The aim therefore is to provide both a comprehensive picture of the current situation and an informed analysis of the likely impact of the government's legislative programme for the political management of local authorities.

We would like to acknowledge our indebtedness to a number of people who have helped us in the preparation of this book. First, we are grateful to all the local political leaders who were prepared to be interviewed by one or both of us in the various research projects that have been drawn upon in this book. In particular, we acknowledge the time and help willingly provided by Sir Peter Soulsby, to whose leadership career in Leicester the whole of Chapter Seven is devoted. Various academic colleagues have influenced our thinking, in particular John Stewart, Chris Game and Peter John. We are indebted to Melvin Wingfield for allowing us to use some of his interview material about Rutland in Chapter Eight. Thanks go to Dawn Louise Rushen at The Policy Press for her efficient and approachable management of the publisher–author interface. We are also grateful for the constructive comments of the two anonymous academic referees used by the publisher. Last but by no means least, we acknowledge the space and support provided by our respective families, Karen and Callum, and Sue, Chris, Andrew and Jamie, without which this project could never have come to fruition.

Steve Leach and David Wilson
De Montfort University, Leicester

Introduction

The changing context of local political leadership

In 1979, Chris Game wrote: "The concept of 'political leadership' has received scant treatment over the years from social scientists of almost all persuasions. Those interested in the operation of British local government have proved no exception" (Game, 1979, p 395). In the intervening 20 years nothing much has changed. While literature on local political leadership in the USA abounds, studies of local political leadership in Britain remain few and far between. Jones and Norton (1978) edited a largely descriptive study of 15 leaders; in addition there has been a scattering of case studies, biographies and autobiographies. Most recently there have been contributions by Stone (1995), John (1997), Hambleton (1996, 1998), Stoker (1998) and Elcock (1996, 1998); but apart from an emerging literature on elected mayors the cupboard is remarkably bare, invariably comprising material relating to a specific locality or individual (see, for example, Beecham, 1996; Doyle, 1996). This book moves the debate on both by providing an analytical framework and by drawing on a wealth of empirical material based upon 120 interviews with political leaders and chief executives during projects carried out over the period 1990-98.

At the outset, it needs to be recognised that the contemporary local political scene is very different from that of even 20 years ago. Elected local government is now but *one* element of local governance (see Wilson, 1998). It works alongside a mosaic of quasi-government agencies such as health trusts, housing action trusts (HATs) and Training and Enterprise Councils (TECs). It is also involved in a range of partnerships with private sector bodies and other public sector and voluntary organisations which are essential to deliver new government programmes – for example, health action zones and education action zones. Peter John has encapsulated the new reality:

> Leadership is crucial to the new urban governance. The politics of decentralisation, networks, participation, partnership, bureaucratic reform, rapid policy change and central intervention need powerful, but creative figures to give a direction to local policy-making. In a

time of institutional fragmentation and complexity, leaders make the shifting framework of individuals and organisations work together. (John, 1997, p 37)

Leadership is a complex concept, one that will be discussed in Chapters Two and Three, but in the 'governance' context it particularly requires skills such as persuasion and negotiation. The last 20 years, however, have not only seen a fragmentation of local service delivery, but also a centralisation of power, often at the expense of elected local government. As Hambleton observes:

> The current debate is not just about developing new ideas in relation to local authority leadership, councillor empowerment and community involvement. It is also about the creation of a new balance of power between central and local government, a balance which strengthens the authority and the capacity of the locality. (Hambleton, 1998, p 3)

Value for money, efficiency, effectiveness and performance indicators have come centre stage. During the 1990s this has provoked much heated discussion about possible new patterns of local political leadership, developments that are charted in this chapter. In this context it is also important to recognise that the way people get involved with and understand politics has changed:

> The role of the media has increased in importance in the presentation of issues and personalities. Single-issue and cause politics have become more prominent. The public is looking for politicians to reach beyond the boundaries of party politics. Local government needs to be able to participate in the modern form of politics. (Stoker, 1998, p 4)

Political leadership has become a much more explicit and widespread feature of British local government than it was 20 years ago. Most authorities now designate a 'leadership' position, the exceptions being the small number of independent-dominated councils and hung authorities where there is little in the way of formal inter-party cooperation. Councils now work with an increasing number and range of organisations to achieve their objectives. In this new world of partnerships and networks there is a strong case for a figurehead, and it is this argument, among others, that underpins the move towards new political management structures. In Part Three of this book we examine and evaluate the current Labour government's proposals for local government reform which promise to strengthen the role of local political leadership. But first it is important to unpack the concept of leadership, examine theoretical perspectives and develop a framework for analysis.

Structure of the book

The book is structured in the following way. Chapter One introduces and develops a framework for analysis and examines the complexities of the concept of leadership, focusing on the intrinsic tension between leadership *behaviour* and leadership *position*. In Chapter One, and indeed throughout the book, empirical material is drawn upon from research by the authors during the period 1990-98. In the context of our conceptual framework, this chapter also identifies four key leadership tasks: maintaining cohesiveness, developing strategic and policy direction, representing the authority in the external world, and ensuring programme implementation.

In Chapter Two the conceptual framework is further developed. The symbiotic relationship between political culture and local leadership behaviour is explored, using material from the interviews which form the empirical base of this book. The concept of a 'political career' is introduced to help develop an understanding of the way in which individuals who aspire to leadership (or, in some cases, have leadership thrust upon them) actually achieve their ambition. The way in which leadership behaviour reflects the political culture of the time and place, but can in certain circumstances change that culture, is explored and illustrated. The series of implicit bargains between leader and group and leader and chief executive, which help to sustain the leader in his or her position (or which, if not fulfilled, tend to lead to a vulnerability in the leader's position), are also examined.

Chapters Three to Six sequentially discuss in more detail the four key leadership tasks already identified: maintaining cohesiveness, developing strategic and policy direction, external relations and task accomplishment. Again, a wide range of interview-based examples are used.

In Chapters Seven and Eight we look at leadership in practice through a number of case studies. Chapter Seven concentrates on the political career of Sir Peter Soulsby, leader of Leicester City Council from 1981 to 1999 (with one break of 18 months in 1994-95) largely on the basis of in-depth interviews and personal diary material. Chapter Eight provides a range of other case studies, exemplifying different types of leadership situation: a low-politicisation authority, a hung authority and majority-controlled authorities of different party control.

In the final part of the book, we explore the way in which the agenda of change set out in the 1998 White Paper has emerged. These proposals, once on the statute book, are likely to transform the nature of political leadership in British local government by altering both the priorities between leadership tasks and the scope for leadership action within them. We conclude by developing an analysis of how leadership is likely to operate in the new system.

Part One
Understanding local political leadership

ONE

Concepts and theories

The concept of political leadership

In the Introduction we used the term 'leadership' in a common-sense, generally understood way. Leadership is the way in which leaders (ie those elected or appointed to a leadership position) behave. We noted for example that, as the role of local authorities has changed in recent years from 'direct provision' to 'enabling', so the requisite leadership skills have changed, with persuasion and negotiation developing a much higher profile. Leadership, as we have so far used the term, comes across as a synthesis of position and behaviour.

It is, however, necessary to be more explicit about the concept of political leadership that will be used in subsequent chapters. The identification of 'position' and 'behaviour' as key elements in the concept of leadership is helpful up to a point, but begs a lot of questions. All that has been written about Liverpool City Council during the early 1980s, when the Militant Tendency dominated the local party network, makes it clear that, although John Hamilton held the position of party (and local authority) leader during this period, he was a figurehead who displayed very little in the way of leadership *behaviour*, in the normal understanding of the term. His deputy Derek Hatton was the 'de facto' leader in terms of influence within the group (and visibility in public arenas), despite his not holding the leadership position (Hatton, 1988; Parkinson, 1985). The ESRC research project 'Changing forms of local politics' identified further examples of this mismatch between position and 'ability to influence' (see Hall and Leach, 2000). Thus, there are clearly situations in which leadership *position* and leadership *behaviour* can become detached.

Indeed, there are party groups in which the significance of the leadership position is deliberately played down. There is a formal leadership position, usually because of custom and practice within the authority. But it is explained by group members that leadership behaviour – the influence (or persuasion) exerted by one individual over group colleagues to follow a particular course of action – can be displayed by anyone in the group. This stance, which is most commonly found in Liberal Democrat groups, uses leadership position as a formal convenience and otherwise, in effect, encourages the fragmentation of leadership behaviour among many.

We should therefore avoid the assumption that leadership behaviour is what is exhibited by individuals in leadership positions. Clearly, there are many recent examples of 'dominant leaders' in British local government, where leadership behaviour is strongly (though rarely exclusively) associated with leadership position. But the extent of the synthesis of leadership position and behaviour has to be verified empirically authority by authority. It cannot be assumed. Our approach follows Weale's advice (1999, p 187) that, in studying democratic practice, the analysis of institutional rules (both formal and informal) should be conducted alongside a consideration of agents' actual behaviour within such institutions.

Influences on political leadership

Peter John (1997) draws a helpful distinction between four different types of influence on a leader's style and behaviour. First, there are *psychological–personal* factors or personality characteristics of leaders which persuade others to follow their lead. Charisma is a familiar example of such a personality trait from the work of Max Weber (see 1978 edn). Trait theories of leadership argue that it is the possession of such personal qualities (and skills) that explains leadership behaviour. Second, there are *institutional factors*, reflecting such formal mechanisms as legal powers (of the office holder), financial levers that can be applied and the framework of organisations within which the leader has to operate. Third, there are *party organisation and system* factors, reflecting the influence of party politics and in particular the extent to which formal power is distributed within national and local parties and the scope (and constraints) this provides for the local authority leader; both sets of factors place an emphasis in different ways on the significance of position, and the rights and constraints associated with position, in the analysis of political leadership. Fourth, there are factors associated with *political culture* which surround the local political system and which encapsulate, inter alia, assumptions about how leaders are expected to behave and, crucially, the extent to which there is a tradition of deference to the leader irrespective of formal powers or personal qualities.

John (1997, p 12) argues that these four factors have varying effects on the character of local political leadership and he identifies them as a set of variable and contingent conditions "for the creation of capacious and imaginative leadership". Our perspective is similar, but we would wish to stress the particular importance of the relationship between political culture and leadership behaviour. Institutional and party organisation and system factors are important in setting a framework context in which leaders develop their roles. However, the main driving force in the experience of the leaders we interviewed is the relationship between the leader's own aspirations and political and organisational culture. Personal and psychological qualities may influence the ability of the leader to exploit opportunities that become apparent in the culture-influenced 'negotiations' that are a key element in the relationship. We would, therefore, regroup the influences on leadership behaviour identified by John, as are presented in Figure 1.1.

Figure 1.1: Influences on leadership behaviour

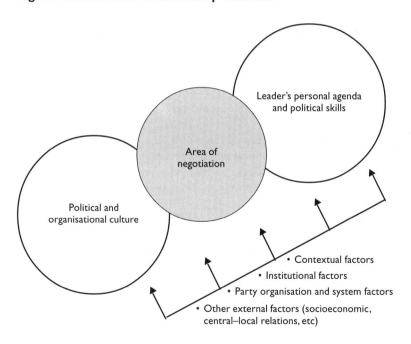

Conceptual framework

Drawing on this analysis, the key distinctions we wish to emphasise in this book are as follows:

- the context of leadership;
- leadership position/leadership behaviour (skills, values, task orientations);
- leadership tasks;
- leadership style.

These distinctions, and the relationships between them, are most fruitfully explored in a series of six propositions, set out in summary form below and then explored in more detail in this chapter and the next, which constitute our conceptual framework for analysing 'political leadership'.

1) Leadership is primarily a *behavioural* characteristic, concerned with the ability of an individual to influence or persuade others to follow his/her initiative.

2) The ability to exercise such behaviour is considerably facilitated by the holding of a formal *position*, through the authority bestowed by that position and the informal group norms that shape perceptions of the role of leader and of leadership.

3) Leadership behaviour is not displayed in a vacuum, but rather is typically oriented towards a *discrete number of key roles* (or tasks) associated with the short-term and long-term well-being of the party and authority.

4) These roles or tasks may vary in significance or priority in relation to the *context* of local political action, for example, as the role and purpose of local authorities change, as the rules regarding internal political management structures change, or in response to changes in local political culture.

5) Leadership behaviour can be helpfully seen as having three key components: the *values/ideology* which influence the leader's personal agenda; the leader's *task orientation* (re the priorities accorded to the key role or tasks of leadership) and the *leadership style* (the way in which the leader operates, in both public and private settings, towards other key actors). All these elements are culturally constrained, but may themselves be used to change political culture.

6) The exercise of political leadership through position is largely *culturally defined*, and in effect is a matter of regular negotiation and renegotiation

within (and sometimes between) leader and party group and between senior politicians and officers.

The first four elements of this framework are dealt with in this chapter; the final two elements are discussed in Chapter Two with its specific focus on political culture and leadership behaviour.

Leadership as behaviourally defined

The first element of our conceptual framework focuses on leadership as behaviour rather than leadership as position, although we recognise that position often provides a strong basis for leadership behaviour. By leadership behaviour, we refer predominantly to explicit actions taken to persuade others (in this case party colleagues or, in a hung situation, other party members) to follow particular lines of action that they would not necessarily be predisposed to follow. In other words, although leadership behaviour can traditionally be defined to cover actions where the leader does not need to persuade (because he/she has authority to act – for example over a decision that has been formally delegated to him/her) and to cover the formal initiation of action where there is known to be consensus, these expressions of leadership behaviour are of much less interest to us in this book. For us, the essence of leadership is the ability to inspire or persuade others to follow a course of action where there is at least some initial resistance to following it.

This conception of leadership reflects that of Burns (1978), who argues that, although leadership is a form of power, it is different from 'naked power-wielding': it is a way of making something happen that would not otherwise take place. Leaders may engage in persuasion, offer inducements, rely on emotional appeals and even mix coercion with other incentives, but they must never lose sight of the fact that their followers are persons to be motivated.

It is acknowledged, however, in line with the helpful distinction drawn by Bachrach and Baratz (1962), that effective leadership behaviour may be deployed in more subtle ways, namely via the art of 'non-decision making'. This term refers to the process whereby potentially contentious items are 'defined out' of the formal decision-making process through agenda manipulation or through the 'law of anticipated reactions'. (An issue is not raised because individuals feel there is no prospect of it being taken seriously.) In our view, leadership behaviour can appropriately be defined to include 'non-decision making'. Our interviews provide ample evidence of leaders' own awareness of the significance of this distinction.

It follows from this element in our definition that leadership behaviour may be exhibited by senior officers in local authorities as well as by leading politicians. Chief executives in small rural district councils often take the initiative and seek to persuade elected members to take particular courses of action, and also seek to influence external agencies to cooperate in programmes that will benefit the authority. This is clearly leadership behaviour, on our definition, and is apparent to a greater or lesser degree in all authorities. In a book about political leadership, 'officer leadership' is by definition of less concern, although areas of overlap between chief executives and political leaders, for example, are very much within our remit, as is the exercise of 'non-decision-making' skills by officers to prevent 'political' issues reaching the agenda.

It also follows from this element in our definition that leadership behaviour will invariably be, to a greater or lesser extent, a *shared* phenomenon. Just as cabinet members in a national government exercise leadership, so too do the powerful chairs of committees in local government. In all politicised authorities that we have come across, there is some form of informal cabinet, comprising the leaders and other committee chairs or party group position-holders. In addition, we know of no party group run on such authoritarian lines that there is no effective scope for backbencher members, on occasion, to raise issues and persuade a majority of their colleagues (including the formal leader) to take a previously unconsidered action.

However, it is important to retain an authority-wide focus here. Leadership in behavioural terms can be exercised by officers at sectional and departmental level as well as over corporate issues, and by members in working parties, committees and indeed local community forums. Our primary concern in this book is with the *corporate* agenda facing a local authority, and the extent to which political leadership is concentrated (in an individual) or dispersed (among several) in relation to this agenda. The exercise of leadership at committee/departmental level is of less importance in the context of this book, although we recognise that certain service issues (eg a secondary school review) often move on to the corporate agenda and are of concern to the corporate (as opposed to service-specific) party leadership.

Formal position as a basis for leadership

Despite all the reservations set out above, much of this book (including the vast majority of examples) is about the behaviour of individuals in leadership positions. This comprises the second strand of our conceptual framework. It is unusual, although not impossible, for formal leaders to become marginalised as far as leadership behaviour is concerned, and it is much more common for them to play a dominant role in behavioural terms. There are both cultural and structural reasons for this situation. All party groups (including the Liberal Democrats) accept that conferring a leadership position on someone gives them the right to initiate proposals; indeed, there would be surprise if a leader did not do so. In many party groups, particularly Conservative and traditional Labour, there is a predisposition to follow a leader's initiative unless there is a very good reason (eg a very divisive political issue) for not doing so. In this way, the leader's authority and potential influence is strengthened culturally. It is also strengthened structurally through a range of advantages that the position of 'leader' enjoys, for example, privileged or 'advance warning' access to politically salient information (via the chief executive) and de facto 'leader's action' opportunities, for example when a crisis arises in which there is no time for the leader to clear a preferred course of action with the group. Of course, such structural advantages may not necessarily be exploited; but they are there to be taken advantage of by an astute leader (see Chapter Four).

Key tasks of leadership

We argued earlier that a discrete number of key roles or tasks face leaders in local authorities. An analysis of leadership behaviour must incorporate some conception of leadership tasks, and it is this that comprises the third part of our analytical framework. This emphasis of the centrality of *purpose* in the analysis of leadership behaviour is echoed by Clarence Stone:

> Leadership revolves around purpose, and purpose is at the heart of the leader–follower relationship. Indeed, in some cases a compelling statement of mission not only gives direction to a group, but is its formative experience, shaping the identity of group members by highlighting a shared aim. (Stone, 1995, pp 96-7)

What is the nature of those tasks? The emphasis for the purposes of this book, the corporate 'leadership agenda' of the local authority, has already been noted. How may this agenda be characterised? Task-orientated leadership analysis is a well developed field of study in organisational behaviour. Selznick's conceptualisation of four functions of institutional leadership provides a useful starting point here: his functions are the definition of institutional mission and role; the institutional embodiment of purpose; the defence of institutional integrity; and the ordering of internal conflict (Selznick, 1957). However, these headings were intended as a general perspective for the study of leadership in *any* administrative organisation, and require modification in the specific situation of a 'political' organisation such as a local authority.

One of the most influential studies of political leadership in America – the Kotter and Lawrence (1974) study of elected mayors – identifies six behavioural models of political leadership, of which the authors argue two are concerned primarily with the setting of policy, two with its execution and two with organisation and service management. They are thus able to identify three key mayoral processes: agenda setting, task accomplishment and network-building and maintenance. Game (1979) argued that these distinctions formed an appropriate basis for studying political leadership in British local government.

If the last process – network-building and maintenance – is subdivided into *internal* (maintaining cohesiveness) and *external* (representing the authority in the outside world) elements, then we have a categorisation of leadership tasks that seems to us to be particularly helpful in the British context. These tasks, which can be summarised as maintaining cohesiveness, developing strategic direction, representing the authority in the outside world and ensuring programme implementation, are outlined here before being discussed in more detail in later chapters.

Maintaining cohesiveness

The complexity of the local authority as a politically led entity means that the task of maintaining cohesiveness has a number of different elements. Assuming that there is majority party control (hung authorities will be dealt with at the end of this chapter), the leader will invariably be concerned primarily with the cohesiveness of the party *group*. But he/ she will necessarily also be concerned with the cohesiveness of the *authority as a whole* (ie with the ability of members and officers to work together) and with the cohesiveness of the *local party network*, particularly the relationship between party group and local party (most important in the Labour Party, least so for the Conservatives). Whether one is considering the party group or the wider network incorporating the group and the local party machinery, there are likely to be a variety of political perspectives. Factions may also emerge. In such contexts maintaining cohesiveness can be a particularly challenging task; this is further developed in Chapter Three.

Developing strategic and policy direction

There is in all local authorities a leadership task of strategy/policy initiation or agenda setting. (What kind of authority are we? Where are we going? What kind of policy should we have in relation to economic development?) This task, which is more explicit and better developed in some authorities than in others, is of growing importance in a world of 'community governance' and financial constraint. It is a task that may be exercised proactively or reactively (as in a crisis). At party group level, policy direction, as set out in a party manifesto, will typically involve a much wider range of party and group interests than those of the leader himself/herself (although the leader may possess a de facto power of veto). At authority-wide level, the main source of strategic policy initiation is likely to be the leader/chief executive axis, particularly where 'reactive' strategic decisions are required. Many strategic decisions, particularly in large all-purpose authorities, are made in this kind of reactive mode, with the leader being centrally involved, as Chapter Four will demonstrate.

Representing the authority in the external world

This leadership task has increased in significance in recent years. As we have seen, local authorities now have to work with a range of other organisations to achieve their objectives. The fragmented structure of community governance means that, on many of the issues facing local authorities, they are in partnership with other public bodies. This means that it is important for leaders to maintain contacts with a wide range of individuals and organisations in establishing the role of the local authority in community leadership.

The internal dimension of the public representational role is the expectation in most authorities that the leader will represent the majority party's views in public debate with other parties. The significance of this role varies from authority to authority. If there is a sizeable competent and an ideologically opposed opposition, the role will be a demanding one for the leader; if the council is dominated by the majority party it will be of much less significance. These issues will be further explored in Chapter Five.

Ensuring task accomplishment

Although in most textbooks this task is conventionally delegated to officers ('members make policy; officers implement it'), in most politicised authorities the division of labour is no longer seen in such cut and dried terms. As Chapter Six will show, although there are clearly limits to the extent to which local politicians can 'ensure delivery' (through limitations of time, if nothing else), there is now a widespread, though contested, acceptance of the principle that politicians have a legitimate interest in task accomplishment (ie in ensuring that what they want to happen does happen). This leadership task has increased in profile in recent years, although the development of the use of contracts, of service-level agreements and of delegation to cost centres has made political involvement in programme implementation more difficult.

One of the most crucial skills of a leader is to judge what relative priority to give to each of the above four tasks. They will rarely all be equally important – indeed, one or other of them may, in some circumstances, have only a very limited relevance. For example, ensuring programme implementation may not be perceived to be an issue in circumstances where the majority party is confident of officers' ability to carry out this task effectively. Leaders have to consider their role in relation to the position of other leading members, and this too will affect the relative priority given by them to different tasks. Thus, much of the task of 'making things happen' often falls upon the chairs of the committees. Likewise, the relative importance of the different tasks may vary over time. Leaders spending considerable time on external affairs (particularly those in which the interests of the authority are not directly affected) may find they have neglected growing tensions within the group.

As we noted earlier, the identification of a leadership *task* does not in itself imply that the tasks will all be undertaken or given the same emphasis by the *political leadership*. At one end of the spectrum, there is the highly politicised authority where all four leadership tasks would be dominated (or, in the case of 'making things happen', managed) by the political leadership, although not necessarily by the formal leader per se. At the other end of the spectrum can be found district councils, relatively unpoliticised in a party sense, in which strategic direction is either absent or officer led: 'making things happen' is delegated to officers (except, perhaps, in relation to development control decisions), and the external relations role is largely a formal one politically. Indeed, in such independent-dominated authorities the chief executive may play an important brokerage role in maintaining organisational cohesiveness at the 'political' level'. Table 1.1 summarises the typical pattern of member/officer responsibilities in relation to the four key tasks identified above.

Table 1.1: Leadership tasks: member and officer roles

Key tasks	Member role	Officer role
Maintaining cohesiveness	Necessarily exclusive in relation to intra-party role. Normally dominant in relation to inter-party relations	Normally limited in relation to political side but may be significant in independent dominated councils, and an important brokerage role in hung authorities. Key role in relation to officer structure
Developing strategic and policy direction	Dominant in conventional terms but may rely heavily on officer advice, especially in less politicised councils	Subservient in conventional terms but may have high degree of informal influence
Representing the authority in the external world	Some specific external representation responsibilities; but beyond that, task may be shared between officers and members	Role varies from minimal (in some political authorities) to substantial (in less politicised councils)
Ensuring programme implementation	Members may see this task as wholly the domain of officers; or may interpret political role in more managerial terms	Officers necessarily play a dominant role (time availability, formal delegation, etc) but members may have significant selective involvement and monitoring role

The changing context of political leadership

The fourth strand of our conceptual framework focuses on the context of local political activity. We have already noted how political culture –

the norms and expectations concerning political leadership operating in the party group and local party – can operate as an influence on leadership behaviour. This is one example of the impact of external or contextual issues on political leadership. There are differences between the three major parties in terms of the relative priority attached to the different leadership tasks, as well as to anticipated or preferred leadership style.

Traditionally Conservative leaders have not placed much emphasis on the task of 'making things happen', which they have been happy to delegate to officers (although 'New Right' dominated groups do not necessarily share this view). Both Labour and Liberal Democrat leaders typically have to place more emphasis on party/group cohesiveness than their Conservative counterparts. Labour leaders in particular often have to devote more of their time and energies to the interface between the party group and the local party than is the case in the other two parties, where the autonomy of the party group on the council is customarily stronger. There is less enthusiasm for an explicit corporate strategic direction within Conservative groups (although all party groups have their implicit strategic priorities). Table 1.2 summarises these party differences.

But other contextual elements are equally important, for example, the legal framework relating to political management structures and processes in local government. Under the current legislation, any formal division of executive and representational functions is extremely difficult. The council is the ultimate decision maker, and while this leaves scope for the operation of 'informal' cabinets (which are widespread) it does not permit formal allocation of executive responsibility either to individual cabinet members or to a cabinet (or executive) collectively. The 1998 White Paper, *Modern local government: In touch with the people* (DETR, 1998b), however, contains proposals that would make formal executive responsibilities possible (see Chapter Ten). Any legislation that 'changes the rules' of political management and decision making in this way is bound to create new opportunities and challenges for political leadership. In the case of elected mayors, for example, the scope of authoritative personal leadership in relation to all of the key leadership tasks (except for 'maintaining group cohesiveness') is considerably enhanced.

Important also is the changing role of local government. In the Introduction we noted the transformation of local authorities over the past 20 years from self-sufficient inward-looking service providers to externally orientated community leaders, with a service commissioning role increasingly replacing the actual delivery (or contracting) role. These changes, which are reinforced by the contents in the 1998 White Paper,

Modern local government (DETR, 1998b), have had profound implications for the nature of the corporate agenda facing local authorities and the implications for leadership tasks (or at least the relative priority accorded to them). In effect the changes have increased the priority of 'providing strategic direction' and 'external representation' and have diminished the capacity to control 'programme implementation', even if the desire to maintain this role remains.

Table 1.2: Leadership tasks: inter-party differences

Key tasks	Labour	Conservative	Liberal Democrat
Maintaining cohesiveness (within party)	High degree of procedural prescription on group behaviour and group–party relationships; strong formal group discipline	Relatively high degree of autonomy of group from party; moderate formal discipline	Relatively high degree of autonomy of group from party; weak formal group discipline
Developing strategic and policy direction	Formally, the decisive role in relation to proactive policy making is with the local party (via manifesto)	Traditionally a group task with leader often dominating	A group/local party dominated process
Representing the authority in the external world	Tendency has been to share task among 'leadership group', but new 'partnership' initiatives typically involve the formal leader	Typically dominated by leader	Preference for sharing of task (within constraints of external expectations)
Ensuring programme implementation	Strong traditions in some areas of systematic or ad hoc involvement, but trend now is away from such detailed involvement	Traditionally a clear member–officer division of labour with minimal political involvement	Acceptance of traditional divisions of labour; but strong tendency to progress-chase

This major change in the role and purpose of local authorities has led some commentators to define local political leadership in a quite different way from that set out above. As local authorities have lost powers and operational responsibilities to central government quangos or the private sector, so the primary focus of leadership has moved from within the authority (ensuring that the organisation carries out a political programme) to a wider network of organisations, within which the local authority is merely one player, and not necessarily a dominant one. If, so the argument goes, local governance is now fragmented among a range of different agencies and actors, then should local leadership not be redefined in a more collective sense, reflecting the replacement of 'hierarchy' by 'network' and the relegation of the local authority leader to one among a group of 'leaders' on whom he/she is dependent in the achievement of local authority priorities? This perspective takes us into the realm of regime theory, which raises these kinds of issues about leadership scope *within* local authorities. As Harding (2000) points out, urban regime theorists argue that a distinction must be made between holding political power and governing, that is, between local government in a narrow sense and 'local governance' in a wider sense. In order to achieve anything beyond straightforward statutory tasks, regime theorists argue, elected leaders need the support of other powerful interests, especially within the business community. Governing coalitions regularise these relations of mutual support; a governing regime is constructed through informal bargaining and the tacit understandings of its members.

Urban regime theory was developed in the USA (Stone, 1995), where local political leaders often have very few formal powers and operate in a very fragmented system. It is only recently that attempts have been made to test its applicability in Britain. Research on urban regimes in this country has shown that, although arrangements approximating to regimes exist in relation to economic development activities (Dunleavy et al, 1995; Harding, 2000), their continuity, coherence and, in particular, scope of activity are much less than was found in many American cities. In Manchester and Edinburgh, Harding shows that the influence of development coalitions is limited to particular production-related strategies and projects, rather than to a whole range of political choices.

This conclusion is supported by our own research. However, although stable, well-integrated regimes with a continuity of leadership priorities, coherent development strategies and clear overall priorities are not common (if indeed they exist at all) in Britain, the need for local authority leaders to work with a range of other local influentials to achieve economic regeneration is illustrative of a range of other policy areas (environmental sustainability, community safety, community health) where inter-agency working has become a necessary condition for progress. Thus, although the starting point for the analysis of political leadership remains the local authority and the dominant coalition within it, one of the key tasks of leadership – representing the authority in the external world – is clearly growing in relative importance and is occupying more and more of local authority leaders' time. This task requires different leadership skills – negotiation, networking, the search for common ground – which, although by no means absent in relation to the other leadership tasks, are likely (except perhaps in hung authorities) to be less important in those cases than more 'traditional' leadership skills.

There are other good reasons for adopting a leadership perspective that remains focused on the local authority, albeit with a greatly enhanced external focus. The first is that, although we acknowledge the extent to which the powers of local authorities have been eroded since 1980, we would argue that this process has not eliminated the scope for political choice within local government. The scope has become more limited, but choice remains in all the key areas of local service responsibility. Within the education service, some authorities seek to maintain small village schools, while others are more ready to adopt 'rationalisation schemes'. In relation to housing, some authorities run elaborate schemes for tenant consultation, sometimes devolving some responsibilities to tenants' associations, while others retain such powers within the authority itself. Many local authority services are discretionary, in relation either to the level of service provided (eg public libraries), or to whether it is provided at all (eg support for the arts). Emphasis and expenditure on areas of concern such as youth and community work, grants to voluntary organisations, park-and-ride schemes, CCTV and recycling show large variations from authority to authority. The community governance/ civic leadership agenda, itself a role that is adopted with different levels of enthusiasm, and interpreted in different ways in different local authorities, involves a whole range of largely non-statutory activities. All these choices have to be brought together and prioritised at budget time, where, even though an upper limit may be imposed, the scope for allocation of expenditure within that limit remains considerable. The agenda set out above consists of items that are clearly 'political' in nature, where the scope and role of political leadership remains relevant. We are a long way yet from the local administrative state.

The second reason follows from the Labour government's explicit recognition in the 1998 White Paper of the 'lead role' of local authorities in responding to the needs of their areas:

> Community leadership is at the heart of the role of modern local government. Councils are the organisations best placed to take a comprehensive overview of the needs and priorities of their local areas and communities, and lead the work to meet those needs and priorities in the round. (DETR, 1998b, para 8.1)

This quotation represents an explicit commitment to the local authority as community leader and reflects a much stronger local authority role than is normal in the more fragmented world of local governance in the USA. It supports our view that regime theory, while it has a partial degree of applicability, especially in the economic development field, does not provide an appropriate basis in itself for the study of local political leadership in Britain.

Conclusion

We have argued in this section that in local authorities 'leadership' is required in relation to four major organisational tasks: strategic policy direction, organisational cohesiveness, external networking and task accomplishment. Although all these tasks are usually recognised, their relative priority varies from one authority to another. While all these tasks can be seen as intrinsically political in nature, the extent to which 'political' leadership dominates or manages them also varies from authority to authority, with only 'maintaining cohesiveness' being (at party group level) an unavoidable political responsibility. Leadership tasks not exercised at a political level may be carried out on a de facto basis by officers. Typically, the formal leader plays a key role in each of the leadership tasks that his/her group identifies as important, but sharing or delegation of leadership tasks is possible and does take place. Leadership tasks are not all necessarily the prerogative of the nominated leader. The exercise of the leadership role may be influenced by, inter alia, personal qualities/ charisma, level of trust, skills, the traditions of the political group's perception of the role (and the relationship between leaders and followers) and the authority's political and organisational culture. Such cultural factors and perceptions are themselves amenable to change by interventions from the leader (or his/her followers) or through changed circumstances; what is an appropriate and acceptable role interpretation at a time of stability may not be appropriate or acceptable at a time of crisis. It follows that different leadership styles can often be identified reflecting patterns in these different sets of circumstances and related negotiations. These arguments are developed in more detail in Chapter Two where strands 5 and 6 of our conceptual framework are discussed.

Nowhere is the emphasis on bargaining and negotiation in the exercise of leadership more apparent than in hung authorities. In majority-controlled authorities, as we have argued, little attention has to be paid to opposition groups, unless they show a potential to embarrass the majority group. If group cohesiveness can be maintained, the other tasks can become channelled through member–officer relationships, rather than through inter-party networks. In hung or balanced authorities, although the four key leadership tasks identified in the third strand of our conceptual framework remain relevant, the way in which they have to be implemented changes. Assuming that a particular party group wishes to achieve as much as it can in a hung authority through cooperative strategies, rather than to operate as a self-styled opposition, organisational cohesiveness often becomes something of a 'balancing act'. On the one hand, the leader will seek to do deals with his/her opposite numbers (a process facilitated by regular leadership meetings between the chief executive and those party leaders who are cooperating in the political management of the authority); on the other, he/she will often find that group cohesiveness (and sometimes the relationship with the local party) is threatened by concerns about some of the implications of this process (in particular, a fear that too many concessions are being made). The tasks of developing strategic/policy direction and ensuring programme implementation also become less straightforward than they are, in principle at least, in majority-controlled authorities. Again, negotiation and bargaining with other leaders will be required in relation to strategic direction, and any concern with implementation is more easily challenged or deflected by officers than is often possible in a majority situation. The responsibility for external representation becomes more diffuse also. It is not surprising that there are several examples of leaders who were effective in a majority control situation but whose temperament and skills were much less appropriate in a hung situation (eg Emily [now Lady] Blatch in Cambridgeshire in 1983).

In authorities with a relatively low degree of politicisation, where independents remain a significant force and where group discipline on the part of such party groups that do exist is typically much more limited and permissive than their counterparts in more similar politicised authorities, there is a premium on negotiation and bargaining in leadership behaviour. In this context, the example of a recent independent leader of Rutland will be discussed in Chapter Eight.

TWO

Political culture and leadership behaviour

Introduction

As argued in Chapter One, political culture is a key influence on leadership behaviour. The final element of our conceptual framework stated that 'the exercise of political leadership through position is largely culturally defined, and in effect is a matter of periodic negotiation and renegotiation within (and sometimes between) leader and party group and between senior politicians and officers'. In this chapter we explore in more detail this complex but central interrelationship between political culture and leadership behaviour.

Given the lack of formal authority enjoyed by political leaders in local government at the end of the 1990s (eg no powers of executive action; no powers to override majority group preferences), a leader's scope for action is constrained by political culture. For example, a leader's ability to commit a local authority to a specific course of action in a set of negotiations with an influential external organisation is premised upon his/her confidence that 'the group' can be persuaded to support that course of action. In some circumstances there will be a high degree of confidence on the part of the leader that such an initiative will be supported; in others he/she may have to be much more circumspect. Essentially, it depends on the local political culture. The leader's judgement will partly reflect the nature of the issue ('is it in line with group policy?') and partly the prevailing view about appropriate leadership style ('is it acceptable for me to stick my neck out?'). In both cases, the influence of political culture works through the process of anticipated reactions. Discussion throughout this chapter explains and develops the fifth and sixth elements of our conceptual framework.

Three specific aspects of the relationship between leadership behaviour and political culture are highlighted in this chapter. First, the circumstances in which individuals achieve leadership positions are examined. Our research provides an interesting range of different paths to leadership from which different typical patterns can be identified. Second, three different relationships between leadership behaviour and political culture are identified and analysed: congruence, reaction and transformation. Third, our analysis of the dynamics of leader–group relationships in the context of political culture is presented. But first, having identified leadership style as a key element in leadership behaviour, it is important to explore this concept in more detail.

Leadership behaviour and leadership style

Leadership behaviour can helpfully be seen as having three key components, which comprise a further strand of our conceptual framework. These are the *values/ ideology*, which influence the leader's personal agenda; the leader's *task orientation*, that is, what priorities are afforded to the key tasks of leadership; and a *behavioural* element, that is, what is the prevailing view of an appropriate leadership *style* – is the leader expected to provide a lead on key policy issues which the group then decides whether or not to follow; or is the leader expected to reflect in other arenas a group view which he/she is not necessarily expected to share?

In relation to neither ideology nor style will the political culture necessarily be uniform. It is not uncommon for ideological subcultures to exist. The phenomenon of 'factionalism' within party groups, which may be based on ideological orientation, ethnic groupings or other specific issues, is familiar. It is possible also that different sections of a party group may have different views about leadership style, sometimes reflected in the pattern of alignment with an existing leader or challenger. At any one point in time there will be a 'centre of gravity' culturally, for example a majority of traditionalists, or a majority favouring 'strong leadership'. But that centre of gravity is always vulnerable to change as the composition of a party group alters (most commonly following a local election), or as the views of those within it change.

Within this mutability, there lies the opportunity for a leader to move beyond the status quo and try to refashion political culture along different lines. The relationship between political culture and leadership behaviour is *symbiotic*. Although values and style are shaped by culture, they can, in certain circumstances, act as agents of cultural change. As we will exemplify, there are certain conditions – the overthrow of a former leader who has lost his/her base of support, a particularly successful election result, or a major success in terms of policy or status – in which the propensity to support the leader is high. Perceptive leaders can recognise such opportunities and use them to provide a cultural steer. Leadership style, and the relationship between leader and group, are potentially negotiable, although the scope for negotiation will vary between parties, between local authorities and in relation to the strength and durability of the dominant culture.

In Chapter One we argued that *task definition* was the most helpful starting point for the analysis of leadership in local government, and we identified four priority leadership tasks: maintaining cohesiveness, strategic direction, external relations and task accomplishment. But we also emphasised that different leaders give different priority to these tasks. The process of *task interpretation* is also the subject of two-way influence and negotiation between 'leader' and 'followers'. A difference of view about task priorities may lead to a leader's downfall. For example, a leader spending what is perceived to be too much time in external arenas such as the Local Government Association (LGA) may be seen as failing to ensure group cohesiveness. Alternatively, a new leader may be elected on the basis (inter alia) that he/she is the right person to give emphasis to a previously neglected task (eg task accomplishment, perhaps expressed in terms of the need to recapture the initiative in what is perceived to be an officer-dominated authority). Thus, in addition to values/ideology and leadership style, task orientation (and prioritisation) is a key element to address in the analysis of leadership behaviour.

Understanding leadership style

There have been many attempts to develop classifications of leadership style since the study of political leadership developed momentum in the 1960s. All in their different ways make a distinction between *responsive* and *authoritarian* leaders. This distinction is clearly compatible with what we have already written about the symbiotic relationship between leadership and culture. Leach and Stewart (1990) identify three broad types of leadership along an individualistic/collective continuum (see Figure 2.1). At one end of the continuum there is *leadership from the front*, where the leader is looked to by the party group to take the initiative in proposing major policy developments which the group will then generally agree and adopt. The style of the *group spokesperson* is essentially the reverse: here the party group is the chief source of policy decisions, the leader's main role being to act as the group's public mouthpiece, first in the council chamber and then in dealings with the media. Somewhere in the middle of the continuum can be identified the role of the *consensus builder*: here the leader actively seeks to build consensus in the party group, arguing for what he/she feels is the most desirable or attainable policy, but positively committed to accepting and publicly advocating the eventual majority group view.

Figure 2.1: A model of leadership styles

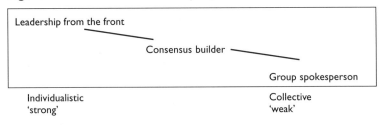

Individualistic   Collective
'strong'   'weak'

Source: Leach and Stewart (1990, p 6)

This is a relatively simple model which concentrates on making broad distinctions, and does not purport to cover adequately the full gamut of leadership styles found in British local government. It is helpful as a starting point, however, in exemplifying the general argument about the interrelationship between leadership style and political culture.

Other writers have drawn more subtle distinctions between different political leadership styles. Madgwick (1978), drawing heavily on Barber's study of American presidents (Barber, 1977) identifies four 'types of leadership' reflecting different combinations of political drive:

1) *chair–broker*, reflecting high political drive and negative policy orientation, and likely to lead to (or reflect) continuity and stability in council affairs;

2) *programme politician*, reflecting high political drive and positive policy orientation, and likely to lead to (or reflect) guided change in council affairs;

3) *quiescent consensual*, that is, low political drive/negative policy orientation, resulting in (or reflecting) inertia and drift in council affairs;

4) *garrulous/impotent*, low political drive/positive policy orientation, resulting in (or reflecting) erratic incremental change.

These distinctions reflect leadership styles that are certainly recognisable from our interviews. They are helpful too in illustrating the crucial difference between *transactional* and *transformational* leadership. For the 'chair–broker', leadership is exercised transactionally (and often with an authoritarian style) to maintain the status quo, which is a similar goal for the 'quiescent consensual' leader, in so far as this style embodies leadership at all, in the terms we have defined it. The 'programme politician', on the other hand, is concerned with *transformational* leadership; he/she is using 'political drive' to try to change the political culture in support of key policy or organisational changes, while the 'garrulous/impotent' leader lacks the political skills to motivate followers. As Burns (1978, p 425) points out, leadership can be seen as the "reciprocal process of mobilising ... various economic, political and other resources ... in order to realize goals independently and mutually held by both leaders and followers". In this definition, the leader's goals may not be the same as those of followers, who may themselves have diverse ends. The leadership challenge lies in motivating followers to make something happen that would not otherwise take place.

Kotter and Lawrence (1974), in their influential study of the behaviour of US city mayors, identify five separate patterns of urban governance, each with its own characteristic style of agenda setting, task accomplishment and network building. They combine an analysis of the behavioural proclivity of leaders (coalition builder, power broker, etc) with the three key mayoral processes referred to above (which, as argued earlier, are compatible with our own four-fold leadership task classification). The patterns identified by Kotter and Lawrence are:

- the ceremonial;
- the caretaker;
- the personality/individualist;
- the executive;
- the programme entrepreneur.

There is clearly some similarity here to Madgwick's classification, with 'positive policy orientations' being a key characteristic of the programme entrepreneur and (probably) the individualist, and 'political drive' being a key characteristic of both these patterns and the executive (whose executive actions may or may not be coordinated within a coherent policy programme).

Peter John (1997) helpfully combines a continuum of responsive/authoritarian behaviour with a continuum reflecting distinctions between the *narrow* exercise of power ('power of') and an *empowering* exercise of power ('power to') which enables all actors to exercise their potential. Figure 2.2 illustrates the typology which emerges.

Figure 2.2: Typology of leadership roles in the new urban governance

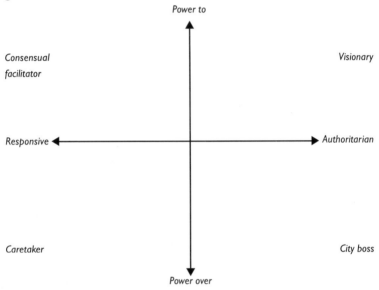

Power to

Consensual facilitator

Visionary

Responsive ← → Authoritarian

Caretaker

City boss

Power over

Source: John (1997, p 8)

John argues that the conditions of governance that operate in British and European local government mean that leaders are likely to resemble one of, or a combination of, the four roles in the grid presented in Figure 2.2. The roles are defined as follows:

- The *caretaker* is the weak political leader who is unable to manage the complex coalitions that have emerged in local governance; probably effective as a city manager and party chief, the leader finds it hard to cope with the complexity of networks and the rapidity of policy change.
- The *consensual facilitator* is far more adaptable than the caretaker counterpart, having learnt about the importance of partnerships and networks, and keeps abreast of national and local policy debates as

they rapidly change. This sort of leader can generate capacity less through the efforts and authority of office, and more through persuasion and finding the best in others. He/she is driven along by the reforming efforts of the many partners in local policy making and responds reactively to central initiatives. This type of leader may be initially popular, but will find it hard to develop a coherent local strategy as local policy is driven by the demands of other powerful local actors, the need to please too many people at once and the fashions of the moment.

- The *city boss*, like the caretaker, does not adapt very well to the new urban governance, as the temptation is to retry tough management strategies in conditions where they do not really work. Where an understanding of networking, complex manoeuvring and innovative policy making is required, the city boss does not deliver. It is not possible to hypothesise which outcome for city politics would be worse. The city boss could aggravate the delicate processes of urban governance; on the other hand, some control over decision-making processes is desirable.
- The *visionary* combines elements of strong leadership with capacity generation. The visionary is the type who can knock heads together, who can break down some of the recalcitrance and divisions in urban politics and who is able to establish more creative policies and effective coordination. Complexity is confronted by the force of the will of such a leader, who can forge a powerful if disparate coalition.

The benefit of John's typology is that, like that of Kotter and Lawrence, it attempts to relate leadership style to leadership tasks, demonstrating in particular that, for the increasingly salient task of managing external networks, two of the styles ('consensual/facilitator' and 'visionary') are much more compatible with this key task than the other two ('caretaker' and 'city boss'). One implication of the above typologies is that, in the analysis of leadership style, three key dimensions may be identified:

- leadership orientation/predisposition;
- attitude to the exercise of power;
- policy/executive orientations.

Leadership orientation/predisposition

This dimension reflects the distinction between a positive attitude to leadership – an individual in a leadership position with a clear personal agenda which may be political or executive/managerial in nature – and a negative attitude – a lack of any kind of agenda of this nature. Thus, whatever other categories they fall into, the 'caretaker' (John; Kotter and Lawrence), the 'ceremonial leader' (Kotter and Lawrence) and the quiescent or consensual leader (Madgwick) clearly fall into the 'negative' category – they may be in leadership positions, but they have little desire to provide a lead in terms of ideas, let alone vision. John's consensual/facilitator type of leader fits somewhere in the centre of this spectrum; he/she has a limited personal agenda, has a sense of responsibility for exercising leadership, but tends to work very much with and through others and to rely on them for ideas.

Attitude to the exercise of power

The key distinction here is between the desire to act authoritatively (power over) and the desire to act through empowerment (power to). The 'city boss' and the 'chair broker' (as defined by John and Kotter and Lawrence, respectively) work through the narrow exercise of power. The 'consensual/ facilitator' (John) and the 'programme entrepreneur' (Kotter and Lawrence) work through a more enabling approach to power (power *to*). The transactional/transformational dichotomy captures the essence of these different orientations.

Policy orientation

This dimension reflects the way in which some leaders have a distinctive strategic/policy agenda which they wish to develop within the authority, while others are more concerned with executive action, preferring a more generalised policy framework which leaves more scope for executive action. The former, in the context of British local government, are increasingly having to work through and with networks external to the local authority to achieve their goals. While this is also important for the leader who is more concerned with executive decisions, this external dimension is normally less central to his/her concerns. 'Programme politicians' (Madgwick), 'programme entrepreneurs' (Kotter and Lawrence) and 'visionaries' (John) all have a strong policy orientation. 'Executives' (Kotter and Lawrence), 'city bosses' (John) and 'chairpeople brokers' (Madgwick) typically have much less so. Figure 2.2 attempts to summarise the key feature of the leadership styles of a selection of the ideal types identified, using the dimensions discussed above.

There is of course a further element of leadership style that is an influential factor in the detailed exercise of political leadership. Leaders are responded to, both within their party groups and in wider council and external arenas, as 'individuals' as well as 'leaders'. In this sense, a number of informed subjective personal factors come into play. These factors could include a leader's ability inter alia to influence colleagues through skills of personal interaction; to make judgements about the consequences of his/her decisions or actions for group dynamics; to engender (or fail to engender) trust, particularly at times of crisis; and to judge when a tolerance of non-conforming behaviour on the part of group members should be exercised and when it should not.

A more detailed analysis of such micro-level skills would introduce a socio-psychological dimension which is largely outside the scope and plan of this book. But we recognise the importance of these more intangible aspects of leadership behaviour, and there are several illustrations of their significance in the case study material.

Developing a 'political career'

The variety of backgrounds, experience and precipitating factors of the group of leaders interviewed is not unrepresentative of councillors generally, with the important exception that leaders are somewhat more likely to have come into council life as 'intenders' rather than 'drifters' (Barron et al, 1991). However, by the time they reach a leadership position, that equivalence with the wider body of councillors has changed. With few exceptions, the achievement of political leadership is not easily gained. Sacrifices often have to be made in relation to work (typically, promotion prospects) and/or personal life (typically, time with family, and time for other personal interests). Few councillors become leaders without recognising that the demands of the job in terms of time commitment, pressure and expectation are considerable. To take such a step implies that by this time their council activity can be seen as a 'political career' as opposed to a spare-time hobby, or accident of fate.

The concept of a 'political career' refers to the way in which, for some councillors, council work becomes an integral part of their 'life-plan' – a career which, although it does not preclude a more conventional 'occupational career', invariably implies major adjustments in the latter to enable the development of the former. For such councillors, council activities would never be described as a 'hobby', a 'sideline' or even a 'desire to be of service'. It has become a much more central feature of their lives – part of their self-image, a major source of their feelings of self-worth, and something as important (or almost as important) as conventional careers or family relationships, in relation to both of which there has been evidence of many casualties, both in this study and in other research. As with conventional careers, promotion or the retention of key positions becomes of real importance, and the loss of council leadership or councillor status can induce a sense of personal loss, paralleled by reactions to job loss or retirement. For councillors who become council leaders, council work and the power attached to formal positions of responsibility are often seen as something that has 'got into their blood'. Indeed, for many of the leaders we interviewed an active political background within their family had helped develop an early interest in politics – sometimes, as in Pat Doyle's case, in line with the family tradition:

> "My roots were Irish Catholic, working-class, under the very strong influence of my grandfather who was very pro-Labour. Although my father never formally belonged to the Labour Party, I attended my first political meeting with him at the age of 16."

Sometimes it might be in reaction to the family tradition, as was the case with Alan Whitehead:

> "My parents were both members of the Conservative Party where we lived in Twickenham. Politics were always discussed and my father used to keep detailed charts of all the general elections. It was certainly a background which encouraged political thought although not the political thoughts I turned out to have! I became a Liberal as a kind of instinctive reaction to my parents' Conservatism."

For some political leaders, such as those who are retired or unemployed, there will be no major tension between political and occupational career. The majority of leaders appear to have found it possible to combine leadership responsibilities with stable (if not always 'normal') family life, a balancing act which is immeasurably more feasible if other family members share the leader's political commitment and enthusiasm. In the shire districts in particular, it may be possible to interpret the role of leader in a way that does not necessarily imply the kind of dominance we have represented. Keith Andrew, Liberal Democrat leader of Chelmsford between 1982 and 1990, combined that job with his career of bank executive without obvious difficulty, and when his banking career took him away from Chelmsford he relinquished leadership and councillor status without any great traumas. However, such attitudes are very much the exception. Power, status and the opportunity for the achievement of political goals in general is as unwillingly relinquished in local government as in central government, and with equivalent problems of loss of sense of purpose for those involved.

Dave Wetzel of Hounslow was (in 1990) more philosophical about the potential loss of leadership than most:

> "I haven't got a plan which says when I'll give up the leadership ... but how hard would I fight to retain it? Not very hard! I would fight if I were challenged by someone I didn't rate. But if I were challenged by a competent young councillor whose views I agreed with, I'd probably relinquish the leadership. If the Conservatives won another election I'd probably want to give up anyway...."

The concept of 'political careers' is of course wider in scope than activities within council work. Sir Richard Knowles was a Labour Party agent long before he became a Birmingham councillor and subsequently the council leader. Of the leaders we interviewed, two – Eric Pickles (Bradford) and Jim Cunningham (Coventry) – became MPs at the 1992 General Election and developed their 'political careers' in that time-honoured fashion. Alan Whitehead (Southampton) followed in 1997. Jeremy Beecham (Newcastle upon Tyne), Peter Bowness (Croydon) and Pat Doyle (Hull), council leaders of their respective authorities for many years since the late 1970s, extended their political careers into the national arenas of local government through election to positions of responsibility in the relevant local authority associations. There comes a time when 'retirement' becomes an acceptable option, to which no stigma of failure is attached in the world of local politics as in 'occupational careers', although age has proved no barrier to the continued exercise of the leadership role in authorities such as Mid-Glamorgan, where in 1982 the 87-year-old leader made way for a 'younger man' of 76. The worst scenario for a leader 'at the height of his or her powers' is defeat in a leadership election (ex-leaders who remain as councillors often, though not always, exhibit a streak of embitterment in their behaviour), with electoral defeat for the party or oneself almost as traumatic in impact.

The *First national census of councillors* (LGMB, 1998) provides some interesting details of the personal characteristics of local authority leaders in England and Wales. Of the 455 council leaders who responded to the questionnaire in 1997 (a response rate of over 95%):

- 84% were male and 16% female;
- 99% were white and 1% ethnic minority;
- 5% were disabled;
- 36% had caring responsibilities (ie for children under 16 or other dependants);
- 56% were full-time leaders.

Comparisons with the overall population of councillors who responded to the survey are of interest here (see Table 2.1). Interesting points of difference are the under-representation of female leaders and the fact that over half the leaders are full-time (compared with 24% of all councillors). Unfortunately, the published survey results do not provide evidence of leader's age, employment status, occupation, education or length of service.

Table 2.1: Characteristics of leaders and councillors

	All councillors	Leaders
% male	73	84
% female	27	16
% ethnic minority	3	1
% disabled	11	5
% caring responsibilities	34	36
% full-time	24	56

Source: LGMB (1998)

Achieving the leadership position

For a number of the leaders interviewed, there was not a recognised 'leadership position' in the authorities in which they operated, and they had had to influence a process of change within the authority in which the leadership role and position became more widely recognised. Doug Robertson described the situation in Surrey in the mid-1980s in the following terms:

> "The role of leader was not well understood at county level. The Conservatives had a very large majority and a lot of independent-minded

members who did not take kindly to being led by *anyone*! The most influential figures were the chair and vice-chair of the county council, the chair of the policy committee and the chair of the majority party, the views of all of whom were 'sounded out' by the chief executive when he felt it to be necessary."

This situation is now increasingly unusual. The vast majority of the leaders we interviewed had become leaders in authorities where the leadership role had long been recognised in formal terms and represented an acknowledged source of power. This raises the question of the circumstances in which the leaders concerned sought the leadership, or were prevailed upon to do so, and subsequently gained it.

In formal terms, the position in all three major political parties is similar. All group officers (including the group leaders) are elected every municipal year or immediately before the annual meeting of the council, which follows the local election (if there has been one). But the fact of a formal election does not necessarily mean that anyone will stand against the existing leader (or indeed against the existing deputy, chief whip, chair of housing, etc). The situation in which a sitting leader is re-elected unopposed is not only possible, but has been very much the norm among the group of leaders interviewed. However, leaders may resign (as Don Robson's predecessor in Durham was somewhat reluctantly persuaded to do in 1989) or retire (as Dick Knowles chose to do midway through an electoral term in Birmingham in 1993) or lose their council seat at an election (as John Clout's predecessor did in North Yorkshire in 1981). In each case a leadership contest would automatically be triggered off – although it is not unusual for there to be only one contestant for the vacancy.

There are thus two main ways in which a non-leader becomes a leader: either by a successful challenge to a sitting leader, or by a leadership contest following the resignation, retirement or electoral defeat of a sitting leader. The former is potentially a more disruptive political act in terms of group cohesiveness, and raises potential problems, if the challenge is successful, for the new leader in working with his/her deposed predecessor. Allowing a nomination to go forward is more acceptable in the second type of circumstance, although even here it may be viewed as disruptive or damaging to group cohesion if a natural successor (eg an experienced deputy leader) has been identified. This is the kind of judgement a leadership aspirant has to make; for the consequences of a failed bid, widely seen to be premature, may be damaging to future 'political career' prospects. On the other hand, if the bid, although unsuccessful, demonstrates a greater than expected level of support, that in itself may generate concessions and placatory action of the part of the incumbent leader, and could weaken his/her position in the long term.

The juxtaposition of group leadership and council leadership depends on the political arithmetic of the council. If there is a party group with an overall majority, an election for party leader is in effect at the same time an election for council leader. If the council is hung, then it depends on which parties are cooperating, and on what basis. In increasing numbers of hung authorities, the position of council leader (though not the leadership role per se) has become meaningless, and councils of this type may decide to stop using the term (Leach and Stewart, 1992). In contrast, a minority group – particularly a small minority group – knows that in electing a party leader it is certainly not electing a council leader, although this does not mean that whoever is elected is not in a strong position if the party arithmetic changes in spectacular fashion. Graham Tope, leader of a Liberal Group of two in the London Borough of Sutton in 1978, was still in position, and widely regarded as the 'natural leader', when the Liberal Democrats formed a 'minority administration' in Sutton in 1986, and later achieved an overall majority.

Of the leaders interviewed for this study, a surprisingly large proportion gained their position through a leadership contest against a sitting leader (particularly if one included last-minute resignations by leaders who recognised that they would be defeated). This mode of accession was much more common among Labour leaders interviewed (although not unknown for Conservative leaders), and provided the most common personal explanation for leadership candidature among the Labour leaders interviewed. They stood for leader, they claimed, not because of a burning personal ambition to become a party (or council) leader, but because they stood for a particular interpretation of Labour principles or ideology in a situation in which there were competing ideologies or principles within the group: if they thought, or were persuaded by others, that their candidature represented the faction's best chance of success, then they stood for that reason.

In John Battye's case, it was the Oldham District Labour Party that 'persuaded' him to stand, as someone who better reflected their political perspective than did other leadership contenders:

> "At the time, I was vice-chair of Finance, and a number of councillors asked me informally if I would stand for leader ... but it was the district

party who actually nominated me without me knowing! I said, 'well that's good of you!' They replied, 'Well you're not going to withdraw are you, because it's the first time we've had the opportunity to nominate a leader'. So I said OK. I thought I might get second place on the first ballot. As it was, I won 17–15."

The reason for challenge is not always ideological in the political sense; sometimes the current incumbent's style is the crucial issue; sometimes it is a growing belief within a party group that the leader can no longer perform key tasks adequately (the 'failing powers' syndrome). In both cases, however, the processes and problems are similar. Sometimes the challenger was widely seen by the faction he/she adhered to as the appropriate person to challenge the incumbent and agreed to stand for this reason, as in the case of the successful challenge by Pat Doyle of Sir Leo Schultz's leadership in Hull. It is possible that these kinds of non-careerist explanations could be rationalisations of a more deeply rooted desire for power for its own sake; but there was little evidence in the interviews of a 'hidden agenda' of this nature.

Other leaders did not need to fight power battles of this nature. Several of the Conservative leaders interviewed took over the mantle of a retiring predecessor in an unobtrusive and uncontested way, sometimes from a position of deputy, as in the case of Peter Bowness of Croydon. Colin Warbrick was widely regarded as the 'natural leader' of the newly constituted Borough of Trafford in 1974 following his previous experience as leader of Stretford and his year as mayor (and had to be persuaded to resume the position in 1984 by the Conservative group). Jeremy Beecham was elected leader in Newcastle upon Tyne when his predecessor, anticipating a return to the leadership position immediately afterwards, stepped down for a mayoral year, and failed to win back the position a year later, much to his disappointment.

Several leaders talked about 'being in the right place at the right time', none more so than John Harman, who was chair of Economic Development in West Yorks Metropolitan County Council (MCC) between 1981 and 1986. He joined Kirklees Metropolitan Borough Council (MBC) in May 1986 and was elected leader in June 1986 (which must constitute some kind of record for shortness of apprenticeship in one authority before becoming leader):

"We had a situation where the group had exhausted itself – two sides fighting each other. There was also the whiff of scandal in the air. One of the parties to the argument saw me as a candidate who could be voted for because I was 'untainted'."

In many other cases, there was a juxtaposition of circumstances that facilitated the succession of the individual concerned into leadership. The important point to emphasise is that such circumstantial factors – in which the new leader 'best fitted' the emerging majority view within the group as to the kind of leader, in terms of style and political orientation, that was now appropriate – is a much more convincing way of explaining outcomes than the idea of individuals with burning leadership ambitions fighting their way to the top. None of the circumstances of succession identified in the research reflected the latter scenario. The few leaders who had set out with relatively explicit leadership intentions, for example, John Meikle, usually managed to do so with little overt opposition. The vast majority had almost all, by the time they became leaders, embraced 'political careers' (in the sense discussed above) but had not necessarily expected, or particularly wished, to become a council leader by that point in time.

Leaders are all, in a formal sense, vulnerable to annual challenges from aspirants to their position. The reality was that relatively few had experienced such challenges. There were no challenges to Peter Bowness during his 14 years as leader in the Conservative group in Croydon, nor to Pat Doyle in his years as Labour leader of Hull. But leadership challenges, particularly when they result in relatively close votes, can have a marked effect in the confidence and authority of the leader and his/her leadership style, even when he/she emerges successfully from the contest. Peter Soulsby of Leicester experienced a leadership challenge after seven years as leader, which markedly changed his approach (see Chapter Seven).

The predominantly circumstantial mode of leadership accession underlines the importance of explaining the relationship between an authority's political culture and its leadership style. Sometimes authorities elect leaders who reflect the traditional political culture, but more typically the election of a new leader represents a reaction against a traditional style or political orientation, as in the case of Alan Whitehead in Southampton. Thus, leadership battles commonly reflect changing patterns of perception within a dominant party group of appropriate leadership style or policy orientation (the two factors are often interrelated) in which one individual – the challenger – is seen to embody the case for change vis-à-vis the case for continuity. This issue is explored in more detail below.

Three leadership–culture relationships

There are in principle three basic forms that the interrelationship between leadership and political culture might take. First, there is the situation in which the political and organisational cultures are relatively stable, in which case leadership role interpretation is likely to reflect and reinforce the traditional cultural ethos. This situation can be characterised as one of the *congruence* between political culture and leadership role.

Second, there is the situation in which instability in the political environment has resulted in a reaction against the prevailing leadership role interpretation on the part of at least some of the political group concerned. In these circumstances there is likely to be a challenge to the current leader (who represents the prevailing style and the traditional political culture) from a leadership contender (who represents the forces for change). Assuming the challenge is successful, we can characterise the new leadership situation as *reactive*, in that it is a response to the mismatch between the predecessor's role interpretation and the emerging dominant political culture.

Third, there is the situation where the leader, through his/her own leadership qualities, persuades a political group that a change in leadership role is necessary (to respond to changes in the political environment) even where this need is not initially widely perceived. In these circumstances, it is possible to characterise the situation as 'transformational'; it generates a change in political and organisational culture (and expectations of leadership) though action taken by leaders themselves. As we will see, the reactive and transformational conditions are not mutually exclusive.

In effect, these three situations reflect different stages in development of political culture, and different forms of negotiation between leader and party group. In the first situation (congruence) a leader is elected (or re-elected) on the basis of a set of shared understandings, embracing both ideology and style. What organisational theorists have called *transactional* leadership is the most likely style of operation. A leader may be conceded power to make certain kinds of decision, and may operate in an environment that expects and will respond to a 'strong lead', but such concessions and expectations are circumscribed by the prevailing assumptions about ideology (or policy content) and style, which the leader steps outside at his/her peril. In relation to the second situation, a leader who gains power through a process of reaction, there will be a clear expectation on the part of those who have voted him/her into power that the new leader will advocate policies and behave in ways that overcome the shortcomings perceived in his/her predecessor. Failure to deliver on this basis will lead to a vulnerability of the new leader to further replacement. In the third situation there exists a degree of scope for innovation, which may reflect either an open-mindedness on the part of the group concerning ideological emphasis and/or appropriate style, or the ability of the leader to overcome initial constraints of cultural expectations. In either case, the style of operation moves towards *transformational* leadership where the leader through his/her own powers of influence and persuasion changes the way in which the group, or a critical mass thereof, perceives the challenges facing it.

In our research, all three situations were encountered. We came across authorities that 'had the leaders they deserved', in that the leader's personal style was both a reflection of and congruent with the traditional expectations and behaviour patterns of the authority. The congruence between Peter Bowness' leadership style in Croydon and the traditional political culture of the authority is a case in point. But we also encountered authorities in which there had been a recent reaction against a traditional style of leadership, a reaction of which the new leader was either an enthusiastic advocate or had been astute enough to recognise. Trevor Burkenshaw's accession to power in Swansea in 1990 was very much a reflection of an adverse reaction to his predecessor's style. And we also visited authorities in which the initiative for a change in leadership style had personally come from the leader, where a new interpretation of the leadership role had generated change in the political culture of the group or authority. Pat Doyle's attempt to make the Labour group in Hull more participative is one example; John Harman's attempt to change the relationship between leading members and officers in Kirklees is another. Changes in political culture associated with either 'reaction' or 'innovation' may either develop slowly and cumulatively, or may accelerate because of a crisis or particular event. A leader may do something that is seen as 'the last straw', a catalyst to the process of dispensing with him/her. Or a leader striving for an innovative role change may be able to use an external crisis to bring about change. For example, the relatively sudden impact of the Poulson affair on leadership styles of Labour-controlled authorities in the North East has been documented, with a consequent move away from relatively autocratic leader or caucus-dominated approaches to more consultative and participative styles (epitomised by Don Robson of Durham County Council). Another example would be the sudden transition in a previously Conservative dominated authority to a situation of no overall control, a change that often generates an awareness that the previously decisive 'leadership from the front' style is less appropriate in the new circumstances, where the softer skills of persuasion, bargaining and negotiation are required, not least in a situation where the Conservatives are allowed to form a minority administration (Leach and Stewart, 1992). It is unlikely, for example, that Lady Porter would have survived for long as leader of a minority Conservative administration in a hung Westminster! More typically, however, the process of changing expectations is more gradual, often reflecting a change in the political orientation of the dominant group. Potential leaders embodying the ascendant values (typically, in Labour groups, 'participatory' as opposed to 'directive') may unsuccessfully contest leadership elections on one or more occasions before the breakthrough is achieved.

Ken Livingstone's account of his political career in local government (Livingstone, 1987) provides a vivid account of the exploitation of a growing incongruence between the political culture of the Labour group on the Greater London Council (GLC) and first the leadership style of Reg Godwin and second the (embryonic) style of Andrew MacIntosh. Livingstone describes Reg Godwin's style in the following terms:

> "He was quiet, undemonstrative and hated publicity, particularly television. His manner was polite in the extreme and he clearly detested the crudeness of politics and the private vulgarities of politicians. Wherever he joined the Labour lunch table in the members' restaurant, people automatically stopped swearing and conversation died away and only polite generalities remained. It was rather as though one had been joined by a frail remnant of the Victorian era.... He completely lacked a firm grasp of leadership and sense of direction. The problem was partly due to his inability to communicate with colleagues, which meant that everyone left his presence with the idea that Sir Reg agreed with whatever they were proposing."

Although it is difficult to imagine this style of leadership being congruent with any current political culture, it was clearly less acceptable to the 1977-81 Labour group in opposition than to its predecessor in power in 1973-77. Although Godwin tried to engineer the election of Andrew MacIntosh as his successor, the intensity of the reaction to the traditional style (together with a significant change in group composition) helped to ensure the success of Ken Livingstone in the leadership election that followed the 1981 Labour victory in Greater London.

Accounts of Ken Livingstone's period of leadership in the GLC – Carvel (1984), Forrester et al (1985) and Livingstone (1987) – are instructive in other ways too. Although undoubtedly one of the most high-profile leaders in the history of local government, Livingstone was by no means a strong leader compared with many local Conservative and Labour leaders elsewhere. He was an eloquent spokesperson for the group; but within the group his style was consultative and non-directive, which was congruent with the political culture of the experienced, imaginative and radical group involved.

The dynamics of leader–group relationships

As we noted earlier, leadership *style* is one of the three important elements in leadership behaviour. The other elements are *values/ideology* (ie the set of political values and predispositions held by the leader) and *task orientation* (ie the relative priority accorded by the leader to the four key leadership tasks). Any one or all of these elements may form part of the 'negotiated order' between leader and group and may indeed have been influential in the leader's election in the first place. The importance of style in this connection has already been illustrated. As an example of task orientation, when Labour gained power in Derbyshire in 1981, the leader David Bookbinder was clear (as were his most influential colleagues) that the key tasks were to seize the initiative from the officers in relation to strategic direction *and* (reflecting their lack of trust in the officers) to ensure the delivery of the party manifesto. External relations was also an important sphere in which the need was seen to replace officer domination by member domination.

But value orientation – or what leaders 'stand for' – can be an equally important influence. There is no doubt that a perception of what Ken Livingstone stood for, as well as his personal style, was a significant factor in securing his election as the leader in 1981. The same point could be made in relation to Alan Whitehead (Southampton Labour group, 1984), Eric Pickles (Bradford Conservative group, 1987), David Bookbinder (Derbyshire Labour group, 1977) and many others. These key values will then influence the stance taken by the leader, particularly in relation to the task of strategic direction.

Once elected, the leader's initial relationship with the group may subsequently be threatened by various factors, some of them concerned with the dynamics of the group and others with the inertia of the wider organisational (as opposed to political) culture. In a council elected every four years, the political ideology of a group is not likely to change significantly, although there may, if the group is finely balanced, be changes brought about through a small number of by-elections, and changes in perception within a group reflecting the experience of governing are not unknown in hung authorities (Leach and Stewart, 1992). However, in a council in which there are elections in three years out of four (eg metropolitan districts and many shire districts), the political composition of a group is of course much more vulnerable to change, and a leader elected in one year because of ideological congruence with a majority of the group may find the morning after the next election that such congruence has disappeared. One possible reaction is a leadership election resulting in the defeat of the existing leader. But in an alternative scenario the leader adjusts his/her behaviour to take account of changes in group composition and ideology. In a strongly factionalised situation this may not be feasible; but in a more fluid situation there are several things a leader can do to survive. If he/she is in a position to influence the election of chairs and vice-chairs, as leaders usually are (although the power to *appoint* chairs and vice-chairs is limited to about 10% of Conservative groups (Gyford et al, 1989, p 182), then, through a process of incorporation of the newly dominant faction, survival may be ensured. In addition, or alternatively, leaders may modify their prioritisation of political beliefs in a way that is acceptable to enough members of the group to ensure survival. The general point to emphasise is the inherent instability of the relationship between political culture and the political ideology element of leadership role.

If the new group leader immediately becomes council leader in an authority with a stable political and organisational culture, then the transition is likely to be relatively straightforward. In other words, if there is no pressure to alter the main tasks of political leadership (which are well established and accepted by members and officers), and there is a traditional view of appropriate leadership style (eg consensus building), then the main impact of the change will be a policy shift, based on the change in ideological orientation which the leader represents. The only real problem occurs if the new leader's style does not fit the key tasks and traditional expectations. Leadership styles cannot always be predicted in advance, although if, as is likely, the newcomer has been a committee chair, there should be some evidence of style and skill; and if there was on these grounds an apparent mismatch, this would be likely to be recognised by councillors in an authority with a clear and stable set of expectations about leadership style (eg 'M has got the right views, but will he be able to stand up to the chief executive?'). However, lack of congruence between leadership role and political culture can arise if a group fails to recognise that the style of the individual they have elected is inappropriate to the tasks they regard a priority (eg external representation) and if the leader proves incapable of making the necessary change of style.

A mismatch between organisational culture and leadership behaviour is particularly likely where emphasis on a new task – for example, on 'making things happen' – generates resistance within the officer culture of an authority. Of the four key leadership tasks, this is the one that is likely to prove the most contentious among the officer elite. 'Developing strategic policy direction' and 'representing the authority in the outside world' would be readily conceded 'in principle' as politically led processes; 'maintaining organisational cohesiveness' is clearly a political task, although chief officers can make a significant contribution in a hung situation. However, task accomplishment or 'ensuring delivery' threatens traditional officer values about appropriate divisions of labour, and is likely to be resisted – directly and/or indirectly – if it becomes a priority for a political leader. In authorities where there is a powerful tradition of officer domination of this task – for example, many of the shire counties – a new leader may find that he/she is 'unable to deliver' – that is, lacks the skills or resources to break down well established ways of doing things.

There are other ways in which a 'mismatch' between leadership style and culture can develop. In hung authorities, where leadership tasks in effect become 'shared' between two or more parties (unless one party is allowed to play a dominant role), there is considerable pressure on the leaders concerned to reach consensus, particularly for decisions that need, if not a 'quick decision', then at least a 'quick steer' for the chief executive (eg an expression of interest in a local site by a multinational company). In many hung authorities there is an informal 'leadership group' comprising the chief executive and the leaders of either the two cooperating parties or, more typically, all three parties, which is designed to deal with just such eventualities. These groups in themselves provide a fascinating learning experience for the different leaders, with a Conservative leader's ability to commit his/her group in advance to a position adopted by the leader contrasting vividly with the need of the other group leaders to consult their party groups before making any such commitments (see Leach and Stewart, 1992, p 70). However, in relation to leadership behaviour, what such groups do is to exert pressure from the organisational culture (through the chief executive) on leaders to behave in ways that may be at odds with the political expectations and culture of their own groups. This can work in a number of different ways. Often a suspicion emerges – particularly within Labour groups – that 'deals are being done' within this leadership group that are 'bypassing' normal group processes. The leader in this situation needs skills of reassurance that this is not in fact the case, or an ability to persuade the group that there are situations in which the needs of the authority as a whole (organisational cohesiveness) transcend those of the group (group cohesiveness). This may be a delicate and difficult 'balancing act', as some Labour leaders have found to their cost. Alternatively, it may become clear to his or her group that the style of a particular leader is not appropriate to the operational requirements of a hung authority. Assertive leaders, intent on exploiting opportunities for party political gain, do not fit easily with the need for the regulation of inter-party behaviour in a hung situation. Thus, unless a party group wishes to play a 'destabilising' role (and hence expects its leader to take every opportunity to do so), it will become increasingly wary if such maverick behaviour persists. The change of leadership in the Cheshire Conservative group in 1986 owed much to this perception; and the all-party leadership group certainly worked much more effectively once Simon Cussins had been elected Conservative leader.

Tensions can arise between a leader's task interpretation and organisational culture (eg if emphasis is placed by the leader on a task that is seen within the organisational culture as non-legitimate) or between emergent and declining political ideologies within the political culture (eg a mismatch between the political values of a leader and those of the majority of the group). An effective leader will ensure in the first instance that the organisational culture does respond positively. David Bookbinder in Derbyshire, partly through a succession of changes in personnel, reached a situation in which the organisational culture reflected both leadership style and political culture (the latter having itself been modified by his own leadership skills).

Leadership behaviour in most politicised authorities is regularly challenged by elements of the prevailing organisational or political culture. A leader may, for example, be persuaded by a chief executive that a new committee structure is necessary for the effective operation of the authority, a change that he/she knows it will be difficult to persuade the group to accept (especially if it reduces the number of status positions). He/she may also be under pressure from the group to organise the replacement of two or three officers who the group feel are not being sufficiently supportive. In this way the leader acts as a conduit of pressures for change, a mechanism paralleled on the officer side by the chief executive.

What this analysis of the dynamics of leader–group relationships clearly illustrates is the *vulnerability* of leaders to periodic challenge. Given the factionalism within party groups, a leader can rarely take for granted the automatic support of all group members. On occasions a group can flex its muscles to remove the group leader. In November 1995, for example, two majority group leaders – Stewart Foster in Leicester and Valerie Wise in Preston – were overthrown by their respective Labour groups. Likewise, in May 1998 two other Labour leaders were ousted: John Ryan at Bradford Metropolitan District Council (MDC) was replaced by Ian Greenwood; and at Tower Hamlets London Borough Council (LBC) Michael Keith was toppled by Julia Mainwaring. Factionalism, particularly within Labour groups, means that leadership contests can never be ruled out. Similarly, allegations against a leader occasionally result in the leader standing down. For example, Alan Baldwick, leader of Dumfries and Galloway, stepped down as leader of an Independent/Liberal Democrat coalition in January 1998, after the council had called in the police to investigate alleged irregularities in his expense claims.

Indeed, former leaders can, in factionalised groups, reappear to challenge the policies of their successor. Marinetto (1997, p 35) shows that, at the time of the poll tax disputes in the mid-1980s, when the leadership and the mainstay of Labour members in Camden were determined to delay setting the rate, a small number of Labour councillors put forward a motion to set a 'legal rate'. In June 1985 "a group of 11 Labour councillors, led by a former leader, voted with the Conservatives and passed a motion to set a legal rate". Former leaders can readily become a focus for discontent against the new political elite.

Leadership challenges in the Conservative Party are less frequent but by no means unknown. Holliday (1991, p 448) discusses one such challenge in Kent County Council in 1984. In that year Tony Hart defeated the sitting Conservative group leader, Bobby Neame. Hart was something of an outsider and was highly critical of the Conservative Party establishment in Kent. Neame was part of that establishment. To quote Holliday:

> "The 1984 leadership election which resulted in victory for Hart may well have registered dissatisfaction with the incumbent leader, Bobby

> Neame, as much as it expressed positive support for Hart's change
> programme: a year previously, Hart had been unable to beat Neame in
> an election to select the successor to Sir John Grugeon, leader since
> 1974."

Essentially, Hart was an outsider who believed in radical change and who
had the good fortune to face an establishment leader whose popularity
was on the wane.

The key challenge for a leader faced with the kind of pressures discussed
in this section is to develop a balance between the three key elements of
his/her role. Leadership style is the most difficult element to change,
certainly in the short term. It is a lot to ask of 'leaders from the front' that
they suddenly develop skills of persuasion and negotiation. Political
ideology (or at least the public expression of it) is capable of modification
within limits, although most leaders can identify a 'bottom-line' political
commitment – issues over which they would resign if defeated. Changes
in task interpretation may cause problems if they require unfamiliar skills
from a leader (eg external representation and public relations), in which
case the question is, can the task be shared within a wider leadership
group (increasingly feasible within Labour groups), or does the political
culture of the ruling group limit the scope for such task sharing?

Conclusion

In this chapter we have explored the complex relationships between political
culture and leadership behaviour. We have argued that each of the three
defined key elements of leadership behaviour – values and ideology, task
orientation and style – are to some extent constrained by the current
characteristics of political culture, but are also amenable to transformatory
action on the part of leaders. In certain circumstances, leaders can facilitate
major change in relation to ideology, task orientation and style. However,
given the lack of *formal* authority and sanctions currently available to
leaders in British local government, they have to persuade, or inspire, their
followers (or to engage them in negotiation) if they are to meet our most
fundamental criterion of leadership: the ability to overcome resistance to
particular courses of action, notably to cause others to agree to something
they were not necessarily initially predisposed to.

THREE

Maintaining cohesiveness

Introduction

There are four major areas of concern for local party leaders in relation to the task of maintaining cohesiveness both within the party and within the authority. First, all have to pay attention to the *cohesiveness of the party group* within which the existence of a smaller executive is invariably an important influence. Second, the *cohesiveness of the local party networks*, including the group, is a major concern. Third, leaders of majority parties have a major responsibility for the *cohesiveness of the authority as a whole*, a responsibility in which relations between members and officers and the effectiveness of political management structures will play a large part. Finally, organisational *cohesiveness in a hung situation* is a potential responsibility of all parties (except perhaps those playing an explicitly oppositional role); in this context inter-party relations become an important dimension of organisational cohesiveness.

Although a leader may share or delegate any of these tasks, he/she would be expected to play a major role in each. It is difficult to conceive, for example, of a leader not feeling that group cohesiveness was a major responsibility. Similarly, although some of the detail of group–party interaction could be delegated, the local party would normally expect to deal with the leader on crisis issues or over key stages of the manifesto process. Political management structures are typically built around a core executive, the fulcrum of which is invariably the leader–chief executive relationship. Inter-party relations in a situation of no overall control will almost inevitably require a major input from the leader. This task can be a dominant and time-consuming one for the leader, and one rarely amenable to delegation.

In Chapter One we made it clear that the first leadership task identified by Selznick – maintaining organisational cohesiveness – is, in a politicised local authority, a complex and multi-faceted one. At the outset, however, it is important to explore this concept of cohesiveness.

What is cohesiveness?

Whether one is considering the party group, the wider network embracing the group and the local party machinery, or the political management structure of the authority as a whole, there will inevitably be a variety of political philosophies (or at least emphases) and some form of 'sub-group' structure based on such differences. Such differentiations, along with those of gender, race and social class, do not necessarily constitute a problem, but they may in certain circumstances provide a basis for challenging the cohesiveness of a party group, as might other issues such as patch and other local allegiances.

Cohesiveness sounds as if it implies consensus and a lack of conflict: a cohesive group is one that is 'united' and in which there is 'no trouble'. In fact, the concept is potentially much wider in its scope. In many situations consensus or unity are unrealistic and indeed undesirable goals. Differences of view can make a positive contribution to the political energy of the group (and hence to the achievement of other important objectives, such as 'strategic direction'), so long as they do not degenerate into schisms. There will be periods when groups need to be proactively 'enthused' (eg after a national election defeat of their party) rather than merely 'held together' as a coherent unit. Among the skills of leadership are the ability to sense when an infusion of enthusiasm is needed, and the ability to encourage differences of view but to keep the ensuing tensions 'within bounds'. Thus, the leadership task of maintaining cohesiveness does not imply just 'ensuring that things go through group' or disciplining errant members who do not accept group decisions: it may also imply the encouragement of the expression of differences of view and the recognition that conflict can be productive as well as destructive.

Cohesiveness within the party group

The starting point in a leader's task of maintaining cohesiveness is the party group. If a leader cannot ensure that the group 'holds together' as a unit, and is perceived as a coherent entity by other groups, then the other component tasks of maintaining cohesiveness become infinitely more difficult. It is not just a case of ensuring that group discipline is maintained in relation to council and committee meetings, although this is of course important: there is, as we have seen, a more important underlying task of ensuring that, where internal differences exist within the group, they are contained within an overall group identity and, ideally, are seen as a healthy stimulus to internal debate rather than as a problem. Differences of view may harden into factionalism, or may provide a positive dynamic that strengthens rather than weakens the group. A lot will depend on the way the leader handles any differences.

Although leaders cannot by themselves resolve such potential dilemmas and guarantee cohesiveness, they are in a particularly strong position of influence. After all, a leader invariably represents an expression of the balance of forces within the group when elected, and for a while this is likely to give him or her an authority beyond the status of leader per se (which is in itself considerable). There is a tradition in all parties of rallying round a leader once a leadership election has been resolved, and if the leader's performance in external arenas is impressive, that too strengthens his/her authority. The unseating of incumbent leaders is not undertaken lightly in any of the parties, and changes through retirement, resignation and electoral defect are much more common than a successful challenge to a sitting tenant. In all these ways, a leader has a potentially powerful integrative role. Nevertheless, it must be recognised that leadership policies need to reflect the core political values of the ruling party group. Green (1981, p 74), despite his general emphasis on the power of the leadership, notes how "traditional party values provided limits" to their influence, so the Labour Party leadership in Newcastle upon Tyne could not afford to challenge basic party commitments to council housing or to a 'no redundancies' policy.

There is, however, a further important structural element to consider. The more a party group on the council extends in size beyond a relatively modest level of around a dozen or so, the more likely it is that there will be an important intermediate hierarchical level within the party group which sits between the leader and the wider group. Although groups of a dozen or less will still elect members into a range of formal positions (group secretary, group chair, chief whip, etc), there is little need for a separate group executive meeting apart from attempting to orchestrate the operations of the group as a whole. Moving beyond this scale, however, it becomes increasingly likely that some form of group executive will become a formalised and influential body in its own right. When a party group exceeds more than about 40, it becomes ever more difficult for a leader to have a *direct* relationship with the group as such. The relationship is increasingly likely to be mediated through the group executive, hence the group executive itself comes to play an increasingly significant leadership role. Indeed, it is unrealistic to expect that the leadership task of a large majority group within a large local authority could be dominated by the leader in a way that is possible in a small shire district.

However, there are a number of different possible relationships between the leader and the leadership group. In the Labour Party the leadership group is likely to include the party office holders (collectively, the group executive), all of whom are likely to be chairs (or party spokespersons) in their own right and who will usually also form the bulk of the party group's representation on the Policy and Resources Committee. In a minority of Conservative groups, it is still acceptable for the leader to select the chairs of committees who would then be likely to dominate (or even constitute) the leadership group or informal cabinet. This power of patronage provides the basis for strong proactive leadership, particularly in the light of the more ready acceptance by Conservative group members of this style of leadership. Such powers are very rarely available to Labour and Liberal Democrat leaders.

In some authorities, a decision reached by group executive is regarded as binding upon its members when the recommendation is put before group itself. Thus, if a Labour leader can convince the majority of a group executive of 10 of the need for a particular decision, then that immediately generates 10 votes in favour (even if four group executive members voted against) at the group meeting itself; in a group of 30, the implication is that only a further six votes in support would be required. In these circumstances, a good deal of the leader's energies are likely to be focused on persuading the group executive rather than the group itself, both through discussions and through the more informal pre-meeting processes of lobbying, arm-twisting and manipulation.

If, on the other hand, a majority decision reached by group executive members is not binding upon its members at the subsequent group meeting (a situation that is most likely within Liberal Democrat groups), then the subsequent arithmetic – and need for further lobbying, arm-twisting, etc – looks very different.

In a situation where leaders cannot select chairs or otherwise strongly influence the composition of the leadership group, there may be a greater likelihood of support for a leader's initiative from the wider group than from the group executive itself, a discrepancy that can be exploited if a group executive's decisions are not binding upon its members, but can prove a source of real frustration for the leader if they are (although 'reversals' can sometimes be engineered).

The crucial point is that in a relatively large party group the leadership elite, whatever form it takes, becomes a crucial point of reference for the leader, both as an arena in which leadership has to be exercised successfully if it is to be effective, and as an arena through which leadership tasks are likely to be shared. In some circumstances it is possible for a leader to dominate a leadership elite, through either power of patronage or force of personality or tradition, in which case the leadership elite can become a part of the process by which the leader ensures group cohesiveness. If he/she can dominate the leadership elite (and where a 'recommendation' agreed there is seen as binding upon elite members), then such recommendations are highly unlikely to be subsequently overturned by the party group. In other circumstances, however, where a leader lacks such powers, the scope for personal leadership may be greatly diminished, with a greater probability of leadership preferences being overturned either by the elite collectively or, subsequently, by the party group (in a situation where decisions reached in the leadership elite are not viewed as binding on those involved). At the extreme, a nominal leader may become heavily constrained by the influence of the leadership elite, exercised either collectively or through powerful individuals or factions working within it. It is thus not impossible (though it is admittedly unusual) for leaders who are little more than 'puppets' to emerge in politicised authorities, with the real power being exercised elsewhere within the leadership elite. Such dynamics can really be understood, however, only on an authority-by-authority basis.

For party leaders there are always important choices involved in recognising and balancing different geographical and factional interests in the allocation of offices, particularly committee chair and vice-chair posts. As we have seen, for those leaders with the power of patronage, it is both an important explicit resource in relation to the task of ensuring group cohesiveness, and an annual tactical opportunity to strengthen their own position. However, all Labour and Liberal Democrat leaders interviewed argued that they could influence the allocation of offices – the nomination by or known support of a leader was widely recognised as, at the very least, a considerable advantage to the candidate so favoured. In Derbyshire in the 1987-89 period the Labour leader, David Bookbinder, was allowed to determine, and subsequently change, the specific responsibilities of chairs elected by the group (ie without specific portfolios being identified in the electoral process). The involvement of leaders in such processes is an important feature of the role. In politically fraught situations, the judgement of the leader may be crucial in determining whether rifts are healed or deepened.

The concept of 'group cohesiveness' can incorporate the existence of a small number of rebels, particularly in situations where the group concerned has a sizeable majority on the council. The most difficult situation for a leader is that in which there is a recognised and increasingly self-contained faction – a group within a group – which, even if it chooses to stay within the pale in terms of group discipline, is known to have fundamental ideological differences with the majority of the group. This situation was faced at different times by Alan Whitehead in Southampton, Joan Twelves in Lambeth and Peter Soulsby in Leicester. It is most likely to have become an issue in Labour Party groups because of the intensity of the ideological splits in the party in the 1979-87 period, but it has occurred, usually less openly, in Conservative groups in the same period (for example Maidstone, Thanet, Wiltshire). The options for a leader, the plausibility of which will vary with the specific history of the situation, are to attempt a reconciliation (ie keep the differences 'within bounds') which may involve tactics such as offering positions of responsibility to selected members of the rebel faction; to ignore the problem (which is feasible so long as the remainder of the majority group still constitute an overall majority, or the rebels continue to vote with the group on the vast majority of occasions); or to persuade the remainder of the group to discipline the rebels, which is a particularly high-risk strategy if it leaves the remainder of the group in an overall minority on the council. The second and third strategies clearly do not resolve the problem, but merely postpone its resolution; none the less, there are circumstances where leaders see one or the other as the only realistic course of action. There is, in fact, a fourth possibility – the threat of resignation if a rebel faction does not modify its behaviour at least in public arenas. This is the strategy with the highest risk of all in personal terms, particularly for a leader with a developing political career; for there is always a possibility that the threat will not achieve its purpose and the leader will then have to carry it through. It is not surprising, therefore, that it is rarely used.

In principle, group cohesiveness can be a particularly severe problem for Liberal Democrat leaders, given their lack of disciplinary sanctions. However, in practice, particularly when Liberal Democrat groups gain power or achieve a share in power, the group normally holds together on a voluntary basis. The lack of strong ideological schisms within Liberal Democrat groups is clearly an influential factor here; in the days of the Liberal–SDP Alliance, splits were more likely. One corollary of the lack of formal sanctions is that the capacity for moral leadership is highlighted in Liberal Democrat leaders – 'you ought to do this' rather than 'if you don't do this we'll discipline you'.

Leaders of Conservative groups have traditionally been given more latitude to lead the group in a preferred direction, although this latitude can be exercised only within acceptable limits. Saunders (1980, pp 221-2) recounts the demise of a committee chair who offended Croydon's majority Conservative group by proposing to abolish grammar schools in the area. The voluntary collective submission to a leader's preferred direction is much more likely to work in conditions of a broad ideological consensus within the group. In 1997, for example, in Leicestershire County Council, making the budget proved to be extremely problematic and effectively focused on the chief executive plus the leaders of each of the three major parties in what was a hung authority. The leader of the Conservative group, Bob Osborne, maintained that pressure of time and the sensitivities associated with a possible 600 redundancies "made it impossible to have group meetings to look at it in detail. If I were a backbencher I think I would resent it. I did have to apologise to my group for the lack of consultation". There was, however, no question of any challenge to the leader's authority. Osborne operated within parameters he knew were acceptable to the Conservative group as a whole.

Organisational cohesiveness

What the task of 'maintaining organisational cohesiveness' actually involves will differ depending on circumstances. All leaders of party groups in local authorities have to pay attention to the cohesiveness of the group and to the cohesiveness of the local party network (embracing local constituency parties, party agents, Members of Parliament [MPs] and, in the case of the Labour Party, the local government committee for the authority's area). For 'opposition' parties in an authority in which there is a majority party (or coalition), this is the major sense in which cohesiveness is important. Indeed, one of the most important tasks of an opposition leader is to oppose effectively, and the quality of his/her performance is likely to be judged on the basis of the ability to embarrass or make things difficult for the governing party in public arenas. The extent to which an opposition leader can create a sense of divisiveness within the politics of the authority is important for the cohesiveness of the opposition group; and one of the most important tasks – possibly *the* most important – is to maintain the credibility of the opposition (particularly important where there are two 'competing' opposition parties) as an alternative to the party in power. Thus, in Rochdale, where the parliamentary contest has in recent years been in effect between Labour and the Liberal Democrats, pacts between these two parties on Rochdale MBC have been conspicuous by their absence during the several periods of 'balance' in this authority. Explicit Conservative–Liberal Democrat pacts in the South West are uncommon for similar reasons. In a politicised authority, inter-party cohesiveness is not a priority for an opposition leader, except in special circumstances. Generally the reverse is true.

The hypothesis that the key leadership task of an opposition leader is to oppose effectively has to be modified in certain circumstances. There are authorities in the more rural parts of Britain where there is a good deal of inter-party consensus on 'what is best for the authority'. (For example, in 1997 a 'South Holland First' policy united all political groupings in that district authority.) In circumstances of inter-party consensus there is a potential channel of influence between an opposition leader and a council leader which would be jeopardised by too strident an oppositional stance in public arenas such as full council, although the ritual of political point scoring on such occasions may be mutually acceptable. An opposition leader in such authorities has to balance the political benefits of potential informal influence with the likely costs to group credibility and cohesiveness of too laid back an oppositional role in public. The judgement involved is sometimes a delicate one. Even in the more politicised urban authorities, where the ritual (and usually the substance) of public opposition has long been the norm, there may still be opportunities for informal influence which are worth safeguarding, particularly in circumstances where the chances of the opposition gaining power in the foreseeable future are remote.

In politicised authorities under majority party control, a cosy inter-party cohesiveness is of as little value to a council leader as it is to an opposition leader. As with opposition leaders, one of a council leader's main resources for maintaining or strengthening cohesiveness at group or party network level is his/her ability to perform effectively in public debate. For this purpose an antipathetic and credible opposition has its advantages, offering opportunities to demonstrate leadership qualities in public debate. Small ineffective opposition parties are sometimes seen as problematic in this respect, encouraging factionalisation within a (large) majority group, and providing few chances for 'leadership' in public debate. The ideal is a sizeable opposition (but not too large to threaten the ruling group's majority), which is reasonably effective as an opposition but not so effective that the council leader cannot appear to demolish their arguments. In a balanced situation, the debating abilities of the leaders can strengthen both their positions and the cohesiveness of their respective party groups.

However, there will be times when a strong case for organisational cohesiveness, that is, a 'united front' involving both or all major parties, is perceived as highly desirable by a council leader. A public scandal, for example, an incidence of child abuse in a council-run home, would be one such situation; an opportunity to gain extra resources (eg a 'City Challenge' bid) another. Delegations to a government minister, for example, over the unfairness of a government grant are widely seen as likely to be more effective if an opposition leader is involved, particularly when the latter is of the same political complexion as the national government. If the future survival of a local authority is at stake through reorganisation, there is a particularly strong pressure for inter-party cooperation (eg West Yorkshire 1983, Cleveland 1993). Thus, even in politically polarised majority-controlled authorities, there will be times when a council leader will wish to solicit the support of the opposition, because a crisis (or opportunity) requires the demonstration of organisational cohesiveness on a cross-party basis. Hence an important feature of *council* leadership is the ability to maintain channels of communication with the opposition which can be activated when the demonstration of organisational cohesiveness in a wider sense becomes desirable. The ideal position for a council leader is the coexistence of a confrontational climate in council debate (in which the leader can excel), which benefits group cohesiveness, with an informal personal link with the main opposition leader, which can be activated at times of crisis.

Cohesiveness in a hung situation

In a situation of no overall control, the relationship between group leaders becomes of crucial importance in a number of different ways. If a group decides it wishes to play an oppositional role in such circumstances, then the behavioural implications differ little for that group and leader from what they would be in a situation of majority control. If, on the other hand, a party group wishes to be involved in running the hung authority in a proactive sense, then the leader will necessarily have to deal with at least one other group leader informally. The existence of such informal channels, sometimes based on personal friendship, can be vital in the initial formation of an administration, involving, for example, either the sharing of chairs or the preparedness of one party to support the nominations of another party for the chairs (see Leach and Pratchett, 1996, pp 15-16).

Equally, once an administration based on some level of inter-party accommodation and understanding is established, the link between leaders continues to be of considerable importance. Mention has been made of the tensions between the leadership task in a leadership group on which two or three party leaders are represented, and the leadership task of maintaining group commitment to these arrangements. In this respect, group cohesiveness and authority-wide cohesiveness pull in different directions. The maintenance of the former may threaten the latter, particularly if group members feel that too many compromises are being made, and vice versa. The authority's officers, especially the chief executive, will emphasise the importance to the authority of having stable decision-making arrangements. Backbenchers remote from the higher circles of power will focus on the achievement of the party's programme and the adverse longer-term political consequences of 'deals' or 'pacts'. Again, the different pressures are focused on the leader, and it is his/her judgement that will decide where the emphasis should be placed. The conflicting demands are a particular problem for Labour leaders, where there is a strong expectation of 'govern or oppose' and normally a strong expectation of group participation, both of which threaten the effectiveness of the leadership group. Conservative groups are more likely to back the leader's judgement although not automatically so. For example, when Hertfordshire became hung in 1985, the Conservatives decided to hold on to the committee chairs if they could, partly to ensure the continuation of their secondary schools rationalisation programme and partly for other policy reasons. By making a number of procedural concessions, they received the support of the Liberal Democrats, a situation that prevailed until April 1987, when the announcement of a general election was widely expected. In this period there was growing pressure on the group from the Conservative constituency associations and from local Conservative MPs to give up their chairs. Ultimately the group was persuaded to follow this advice, but reluctantly, by a small majority, and with the leader advising against (see Game and Leach, 1995, p 38). Liberal Democrat groups, although highly democratic and participative, are usually predisposed to making a hung authority work, and will allow a leader a reasonable degree of latitude. The consequences of the attitude and actions of the leaders involved can be crucial for the overall cohesiveness of the authority.

Leach and Pratchett (1996) draw a distinction between 'integrated' and 'fragmented' forms of hung authority. *An integrated hung authority* will tend to have the following features: regular meetings of the chief executive and the party leaders; a well established system of party spokespersons, with equal rights of briefing from chief officers; and a set of agreed conventions for reference back of items delegated to committees, urgent business, access to agendas, etc. There will be a commitment to open government. There are also likely to be arenas in which discussion between the parties can take place more informally than in a committee (eg working parties, management groups, representative panels). There may be a formal statement of the common ground between two (or sometimes three) of the parties concerned, to guide medium-term planning and budgeting.

In contrast, where all or most of the above conditions are absent, a *fragmented hung authority* is likely. In fragmented authorities there will be no regular leadership meetings. There will be disputes over procedural issues, reflecting disagreement on conventions. Standing orders will be regularly challenged. Council meetings will be disrupted or extremely long or both (particularly at budget time). Informal discussion arenas are likely to be absent or not well developed. There will be little pattern to the adoption of policies and making of decisions, and almost no medium-term or longer-term planning. Many of the hung authorities have high levels of overt inter-party conflict and fall into this category. Indeed, if there is no predisposition to cooperate at the political level, there is little that even the ablest chief executive can do about it. At best, they can mitigate the worst effects of this form of hungness.

In the first case, the task of organisational cohesiveness has been achieved in a way that is compatible with group cohesiveness. In the second case, group cohesiveness has been maintained at the expense of organisational cohesiveness, and the leadership tasks of the authority are either carried out or orchestrated by officers, or are neglected. Strategic direction is a particularly likely casualty and external relations may by neglected also because so much energy is being dissipated on internal political and procedural wrangles.

The switch from a majority control situation to one of no overall control may in certain circumstances help a leader resolve problems of internal group cohesiveness that spring from factionalism. Alan Whitehead, Labour leader of Southampton in 1984-92, argued that the year in which Southampton was hung (with Labour retaining the chairs) following a three-year period of Labour control was advantageous in this respect.

The local party dimension

So far we have emphasised the significance of group cohesiveness in the leadership role, but the task of local party cohesiveness extends beyond the party group to the local party apparatus.

Although in organisational terms the 'party group' and the 'local party' are separate, in practice there is likely to be a good deal of overlap of membership. Within any one local authority area, there will be located in whole or in part one or more parliamentary constituencies. Each of the three major parties has a level of organisation focused on the constituency – the 'constituency party'. In addition, there is a separate piece of party apparatus for the Labour Party which mirrors the definition of the authority itself – the 'local government committee'. Liberal Democrats can now establish local parties on local authority boundaries if they so wish. In each party, local councillors are often active at constituency level and not infrequently hold office at this level; some indeed have been parliamentary candidates for a local constituency (and in a few cases – eg Graham Tope – MPs). Similarly, in relation to the Labour Party, councillors may be active members (and office-holders) of the Local Government Committee (LGC) and will typically be well represented during the time when the local party manifesto is being drawn up. In addition, 'observers' from the LGC (or equivalent) have the right to attend all-party group meetings with a level of representation equivalent to one third of the party group membership. In the Conservative and Liberal Democrat Parties the arrangements are more flexible, but the attendance of constituency chairperson, party agents or similar local party activists at group meetings is by no means uncommon. With such patterns of overlap, there may in all parties be very little difference in ideological or policy orientation between party group and local party. However, there are still situations in local Labour Party networks where the differences are overt and observers from the local party have been marginalised at group meetings.

No party leader can ignore the local party network, and in the case of the Labour Party in particular major differences of view can and do become problematical. The LGC, or its equivalent, has a particularly important role at election time, in relation both to the manifesto and to the selection of candidates, although here its influence has been reduced since its power to remove sitting councillors from the list of approved candidates was withdrawn in the late 1980s. It can also nominate individuals for party group leadership, a practice that had benefited at least two of our interviewees: John Battye of Oldham and Alan Whitehead of Southampton. Graham Stringer, the Labour leader of Manchester City Council from 1984-97, was also helped in his leadership bid by his power base in the city party (see Wainwright, 1987).

Where district parties (or LGCs) have been influential in helping a leader to gain power, there is typically a strong predisposition (and at the very least a moral obligation) on the part of the leader to keep in close consultative contact with the LGC. But even for Labour leaders who do not owe that kind of special allegiance, the benefits of taking the relationship with the LGC seriously are often clearly perceived. In cities with a long tradition of party activism there is always the potential for an important difference of view, particularly over a manifesto issue, which could be damaging to party cohesiveness. Such differences can often be 'managed' if identified early enough. It is when they take a leader by surprise that problems arise; hence the preparedness of busy leaders (and other members of leadership group) to put in time with local parties.

The potential flashpoints for Labour leaders are the formulation and interpretation of the local party manifesto. If the document that emerges is strongly influenced by the pragmatism of experienced councillors, leaders and leadership groups can normally live with it; indeed, they may feel a positive sense of ownership. If, however, the manifesto formulation process is dominated by a group of party members with a different ideological stance from that of the leader, then the document that is produced is unlikely to be acceptable to the leadership. The power balance of the relationship is then likely to be tested through a series of conflicts over the implementation of the manifesto, a process well illustrated by the pressure from local parties on party groups in 1984-85 to resist the government's rate capping limits in the 17 Labour-controlled authorities directly affected (Stoker, 1991). Local party pressure was influential in the decisions of the majority Labour groups (and ultimately councils) in Lambeth and Liverpool to delay setting a rate beyond the legal deadline, which resulted the following year in the surcharge and disqualification of the councillors concerned. That experience certainly strengthened the resolve of other Labour groups to resist local party pressure that might have similar consequences; but in areas where there was a different dominant ideology in party group and local party, respectively, the problem for leaders in managing the relationship remained. Marinetto (1997) provides a particularly fascinating insight into Labour leadership problems in Camden during the 1985-86 period.

Ultimately, if conflict becomes so firmly established that a negotiated compromise is unlikely, it is possible for a leader, and a party group, to effectively ignore the views of a district party, while going through the motions of consulting it where consultation is formally required (in the same way that a minority faction within a party group can be marginalised). In Walsall in the mid-1990s both forms of marginalisation were to be found (see Hall and Leach, 2000). But such situations are inherently unstable, and a strategy of marginalisation is high risk for a leader, given the influence – admittedly, in decline – that an LGC can have on the nomination of candidates. It is at this level that most deselections have been initiated.

Most Labour leaders interviewed had not had to face such breakdown in party–group relationships, in some cases because they had put in time and effort to limit the possibility of this happening. In cases where local party machinery is either virtually moribund or dominated by a leader's colleagues or allies, the task of maintaining group–party cohesiveness is not necessarily a demanding one. County parties in particular are relatively low-profile, springing into life every four years at election time but often virtually inactive between elections. In metropolitan local authorities, and in about one third of the shire districts, local elections are held three years out of four, which means that the district party is more likely to operate on a 'permanent' than an intermittent basis.

When a Labour group is in opposition, it is easier in one sense to maintain group–party cohesiveness because the group does not have the responsibility for actually taking decisions, and hence implementing, modifying or ignoring elements in a manifesto. There may still be ideological differences but they are not actually tested. When a Labour group is in a position of power, however, such differences are likely to become much sharper, particularly in relation to key budgetary choices.

Although the management of the group–party relationship is by no means the exclusive concern of the leader, it is an important task. A leader who loses the confidence of a local party for whatever reason is in a vulnerable position, given the centrality of such bodies in local political networks. Liverpool in the 1980s is a reminder that it is possible for the power of the local party to become absolute. As Parkinson explains:

> The district Labour Party has got in the 1980s what it never had in the 1970s, the power to actually determine the council group's policy. When adopted as candidates, members have to agree to follow district Labour Party policy if elected. If they don't agree, they do not become

candidates. The group does what the district Labour Party tells it to do.
(Parkinson, 1985, pp 26-7)

As Hall (1996, p 147) shows, the process behind the suspension of Walsall Borough Labour Party in 1995 and the subsequent fracturing of the Labour group into one official 'Labour group' of 19 members and one unofficial 'Labour group' of 15 members came about because of the influence of a Left-wing dominated Borough Labour Party which pushed a policy of local decentralisation which was far more radical than the official Labour group leadership would countenance. The Borough Labour Party lost its power to act as a shield for Left-wing councillors when the National Executive Committee (NEC) suspended it. Drastic action by the national Labour Party secured the position of a 'loyal' local leadership under threat from Dave Church's 'unofficial' Left-wing group.

For local leaders of the other parties pressures from local party machinery are typically much less significant. In so far as they impinge, it will be on an occasional rather than a regular basis. In the Conservative Party there has long been a tradition of granting the party group on the council considerable autonomy to govern (or oppose) as it thinks best. There is no equivalent requirement for regular reporting by a Conservative leader to a local party forum – and, indeed, unless the authority is coterminus with a parliamentary constituency, no forum which would be appropriate. A Conservative leader may be bombarded by advice from Central Office or buttonholed by local party activists from time to time, but otherwise is unlikely to regard group–party cohesiveness as a demanding objective. Yet the power of Conservative local parties to deselect sitting councillors does exist, and does in conflictual circumstances take place. The most likely exception to this pattern is at the time of a general election, when any policy or practice of a Conservative-controlled authority that is perceived by other party members (particularly sitting and prospective MPs and party agents) to be likely to jeopardise the election prospects of parliamentary candidates will come under particularly close scrutiny. As we have seen, the operation of Hertfordshire's minority Conservative administration in the runup to the 1987 General Election provides a good example of this phenomenon.

Otherwise, although ideological clashes locally within the Conservative Party did become more significant in the 1980s, reflecting differences between traditional and radical Conservative approaches to local governance, these clashes were normally contained within the party group, only occasionally spilling over into local party arenas. Where this happened, it was often sparked off by a particular policy issue such as the move towards grant-maintained schools, or the advent of local government reorganisation in the mid-1990s. In Wiltshire, education policy was so fractious that there were major internal splits within the Conservative group.

Liberal Democrat leaders also reported few problems of group–party cohesiveness at the local level. This is partly because until the late 1980s there were still relatively few authorities that were controlled on a majority basis by the Liberal Democrats, and hence few opportunities for challenges over the policy decisions a Liberal Democrat group was actually making. But it is also because of the much more limited propensity for factionalisation and fragmentation within local political networks in the Liberal Democrat Party. Equivalent ideological cleavages to the Right–Left divisions within the Labour Party and wet–dry forms of conservatism have not often emerged. In addition (as in the case in the Conservative Party), there is usually no piece of Liberal Democrat Party machinery coterminous with the local authority. In these circumstances group–party cohesiveness issues for Liberal Democrat leaders are typically centred in personality differences or one-off policy issues such as a controversial planning decision.

The chief executive–leader interface

The public perception of a local authority's organisational cohesiveness normally focuses on relationships within and between party groups and local party networks. It rarely extends into the domain of officers and member–officer relations, unless there is a particular *cause célèbre*. The conventional wisdom – still quoted by many officers – is that officers are there to 'serve the administration', whatever its political complexion, to help it achieve its objectives and ensure the smooth-running of the authority.

Although it is true that leading officers rarely enter into public conflict with leading politicians or one another, and so in that sense the public face of organisational cohesiveness is rarely compromised, the pattern of relationships between members and officers is as important a dimension of cohesiveness as it is of the other three key leadership tasks. And although the task involves a much wider group than the leader and chief executive, the relationship between these two individuals acts as a fulcrum for the wider set of relationships – so much so that the achievement of organisational cohesiveness can be made much more likely by an effective leader–chief executive relationship, and its achievement fundamentally hindered by an unsatisfactory or ineffective one. To quote Islington's chief executive, Eric Dear:

> It is vital that the Leader and the Chief Executive are seen to be on the same side and that it is the winning side. In my view the Council cannot work effectively unless the Leader and Chief Executive understand and complement each other and respect and are comfortable with each other. If they are not and cannot reach that position, then one of them needs to move on. (Dear, 1996, p 5)

Geoff Filkin, when chief executive of Reading, emphasised (1990, p 46) that "the Leader has a role in affirming the Chief Executive's responsibility over Chief Officers and their services". Reciprocity is the order of the day. As Camden's chief executive saw it (in 1995), "you are the political interface, particularly with the leader" (see Marinetto, 1997, p 13), a point emphasised by Coventry's chief executive in 1997, Iain Roxburgh: "The relationship between chief executive and leader shapes the way the authority is run. I wouldn't have the job if I didn't think I could work with the leader".

The crucial nature of the relationship between leader and chief executive was widely recognised by both types of respondent. Their roles are mirror images of each other. The leader is concerned about cohesiveness, strategic direction, external relations and task achievement largely, though not wholly, from a political perspective, while the chief executive is concerned about similar objectives though from an organisational perspective. The leader normally relies on the chief executive as a key ally in task achievement, relying on him/her for support and cooperation; and the chief executive adopts a similar position in relation to the leader for the parallel organisational tasks. When the relationship works effectively, there is an influence felt throughout the political/ organisational culture – as indeed there is if it does not. Norton (1991, p 38) showed that over two thirds of chief executives (69%) met the leader at least twice a week, and more than one in five met him/her at least daily. Some 71% of chief executives described their relationship with the majority group leader as very good; under 5% described the relationship as less than good.

But if the roles are in one sense mirror images, there is also an asymmetry about them, as implied above. For a leader is concerned primarily about the objectives of one element in the world of the local authority, namely the majority party group (assuming there is one), whereas the chief executive is concerned primarily about the welfare of the organisation as a whole – all the party groups and the council's body of employees. The different emphasis is not necessarily problematical: it is possible, and indeed not uncommon, for the two agendas to be mutually compatible and achievable. But there are potential problems. For example, the organisational cohesiveness of the officer structure is of little concern in principle to a leader so long as the majority group's political objectives are being achieved, though it is of crucial importance to the chief executive. And correspondingly, the problems a leader may be having with a local party are of little concern to a chief executive unless the problems impinge upon the clarity and consistency of political direction. The leadership role of the chief executive is particularly significant at time of change. As the Audit Commission argues:

> He or she must be both the authority's centre of continuity and its agent of change. This means managing the interface between politics and management, converting policy and strategy into action, developing processes, people and management skills to ensure that the authority is capable of delivering its strategy, reviewing its performance against stated objectives and thinking and planning for the future. (Audit Commission, 1989, p 16)

Leach et al (1994, p 123) argue that "The Chief Executive has a crucial role to play in the process of transformational leadership". This must be done in conjunction with the leadership of the political group in control. The advent of a large number of hung authorities in the 1990s has meant that the political–management role of the chief executive has become particularly important. Local political leadership ideally requires good working relationships between senior officers and senior politicians – an aspiration that cannot always be achieved. For example, when Ken Livingstone became leader of the GLC, officers identified as having no sympathy with the objectives of the new administration were encouraged to leave. Livingstone put it bluntly: "Most of the senior officers I was determined to get rid of – because of their simple inability to understand what we were about, their incompetence, racism or Tory sympathies – were gone within two years" (Livingstone, 1987, p 144).

Many aspects of the relationship between chief executive and leader are centred on the other key tasks (see Chapters Four to Six), but in relation to organisational cohesiveness there are three issues of particular interest: first, the barrier to organisational cohesiveness which can emerge from a difference in orientation between the chief executive and the majority party leader; second, the need for clear and consistent rules governing the respective responsibilities of members and officers; and third, the particular pressures of a situation of no overall control.

Painter and Isaac-Henry (1999) argue that, in general, the effectiveness of managerial leadership is highly dependent on political leadership. In the mid-1980s, for example, it was the new Conservative leader of Kent County Council (Tony Hart) who initially embarked on a programme of radical managerial reform, and who in 1986 chose a new chief executive (Paul Sabin) of similar mind to implement the programme. In Kirklees, John Harman, the Labour leader, was the inspiration behind the managerial changes in that authority; he, too, appointed a chief executive to help translate his vision into reality.

The relationship between the chair of a committee and the head of the related department can be an extremely powerful force in local authorities. David Bookbinder, leader of Derbyshire County Council from 1981-92, has described the phenomenon in characteristically colourful terms as a process of chairs becoming 'officered', that is, developing a set of priorities similar to those of the chief officer. Bookbinder observed:

> We have a term – being officered. The officer will get hold of the Chair at a pre-committee meeting, explain to the Chair what they want to do, give them a report, and the Chair will instruct the committee members to deliver what is on the paper. But a member's role is not to say yes or no to the recommendation at the end of the report. We want to say what goes into the sausage machine. We are supposed to be the creators, elected on a political philosophy. (Willis, 1990, p 24)

The potential threat to organisational cohesiveness is indirect rather than direct. The main threat is to the task of developing a strategic policy direction (see Chapter Four). However, the successful resistance on the part of chief officer–chair partnerships, either individually or more seriously collectively, to the development and implementation of strategic priorities can sometimes spill over into a threat to organisational cohesiveness in the political management structure.

The member–officer interface comprises a complex and varied set of mechanisms for passing information of various kinds (including formal and informal 'instructions' from members to officers, but not vice versa).

There are several different possible interpretations of the legitimate scope of member 'involvement', varying from the traditional 'hands-off' approach of the Tory-controlled shire county to the much more intensive (for officers) 'hands-on' approach of some Labour-controlled London boroughs, metropolitan district councils and unitary authorities which involve a great emphasis by Labour groups on the key task of 'making things happen', or task accomplishment. The important point in relation to organisational cohesiveness as opposed to majority group cohesiveness is not what model of member involvement is operating, but how it is regulated. Officers in authorities with a political 'hands-on' philosophy (which include several Conservative and Liberal Democrat examples, as well as Labour) have long been accustomed to detailed member involvement. It is not in itself a problem. Where it becomes a problem is either in situations where there are aspects of detailed involvement, systematically pursued by members, that are incompatible with officers' sense of their own professional administrative role (eg regular requests by chairs to change the content of reports to 'reflect political priorities') or, more commonly, where established norms of member–officer role distinctions break down on a piecemeal basis with the extent and nature of involvement varying among committee chairs (and involving examples of practices unacceptable to officers). Both situations threaten organisational cohesiveness in the officer sphere; both make the chief executive's task in this respect extremely difficult. The problem for the chief executive is to persuade the leader of the negative consequences 'for the authority' of such practices and the need for regulation, given that it is not necessarily a problem from the majority group and the leader's own perspective. The problem for the leader, assuming that he/she is so persuaded, is to convince the group members concerned (typically powerful committee chairs) that organisational interests in this respect should transcend political preferences. If the leader is not persuaded, or cannot act effectively to bring about the required changes, then the overall relationship between leader and chief executive will inevitably suffer, which in turn will further undermine the level of organisational cohesiveness and the prospects for restoring it.

The problems caused for certain officers by hands-on role interpretations by committee chairs may not even come to the attention of a leader if the chief executive is not prepared to act as a champion for the aggrieved officer. In these circumstances the status of the leader may not be affected within his/her own party group, but organisational cohesiveness in the wider sense will suffer. If a set of assumptions and operating procedures concerning the member–officer role division can be agreed which is acceptable to both leading members and officers, even if it is different from that which prevailed under a previous administration, the problem of organisational cohesiveness will be resolved, at least until the next challenge. That is the real 'leadership task' in this problem area for both council leaders and chief executives. For many authorities the problem has not arisen. In those where it has, some leaders have been able to resolve it quickly, some with more difficulty and over a longer period of time, whereas for others resolution was not achieved until the composition of the majority group itself changed.

In a hung authority organisational cohesiveness is potentially threatened if a set of assumptions and operating procedures for dealing with the situation – in which no one party can govern the authority in a traditional sense – cannot be agreed. Lack of organisational cohesiveness is nowhere more apparent than in the 'fragmented' form of hung authority described above. Fragmented hung authorities represent something of a nightmare scenario for chief executives, which is perhaps why the scope of their brokerage skills is sometimes extended deep into the political arena. But if the chief executive is to succeed in this task, he/she will need the support of at least two of the political leaders (and, ultimately, political groups) concerned.

The question of how to act in a hung situation presents, as we have already recognised, something of a dilemma for political leaders. Leach and Stewart (1992) show that there are four distinctive political objectives that a party group has to consider in a hung situation: programme achievement, future electoral success, party distinctiveness and status rewards. The first and last of these objectives point towards inter-party cooperation and power sharing; the second and third point towards non-cooperation and opposition. Although the party group and local party are likely to have strong (and possibly different) views about the respective merits of cooperation and non-cooperation (ie to favour a particular weighting of political objectives), the leader will usually have some scope for manoeuvre; certainly his/her advice would be seriously considered. Leaders will also come under pressure, particularly from more proactive chief executives, to cooperate on forming some kind of stable decision-making arrangements and to agree explicit procedures (cf the problem of the member–officer interface above). Whatever response they make – and the potential gains and losses in relation to the political objectives are ultimately a matter of political judgement – the leadership task then becomes one of persuading the group of the desirability of the option and, assuming the advice is accepted, making the arrangements work. Taking part in a shared administration involves a periodic need to keep group cohesiveness and organisational cohesiveness in some kind of balance.

Conclusion

Different leaders have followed different strategies regarding the stance of the party group in a hung authority, and often have had to make major changes in strategy to respond to the inherent instability of the hung situation. In particular, the issue of when to withdraw cooperation, or go into opposition, has arisen regularly. The problems of political leadership in hung authorities differ markedly in nature, depending on the local political culture. It therefore follows that there can be no universal panacea in the context of maintaining group and organisational coherence. Thus, regular 'leaders' meetings' might be helpful in one context but not in another; written conventions similarly. A crucially important leadership skill is an ability to read the range of possibilities *in the circumstances* and to work to extend the scope of what is possible.

FOUR

Developing strategic direction

Introduction

All the writers who have developed classifications of leadership tasks (see Chapter One) have identified a task that reflects some conception of the idea of institutional purpose. Clarence Stone (1995, pp 96-7) argues that "leadership revolves around purpose ... indeed ... a compelling statement of mission not only gives direction to a group, but is its formative experience". Selznick (1957) identifies both 'the definition of institutional mission and role' and 'the institutional enhancement of purpose' as functions of institutional leadership. Kotter and Lawrence (1974) identify agenda setting as a key mayoral process, and argue that this can (and perhaps should) take the form of 'long-range proactive rational planning'. All these writers, despite different terminology, are making similar points. The development of an institutional sense of direction (or organisational purpose, strategy or mission) is a key leadership task, and something that good leaders would be expected to take seriously.

The fact that various academics define a leadership task as important does not of course mean that it will be perceived as such by a particular local authority leader. The history of local government has involved the gradual accumulation of specific service functions (education, social services, public sector housing, town planning), a process counteracted since 1945 (and especially since 1985) by the loss of service functions (or particular elements thereof, such as higher education). This service emphasis means that there have been many examples of local authorities that have seen running services as their key task, and have not necessarily perceived the need for a *corporate* strategy. Service policies or strategies have long been a familiar part of the local political process, with the formal responsibilities for policy being widely accepted as a member role (even if on many occasions policy has been heavily influenced by officer advice), while formal responsibility for its implementation is accepted as an officer role (even though many members are much more at ease with issues of policy implementation and regularly stray into that arena). But the need for a corporate strategy above and beyond an authority's individual service strategies and policies was frequently unrecognised until recently, especially in the more traditional shire counties and rural shire districts. This perception that a corporate strategy was not necessary was typically shared by leaders and party groups alike. Thus, particularly in the interviews that we carried out with leaders in 1990 and 1991, while recognition of the importance of maintaining group and organisational cohesion, external relations and task accomplishment was widespread, recognition of the significance of developing strategic policy direction was often absent.

This is not to say, of course, that such leaders did not play a major part in the strategic decisions facing the authority. All authorities have to make strategic decisions, for example, in the allocation of resources between services in the annual budget, the reaction to external circumstances such as a threatened local plant closure (or indeed the potential closure of a major theatre) or the choice of how to respond to compulsory competitive tendering (CCT) requirements (strive for in-house provision?) or the Local Government Commission (LGC) (unitary status or retention of two-tier?). However, there is a major difference between authorities that react to the need to make such choices in a short-term incremental fashion, and those that do so within the framework of an explicit longer-term corporate strategy, which explores the links between such choices. All leaders are likely to become involved in strategic choices; but many have not in the past given priority to a proactive involvement in strategic policy direction at the corporate level.

Organisational theorists such as Selznick (1957) argue that a need for an explicit strategic direction can be identified in all organisations, and that if it is not developed the organisation will not be as effective (in terms of other performance goals) as if it had one. John Stewart regularly made this argument in relation to British local authorities at a time when this 'service delivery' perspective dominated (Stewart, 1983, 1988). But over the past 10 years it can be argued that the case for a corporate strategic policy direction has become much stronger, and that the strength of this case has increasingly been perceived. If there was a genuine debate about the extent to which a corporate strategy could 'add value' in the 1970s, and early 1980s, the climate in which local authorities now operate has been transformed since that era.

Gone are the old certainties concerning the public benefits of good professional practice, the annual budgetary increment, the self-sufficiency paradigm in relation to service provision and the blurring of client and contractor roles. For much of the 1990s, the climate facing all local authorities included the following elements:

- severe central government-imposed financial constraint, reaching crisis proportions in increasing numbers of authorities and in the vast majority implying the need for real cuts in expenditure;
- the requirement to introduce client–contractor or purchaser–provider distinctions in an increasing range of service areas, resulting in an increasing challenge to the self-sufficiency of traditional service departments and sometimes leading to a business unit dominated form of organisational structure;
- an expectation that local authorities should operate more entrepreneurially, in partnership (or through contracts) with a wider range of external organisations, whether public, private or voluntary sector, to respond to local issues;
- a wider scope and greater degree of explicitness within the local manifestos and policy agendas of all the major parties (although there has admittedly been some retreat in this respect from the 'socialism in one borough' rhetoric of the mid-1980s (see Leach and Collinge, 1998, p 12).

The collective impact of all these forces has been to change fundamentally the case for the introduction of a corporate strategy dimension into the affairs of local authorities, from an 'optional extra' to a necessity. The interplay of the four processes identified above – financial constraint/ crisis, the fragmentation of service roles, the enhanced entrepreneurial dimension involving closer links with external organisations and the growing explicitness and breadth of political agendas – has resulted in the opening up of a number of fundamental choices regarding the very role and purpose of local authorities.

The case for strategic policy direction was highlighted in the influential LGMB publication *Fitness for purpose* (1994), which argued that there are three key dimensions to the choices:

- the extent to which the local authority wishes to exercise a wider role in local governance;
- the degree to which the authority wants to introduce market mechanisms into its operations;
- the relative importance the local authority puts on service to individuals and service to communities, and the meaning it gives to 'community'.

Depending on the pattern of choices made, it was argued, different 'ideal types' of local authority could be identified (eg commercialist, neighbourhood-oriented).

The election of the Labour government in May 1997, and the publication of the White Paper *Modern local government: In touch with the people* in July 1998 (DETR, 1998b) further strengthened the case for the development of strategic policy direction. Indeed, it would now take the most obdurate of authorities and leaders to ignore it. The idea of 'community governance' and 'community leadership' is openly advocated in the White Paper as a 'role model'. Councils are "the organisations best placed to take a comprehensive overview of the needs and priorities of their local areas and communities and lead the work to meet those needs and priorities in the round" (para 8.1). The government intends to ensure that "councils are able to take the lead in developing a clear sense of direction for their communities, and building partnerships to ensure the best for local communities" (para 8.7). There is an intention to introduce legislation "to place on councils a duty to promote the economic social and environmental well-being of their areas and to strengthen councils' powers to enter into partnerships" (para 8.8). There will also be a new duty to secure the development of a comprehensive *strategy* for promoting the well-being of their areas – the *community plan* (paras 8.12-8.16). These measures signal very strongly the government's commitment to 'strategic policy direction'. They provide an incentive for all local authority leaders to involve themselves in this key task. In practice, many of them had been doing so for several years, and the cumulative development of corporate strategies in local government was apparent before the publication of the White Paper (see Leach and Collinge, 1998). The issue now is not whether strategic policy direction is recognised as a key leadership task, but how it is carried out.

Different forms of strategy

Three different elements of 'strategic direction' can be identified:

- *Core values*, which are expressions of the desired *culture* of the authority, the way it wishes to behave in relation to its own staff, the public and outside organisations. The term 'mission statement' is often used to label the document that expresses the core values.
- *A strategic vision*, which sets out the *agenda of problems, issues or objectives* the authority wishes to address, and which transcends the duties and activities in relation to specific services within the organisation.

- *Strategic responses,* which constitute the unavoidable *reactive* element of corporate strategy – how to respond to the *unanticipated* issues which impinge upon the authority on a regular basis (eg the announcement of the intention to close an industrial plant which forms a key element in the local economy).

Leaders would expect to be centrally involved in each of these different processes. As we noted earlier, leadership involvement in strategic responses has been commonplace even in authorities that have eschewed explicit corporate strategies. Although mission statements as defined above are now widespread, it has to be said that they rarely evoke much leadership energy or commitment. Typically, they are drawn up by officers (eg the chief executive), formally approved without much discussion by the council, and then increasingly ignored. Major changes of organisational culture do take place – for example, the widespread move to a greater degree of customer responsiveness in service delivery – but rarely as a direct result of the formal adoption of a mission statement. It is in relation to the development of the substantive vision of an authority that a leader is more likely to be committed, or at least involved. His/her main colleagues in the leadership group are more likely to channel their interests into the strategy and policy for activities covered by the service committees that they chair. The same is true of chief officers or directors. Thus, if the leader on the members' side and the chief executive on the officers' side do not make the running in relation to the strategic policy direction at the corporate level, no one else is likely to do so.

The political context of strategic direction

If a leader perceives the case for an explicit strategic policy direction in the affairs of a local authority, or is persuaded by an articulate chief executive (who occupies a parallel position vis-à-vis other chief officers to that of the leader vis-à-vis his/her 'leadership group' colleagues), that perception may not necessarily be shared by party colleagues on the council. 'Strategic policy direction' is not neutral in political terms. If applied effectively, it can redistribute costs and benefits among different political interests.

Consideration of electoral success may override the consistent application of a corporate strategy, particularly as the next election approaches. That is why it is not illogical, in political terms, for resources to be allocated prior to a local election in a way that seems inconsistent with strategic priorities. It may, for example, be politically more important at such times to develop a higher profile in marginal wards than to follow the logic of a corporate strategy. Indeed, the concept of strategic direction may sometimes encompass specifically party political dimensions, such as winning a local constituency in a general election (see the case study of Lewisham on pages 80-2).

There is a second sense in which corporate strategies may work against political interests. A previous statement of aspirations or intentions may be referred back to with satisfaction if such aspirations are achieved, even if only partially. Such statements, however, may also act as hostages to fortune, in that they make the failure of achievement that much more obvious. Thus, although there are political advantages in explicit statements of strategic direction, there are also dangers, which are a direct reflection of the electoral vulnerability of politicians. Although it may be irrational managerially not to be explicit about intentions, it is not necessarily irrational politically. Political and managerial logic are by no means synonymous. Thus, one would expect, in any discussion about strategic planning, that politicians may wish to leave a greater scope for short-term manoeuvring and to be less explicit about intentions (though no less ready to publicise achievements) than officers would be.

These two exemplifications of political rationality affect leaders and non-leaders alike in a majority party. The group (and party) need the flexibility to switch resources to increase the choices of electoral success; and mismatches between expressed intention and reality reflect badly on both leaders and followers. But there is a third political aspect to 'strategic policy direction', where the interests of the leader and other senior councillors (especially committee chairs) may be more divergent. Until recently, the dominant basis of organisation in the majority of local authorities has been the 'department' (see Leach et al, 1994, Chapter 2). Typically there has also been a link between a 'department' of this nature and a 'committee' whose remit mirrored that of the department, a link that often resulted in a close mutually supportive relationship between chief officer and committee chair. Such departments and committees often operated in a relatively detached way from the rest of the authority. Consider, for example, the degree of autonomy associated with education departments and committees in the shire counties, before the local authority role in education was destabilised by the provision of the 1988 Education Act. Traditionally, highways and housing have often operated in a similarly detached way.

Relationships between such service-providing departments and the local authority's centre could be characterised by two features: the desire on the part of the service department to maximise its resource allocation within the authority's budget process, and its desire to enjoy as much autonomy (or discretion) as possible from central 'interference'. Terms such as 'warring baronies' and 'independent fiefdoms' were coined to characterise such proclivities.

The strength of the profession-based service department/committee system in the workings of local authorities has been challenged and often weakened by a whole range of recent changes – the devolvement of managerial and financial authority to 'unit managers', the organisational separation of client and contractor's role; the introduction of multi-service directorates and the explicit requirements placed on management team members to operate on a corporate strategic basis. However, it would be premature to argue that linked departments and committees have ceased to be significant sub-units within local authorities. First, many councils have chosen not to adopt a directorate system. Second, in those authorities that have adopted such a system, there are plenty of examples of directorates operating as super-departments, concerned predominantly with the range of services within their remit and very little with any wider corporate agenda. In some cases the directorate system amounts to little more than a thin organisational veneer with a traditional departmental system hiding behind it. The political status of committee chairs remains high in most authorities, ensuring that senior members will continue to fight the corner of their particular service committee. Indeed, most council budgets are still drawn up and scrutinised on a committee-by-committee basis. Thus, resource and autonomy battles between different service committees/ departments and the centre are still, in most authorities, a significant force; and service departments still often view corporate strategies as a threat.

Thus, a leader enthusiastic about the explicit development of a strategic policy direction, typically embodied in some form of corporate strategy or plan, will not necessarily find all his/her colleagues to be supportive. They may support the idea of such a plan, or even its publication; but when it comes to threaten the allocation of expenditure with which they have long been associated (eg as committee chairs), it may prove extremely difficult politically to follow through the implications of the new direction, particularly if it means – as it invariably will – the switch of resources from traditional service priorities to new corporate initiatives. Corporate strategy may strengthen the position of the leader (just as it does that of the chief executive) by giving him/her a legitimate basis for intervention in a range of issues – internal and external – that would be more difficult to justify if such a strategy did not exist. But these position-related interests are not necessarily shared by other key actors (members and officers) who, as noted earlier, have much to gain from a limitation of the basis of central intervention in inter-service policy coordination or budgetary allocations.

It is for these reasons that an entrepreneurial zeal is often required of a leader committed to the development of a strategic policy direction. Indeed, it may prove one of the key transformational tasks of leadership to bring about a change of attitude in a party group from hostility or indifference to this leadership task to at least an open-mindedness. This was one of John Harman's achievements (ably supported by Rob Hughes, the chief executive) in his first few years as leader of Kirklees. It was also an aim (largely achieved) of Graham Tope, Liberal Democrat leader of the London Borough of Sutton, during the Liberal Democrats' second period of office (1990-94). Because of the intrinsic importance of identifying and responding to strategic issues relating to the welfare of the authority, a leader who is able individually to dominate (in conjunction with the chief executive) the way in which the strategic agenda is responded to is in a powerful position. This is one of the ways in which there is still a significant difference between Conservative and Labour leaders: the former can and do still exercise more individual power in responding to a strategic agenda than the latter. That does not necessarily make them better leaders, for the real challenge of leadership in relation to strategic direction is to lead in a way that enables the authority as a whole to respond effectively to strategic issues in a manner that is compatible with the prevailing culture of the leader's party group. Alternatively, leaders who are more low-key and consensual in style may not have the skills or commitment to effect the requisite transformation – if, indeed, they are predisposed to attempt it in the first place.

Strategic direction in Lewisham

A pertinent example of a leader with a strategic vision, and the way in which he ensured that the authority moved towards it, emerged from interviews with Steve Bullock, the former Labour leader of the London Borough of Lewisham. The following case study describes how he operated.

When Steve Bullock became leader in 1988, he had two deputy leaders, Clive Jordan and Helen Dawson, with whom 'he totally shared a political agenda'. The long-term strategy was to turn Lewisham into a 'model borough' in the delivery of quality services, with the further political objective of winning the two parliamentary seats in the borough that were at the time held by the Conservatives. (The other seat was held by Labour.) There was a conviction that a borough that was manifestly successful in service delivery terms could be used as a platform to help win these two constituencies. Steve Bullock was aware that this strategic agenda would take a long time to fulfil, and that the challenge was to "manage the political process so that the long-term strategic plan would move onwards". The internal politics of the group (and the goal of group cohesiveness) was less important to him than the long-term plan, "so long as there were enough members who shared the vision to make it work".

In a general sense, all of the group had signed up to the leader's vision. He had presented it to the group when he first became leader, and when he felt they needed to be reminded of its existence, he would "bring it out again and they would vote for it again". Steve Bullock's perception was that most members were concerned "much more about their patches" than about the long-term strategy. Only about 15 members kept the vision to the forefront of their thinking, but this was enough. He could appeal to this grouping to support him in times of crisis and conflict within the wider group.

Steve Bullock did not get too involved in policy formulation, leaving a good deal of that task to his deputies. He saw his key roles as 'keeping control of the machine' (a process in which the chief executive was an important ally) and holding the strategy together by skilled political management. Links with other organisations in the borough were also seen as a priority, particularly when it came to mounting a City Challenge bid, where the support of partners was a key condition for success. The strategy proved successful. Lewisham gained an increasing reputation for the quality of its services and in 1993 was identified by other local authority chief executives as one of the 16 best managed authorities in England and Wales. In the 1992 General Election, both target seats in Lewisham were won by Labour. Steve Bullock stood down from the leadership in 1993.

This brief case study is instructive in a number of ways. It shows how a long-term strategic view may be held quite explicitly by a leader and become the main reference point for subsequent actions (although this is by no means true of all leaders). It shows that key elements in a strategic direction may reflect priorities in relation to an authority's own responsibilities ('delivery of quality services'), but may also have a party political dimension ('helping to increase the chances of electoral success at a general election'). In Lewisham, these two objectives were closely interconnected; but, whereas the former regularly appeared in public statements of the borough's priorities, the latter never did. It was a tacit rather than explicit strategic priority.

The case study also shows the need for a leader to develop a degree of commitment to the strategy within the group, but that across-the-board commitment is not essential. The 15 strategic enthusiasts were enough to sustain the long-term strategy when it was threatened. Indeed, compared with other authorities, that is a very respectable degree of support; other leaders have had to settle for perhaps half-a-dozen colleagues who understood and were committed to a strategic agenda.

Influences on strategic direction

In developing strategic policy direction and, more importantly, ensuring that it impacts upon the council's activities (and budget), a leader has a strong potential ally in the chief executive, and a potentially helpful reference point in the local party, particularly in the manifesto, which the local party may have been instrumental in developing. (In the Labour Party the responsibility for the manifesto is held by the local party.)

The role of the manifesto

One of the starting points for strategic policy direction is the manifesto of the majority party; indeed, as manifestos came to be taken increasingly seriously as statements of local party policy from the early 1980s onwards (particularly in the Labour Party), so they explicitly or implicitly became part of a post-election debate about strategic direction. However, as we have argued elsewhere, party manifestos are different from strategy statements. They are normally either too general or too specific (or involve a combination of both qualities), and certainly too unprioritised (with too little account taken of resource implications) to provide the clarity of direction required to provide effective mechanisms for budgetary allocation or for responding to unanticipated external pressures. Some leaders have ensured that one of the first acts of a newly elected council is to adopt the manifesto of the majority party as 'council policy' (eg David Bookbinder in Derbyshire in 1981). This action, however, blurs the distinction between party manifesto and strategic direction and ignores the detailed work that is necessary to translate the former into the latter. Indeed, it is interesting to note that in Derbyshire there was a view that an effective strategic direction was never actually established over the 1981-89 period to give coherence to the many controversial political actions in which David Bookbinder's administration became involved.

However it is essential that, in authorities where the manifesto is taken seriously, there should be a clear relationship between manifesto and strategic direction if the strategy is to achieve a sense of political ownership. A further task for the leader therefore is to manage the translation process, which is likely to involve negotiation between senior officers (emphasising issues such as resource constraint, legality, practicability and existing commitments) and leading members (emphasising political values and priorities). It is primarily the leader who has the task of ensuring that, while the latter are not sacrificed in the interests of financial availability or legality, they are tempered by what is practicable, so that the strategic direction that emerges has some chance of being effective (ie implementable).

The credibility of the process, and its ultimate likely success, is considerably enhanced if, in this process of transforming a manifesto into a strategic policy direction, the leader can involve and gain the commitment of other members of the leadership group. If this is possible, then the chances of acceptance by the party group as a whole are considerably enhanced.

If the leader encounters resistance from leading colleagues, links with the local party may prove helpful. In 1986, the Rochdale District Labour Party manifesto contained a commitment to decentralisation as a key strategic priority. That commitment was shared by the leader, Richard Farnell. When faced with resistance from committee chair colleagues to the actual implementation of this priority, he ensured (not too blatantly, however) that the district party kept up the pressure on the council to implement decentralisation. That pressure – partly engineered by the leader, partly a force in its own right – was successful in giving impetus to the implementation of this key strategic priority (see Chapter Eight). In other situations, however, a leader is more likely to be seeking ways of resisting pressure from the local party to develop strategies (or respond to strategic choices). Several Labour leaders in the mid-1980s had to resist pressures from local parties on the council to refuse to set a rate (and in so doing to incur the possibility of surcharge and disqualification).

The leader–chief executive link

A more likely initial source of a corporate strategy is, however, the chief executive. Although there are sometimes situations where the leading 'strategic champion' on the officer side is not the chief executive himself/herself, but an assistant chief executive, or head of a policy unit, to whom the task is effectively delegated, the most common situation is for a leader–chief executive partnership to constitute the dominant driving force for strategy formulation.

If the leader is the major potential champion of strategic initiatives on the member side, it is equally true that the chief executive is the major potential strategic champion on the officer side. A 'strategic direction' serves a chief executive's interests (both as a reflection of the significance of the role and as a potential source of influence on the management of the authority), just as the position and influence of a leader is enhanced by such association. Leaders lack the service-based rationale for their role that is enjoyed by chairs of service committees. They need the support of a corporate strategy as a basis for intervention.

The crucial nature of the leader–chief executive relationship is well illustrated in relation to corporate strategy initiatives. At best, the synergy between the two roles can become the 'driving force' for strategy. As Leach and Collinge argue:

> This sense of driving force can be particularly strong in relatively small shire districts, where the combination of a powerful leader with a strategic vision and a chief executive who shares it is a formidable combination indeed. In shire districts, which have a relatively limited range of responsibilities compared with other types of authority, it is possible for both leader and chief executive to have an overall grasp of the authority's business. This capacity is much more difficult to develop in a shire county or metropolitan district, where the demands on leaders and chief executives in this respect are much greater as they encompass education, social services and structure planning in addition to a range of other services. This does not mean, of course, that the effectiveness of the relationship is any less crucial to the welfare of the authority. (Leach and Collinge, 1998, p 59)

Joint participation in strategic direction comprises one of two implicit bargains (based on mutual interest) that underpin the leader–chief executive relationship (the other is 'information exchange' – see Chapter Six). Chief executives will invariably concede the right of the majority party or 'administration' to play the lead role in strategic direction if it so wishes. What they require is that they and other chief officers should have the opportunity to influence the process so that the political choices made are fully informed. Hence the potential benefits of the informal member–officer discussion forums at whatever level they operate. Leaders can benefit in this respect from the edge that briefings from chief executives give them, in the task of persuading the leadership group and party group of the case for a particular course of action. The ability to come up with workable, politically acceptable proposals to deal with problems can only strengthen the leader's reputation and authority within the group.

If there is a mutual acknowledgement of the interdependency of leader and chief executive in relation to this (and other) key tasks, then any problems faced by the leader, or the chief executive, will be more readily acknowledged – problems experienced by a leader, for example, in controlling or predicting the views of an unstable or factionalised group; or problems experienced by a chief executive in retaining the commitment of a maverick chief officer to a strategic direction. Both leaders and chief executives know that they have much to gain from sustaining the relationship and that they would be in an extremely vulnerable position if it broke down.

Strategic direction in hung authorities

In a hung situation, where there is some form of cooperation, however limited, between some or all of the party groups, the main focus for responding to strategic issues is the informal inter-party leadership group, attended also by the chief executive and sometimes other chief officers. Because strategic directional issues are by definition of high political salience, even in hung situations where there is a minority administration (one party holding all the chairs and vice chairs) it will not be possible for the leader and chief executive to formulate responses (even if the leader's party found this acceptable) in a way that may be possible in a situation of majority control. In a situation where no one party or coalition is seen as 'forming the administration', there is a particularly urgent need for the chief executive to have a 'sounding board', where the authority's response to strategic issues can be explored informally and the political feasibility of different responses evaluated. In most hung authorities there is a regular informal 'leaders meeting', which will usually involve all the party leaders, but from which one (oppositional) party sometimes excludes itself. This group is the equivalent of the majority party leadership group. Studies of the operation of hung authorities (see Leach and Stewart, 1992) demonstrate differences in the effectiveness of cross-party leadership groups, which reflect the extent to which all leaders are prepared to take part in a full and frank discussion to strive to reach agreement, and then to try to persuade (at the very least) their groups to accept the preferred course of action. Conservative leaders sometimes express surprise at the problems Labour and Liberal Democrat leaders have in these circumstances of committing their groups in advance. But this 'problem' only reflects differences in the political culture of the different groups; the key leadership task for Labour and Liberal Democrat leaders is similar in principle to that experienced in conditions of majority control, namely to find an acceptable balance between the interests of the authority (in relation to strategic direction) and the interests of the party (in relation to group cohesiveness).

It is hardly surprising that party groups with strong emphasis on internal group democracy will often be suspicious of all-party leadership groups in a hung situation. The potential scope for 'deals', tacit agreements and the orchestration of outcomes by the chief executive is widely and justifiably perceived. Thus, Labour leaders who refuse to commit themselves to options about which there is a consensus at a personal level among all members of an all-party leadership group, and insist upon taking them back to their own colleagues for discussion, are not behaving irrationally: they are attempting to strike an acceptable balance between party cohesiveness and strategic direction. Sometimes even within these constraints the latter can be achieved reasonably effectively. Sometimes, however, party cohesiveness suffers because of an emphasis on the strategic direction, or strategic direction may be sacrificed in the interests of party cohesiveness.

As is true in relation to many aspects of the work in hung authorities, negotiation skills on the part of the leader (assuming a leader exists) are of crucial importance in developing a coherent strategic direction. This outcome is possible in hung situations, as the case study of Robert Parker's leadership in the hung county of Lincolnshire between 1993 and 1997 shows (see Chapter Eight). However, in hung authorities dominated by 'rancorous politics', such an outcome can be almost impossible to achieve.

Conclusion

We have argued that a strategic agenda faces all local authorities, whether they recognise it or not. For a council leader, the challenge is to blend a political agenda (concerned with profile, public image and future electoral prospects) with a strategic agenda that develops a response to the key corporate challenges facing the authority. In identifying and responding to such an agenda, the chief executive is frequently a key ally. A 'strategic direction' will often challenge other interests within the party group, for example, the autonomy (and budget) of service committees (often closely guarded by their chairs) and the need for political flexibility and 'local discretion', particularly as a local election approaches. Thus, the development and application of a strategic direction will often require real skills of political management and presentation. In this process, a leader is considerably aided by a group of strategic supporters, which is unlikely to constitute a majority of the group but can provide an invaluable supportive resource if the strategy hits problems.

FIVE

External relations

Introduction: the changing context of external relations

The late 1990s is worlds apart from the days when local authorities strove directly to provide virtually all services themselves. Today a wide range of organisations is involved in service delivery; hence the 'external relations' dimension of local political leadership has become increasingly important. Local authorities now increasingly work in partnership with private-sector and non-elected local agencies. The Labour government's consultation paper *Modernising local government* emphasised the challenge this posed:

> Councils are in a unique position to take the lead in developing a vision for their locality and provide a focus for partnership in delivering that vision. But they cannot act alone. There are many other agencies and organisations that need to be involved – TECs, Probation Committees, Joint Committees, Health Authorities, executive agencies of Government, housing associations, police liaison committees, SRB partnerships, Magistrates' Courts Committees and many others. (DETR, 1998a, pp 35, 36)

In the world of local governance, a world that has witnessed the fragmentation of responsibility for service delivery, the 'external' dimension of local leadership has acquired new importance. Effective local leadership is not possible without leaders working alongside the plethora of non-elected bodies located outside the world of elected local government, and with the introduction of regional development agencies in April 1999 this pattern has become more, rather than less, complex. This chapter begins by charting the developing significance of 'external relations' at local level.

In the days when local authorities were almost monopoly service providers, 'external relations' was a much less high-profile task than it is perceived to be today. Some authorities had 'public relations' departments but the majority did not. Dealings with the press were as likely to involve chief officers as elected members, many of whom felt vulnerable when exposed to media questioning. Local government was generally less newsworthy in media terms anyway, with the emphasis being on the local rather than the national level, except for the occasional 'big stories' – such as the network of corruption centred on John Poulson (which involved several local council leaders and was publicly exposed in 1970), or the refusal by Clay Cross Urban District Council (UDC) to implement the Housing Finance Act of 1972 (which required them to raise council house rents to higher levels than they were prepared to implement) and the resulting surcharge and disqualification of the councillors concerned.

Up until the late 1970s, it was only at election time that 'external relations' became a key task for the political parties. The need to present a positive image in local media terms (the local media of the time could be equated almost wholly with local press) was the paramount consideration for party leaders. At other times, it was the more negative view of external relations – avoiding embarrassment – that tended to dominate, rather than any attempt to make use of the media in more positive or creative terms. There was, with only a handful of exceptions, little predisposition or perceived need to work with local firms or local representative organisations of industry or commerce, or voluntary associations, except when it was clearly in the interests of the authority to do so (eg in the former case in connection with a joint town centre development scheme, or in the latter if such associations were able to fill a gap in service provision in a way that was financially beneficial to the council concerned). Liaison with health authorities was a 'low-profile' activity, and even relations with other tiers of local government was something that was often regarded as an irritation rather than a positive opportunity.

From the late 1970s onwards, the 'external relations' situation was transformed by a series of changes, although outside the major urban areas these changes were much slower to make an impact. The Inner Cities initiative launched by Peter Shore in 1977 required 'lead authorities' to cooperate with a wide range of external agencies in the formulation and implementation of inner city partnerships and programmes as a condition of making extra resources available to deal with inner city problems in over 20 targeted local authorities. The 1980 Local Government Planning and Land Act required local authorities formally to consult with representative bodies of local commerce on an annual basis in relation to local authority budgets and rate levels. The economic depression and spiralling level of unemployment in the early 1980s inspired increasing numbers of local authorities to seek to play a much more proactive role in the regeneration of local economies. Labour groups dominated by the New Left had a particularly positive attitude towards working with local community and interest groups in local decision making – see Livingstone (1987) on London, and Seabrook (1984) on Walsall. And the increasingly hostile character of central–local relations (at least as far as the increasing numbers of Labour-controlled authorities were concerned) had the simultaneous effects of both increasing the news value of local government in the national media (the 'loony left' stories – largely apocryphal – in the popular press and, on a more serious note, the newsworthy battles over the abolition of the GLC and the MCCs, rate-capping and council house sales) and motivating the local authorities concerned to ensure that what they were doing was at least understood, and preferably supported, by the public.

By the late 1980s the importance of external relations was well understood by local authority leaders. Indeed, almost all the legislation passed during the Thatcher administration required local authorities to take external relations much more seriously, whether with external contractors (CCT), housing associations (1988 Housing Act), urban development corporations, local industry (TECs, City Challenge) or health authorities (1990 NHS and Community Care Act). During this period also the local authority associations continued their increasingly high-profile role which had begun to develop in the early 1980s, both as key actors (and mediators) in the central–local conflict arena and as sources of advice to local authorities about how to deal with the increasingly demanding legislative programme. In a large majority of authorities the amount of political time and energy that was spent by leaders in external networks grew.

Undoubtedly, a good deal of external networking activity is not a leadership task – either in member or officer terms – and can be delegated accordingly (eg via membership and servicing of some of the more routine arrangements instituted in the metropolitan areas following the abolition of the MCCs in 1986). However, in situations in which the authority is seeking to persuade an external agency of significant size and status to cooperate in a joint venture, there is an important symbolic dimension to the status of who attends meetings from the local authority side. The presence of the leader (and/or chief executive) symbolises one level of commitment; their absence and replacement by deputies, another. Thus, although there is some scope for delegation, there is often pressure on leaders to exercise this 'leadership task' on a personal basis, whatever their own personal predilections for this kind of activity. Indeed, in the more urban and politicised authorities, the increasing significance of this task is one of the key influences pushing leaders towards a full-time or almost full-time leadership role. Table 5.1 is a reminder of the extent of the local quango state, part of the world of local governance, which local political leaders are unable to ignore. By 1996 there was at least 10 times as many unelected local executive quangos as there were elected councils.

Table 5.1: The local quango state

Type of quango	Number
Recognised executive quangos (or NDPBs) including urban development corporations and housing action trusts	33
NHS hospital trusts	521
'Non-recognised' local executive quangos	
Careers service companies	91
City technology colleges	15
Further education corporations	560
Grant-maintained schools	1,103
Higher education corporations	175
Housing associations	2,565
Local enterprise companies	22
Police authorities	41
TECs	81
Total	**5,207**

Source: Wilson and Game (1998, p 142)

There are a number of different aspects of the 'external relations' role which require different skills and may have different priorities in the activities of the authority. Useful distinctions can be drawn, for example, between media relations, the national world of local government, and networks with local economic and community interests. These different areas of external activity are considered in sequence[1].

Media relations

Relatively few leaders or local authorities seek the attention of the national media on a regular basis. When they are focused upon it, it is usually because they are seen as symbolic of a genre (the loony left; the 'privatising' right) and because the leader has a media-exploitable persona. Ken Livingstone enjoyed a long period of attention on this basis, as did, in a more limited sense, Bernie Grant, Margaret Hodge, Ted Knight and Lady Shirley Porter. The predictable London dominance of such symbols was challenged only by Derek Hatton, in the very special circumstances of a Militant-dominated Liverpool City Council between 1983 and 1985, and David Blunkett in Sheffield. Significant national media attention was also occasionally experienced by the chair of the Local Government Association at the end of the 1990s (Sir Jeremy Beecham of Newcastle upon Tyne), but that is a reflection of his national position rather than local circumstances.

For most other authorities, national media attention descends only in special circumstances – a crisis such as a serious child abuse case, evidence of serious fraud or financial mismanagement, or a more positive initiative of national interest such as a bid to stage the Olympic Games. In a crisis, the small size, obscurity or remoteness of an authority is no barrier to the spotlight, as the Orkneys (child abuse), West Wiltshire (fraud) and the Western Isles (financial mismanagement) found to their cost. Manchester's Olympic bid gave the authority and its leader, Graham Stringer, a high profile for a period of about six months, but it is difficult to identify many parallel cases. 'Bad news' or a 'crisis' is sadly a much more likely cause for a one-off appearance on the national media agenda. In 1997, for example, three cases involving high-profile scandals in Labour-run councils were given considerable space in the national media, invariably drawing the local political leadership into the fray:

- *Renfrew District Council, August 1997* Two councillors were suspended by the Labour Party in an investigation into allegations that community business FCB was a front for drug peddling and money laundering.
- *Doncaster MCC, February 1997* District auditor sparks off 'Donnygate', with report criticising perks abuses; by January 1999 12 serving or former Doncaster councillors had been arrested in what turned out to be a long-running police investigation into corruption.
- *Glasgow City Council, February 1997* Leader Bob Gould alleged that councillors had traded support in return for junkets; some 17 councillors faced disciplinary action by the Labour Party's NEC.

By far the most high-profile case in recent years involving a local political leader concerned Dame Shirley Porter, Conservative leader of Westminster City Council between 1983-91. In a case much more to do with political power than personal financial gain, Dame Shirley and five councillor and officer associates were found guilty by a local government district auditor of operating a housing sales policy specifically for the electoral benefit of the Conservative Party, thereby costing their council many millions of pounds. In late 1997 the courts upheld the findings of the district auditor against Dame Shirley Porter although she won an appeal in 1999.

Dame Shirley had a distinctive leadership style that fed off the media. It was a very dominant style, as portrayed below:

> "I am synonymous with Westminster City Council. In my years as leader I've tried to change the culture at the Council but ... it's like taking the British Empire and turning it into Great Britain plc. You're changing a cosy establishment of both members and officers."

Her leadership at Westminster City Council was summed up by a badge she liked to wear, saying 'YCDBSOYA':

> I'll give you the polite version. It means 'You Can't Do Business Sitting On Your Armchair'. My father, Sir Jack Cohen, who built the Tesco supermarket chain, gave one to Callaghan and one to Heath, but I haven't had the temerity to give one to Mrs Thatcher yet. (Abdela, 1989, p 186)

The then Prime Minister used to figure regularly in Dame Shirley Porter's networks, and there were some striking similarities between the two women's proactive leadership styles. A skilful use of the media was one such common theme.

Such a highly personalised view of leadership would be much more difficult to sustain in the other two parties, certainly nowadays. Individualistic, let alone autocratic, leadership has become unfashionable and politically risky. Leaders will usually take considerable care to carry their party groups with them, and particularly to talk the language of consensus, teamwork and – to use a favourite expression of Birmingham's longstanding Labour leader into the 1990s, Sir Richard Knowles – 'comradeship'.

In circumstances of sustained national media attention, the 'authority' is invariably equated with its leader, and the latter usually has little choice but to take the burden of responsibility in this connection (unless it is clearly a specialist matter). In the case of a brief spell of national media attention, the appearance of the leader as the authority's spokesperson would normally be expected. Such opportunities do not, however, occur often in the life of a leader, particularly outside London.

Local media interest nowadays normally centres on the local press, local radio and the regional TV news programmes. There is rather more scope for selectivity here. If the 'local press' is a provincial daily/evening paper (eg *Liverpool Post and Echo, Yorkshire Post, Newcastle Journal*) it is more likely that the leader will wish to play a dominant personal role than if the local press is a low-profile (or free) weekly. Increasingly, local authorities are faced with the absence of the former and sometimes the absence of the latter. In the 1960s and 1970s that might have been a cause for relief; in the 1980s and 1990s, however, the reaction is much more likely to be one of regret, particularly where the local authority has a crusading zeal and wants to get its message across. Local media and, in particular, regional television are usually seen nowadays as providing more important media opportunities (some local authorities now have media studio facilities within their premises) and are correspondingly more likely to require the leader's participation, unless there is a deputy who is widely recognised to be more adept at handling such opportunities, the most notable recent example being Derek Hatton in Liverpool.

The general attitude of a leader to the media will depend very much on the juxtaposition of personal skills/preferences of the leader and the political circumstances of the authority. If a newly elected group feels vulnerable in respect of the local media, then there is likely to be a high premium placed on 'getting our message across' or 'putting the record straight'. If the leader relishes such opportunities, he/she will be likely to exploit them beneficially. Even where there is no particular personal enthusiasm for media exposure, many leaders feel a sense of responsibility if a local issue attracts media attention, and so will respond positively. Conservative leaders are less likely to share or delegate this type of responsibility because of the way in which the leadership task is traditionally seen within Conservative groups. Bob Osborne, leader of the Conservative group on the hung Leicestershire County Council in the late 1990s, exemplified this perspective:

"External relations are not important. The Conservative group have not discussed external relations and there is no intention to do so.... The main role of members is to ensure that they are re-elected."

In Labour groups the idea of sharing or delegation is more likely to be acceptable, or indeed even encouraged. In this case, however, leaders are likely to experience resistance from media representatives who are more wedded to the status implications of the formal leadership position, particularly in relation to 'authority-wide' issues. (Chairs are generally acceptable on service specific matters.)

In the more traditional shire counties and districts, and in many hung authorities, the officers may still be permitted to play a dominant role in media relations. Where they do so, it is usually an indication of an officer-dominated authority. Hung authorities are particularly problematic. Referring to Leicestershire at the end of the 1990s, Professor Bob Pritchard, leader of the Liberal Democrat group, observed:

> "One of the weaknesses here in Leicestershire is that we lose out in dealings with the media because we are hung. There is a lack of focus."

Changes of political control can also result in abrupt policy change, but, even in authorities long accustomed to the domination by members of media relations, there may be newsworthy circumstances where there is an important political choice about whether to field a leading politician or officer. In relation to child abuse scandals (in particular where an authority is proved to have 'overreacted') there is an important symbolism in who is fielded to face the media. The appearance of an officer – for example, the chief executive of Rochdale in a situation with the above characteristics – signalled from the politicians' perspective a view of officer rather than member responsibility for the situation. The Labour government's 'modernisation' proposals in the 1998 White Paper elevated the profile of the leader. In this context, with the leaders increasingly becoming the 'public face' of the authority, it is likely that the media will want to target the political leader. Even in 1998, before the White Paper's proposals were implemented, leaders in cities and large towns were carefully pinpointed by the radio, TV and press. The likelihood is of this trend developing further and becoming more widespread as directly elected mayors/executive leaders take root.

The national world of local government

The Local Government Association (LGA)

From the reorganisation of local government in the early 1970s until April 1997 there were three major English and Welsh local authority associations: the Association of County Councils (ACC), representing the non-metropolitan counties; the Association of Metropolitan Authorities (AMA), representing the metropolitan districts and London boroughs; and the Association of District Councils (ADC), representing non-metropolitan districts. The councillor delegates to these bodies were usually senior members of the party or parties that controlled their own local authorities, not infrequently the party leader.

The difficult and initially reluctant decision of the three principal associations to give up their independence and create a new unified Local Government Association (LGA) was a forceful public statement that local leaders were seeking a more politically powerful and persuasive voice for local government as a whole in its dealings with central government. Sir Jeremy Beecham, former leader of Newcastle upon Tyne City Council, was the first chair of this new body, an umbrella organisation with in-built tensions between big and small, metropolitan and rural authorities, alongside the inevitable party political tensions. Some of the most scathing early criticisms of the LGA came from Bury MBC, which formally gave notice of its intention to quit at the end of the first year. John Byrne, deputy leader of the Labour-dominated council, cited fragmentation caused by competing special interest groups and the heavy-handed running of the association by senior members as the reasons for giving notice. Byrne observed:

> "We are far from happy about the way the association is shaping up. The political officers of the association have lost touch. They are undemocratic and not representing all authorities."

In total, seven English local authorities initially refused to join the LGA although one of the seven, Rushcliffe Borough Council, joined a year later. Rushcliffe's chief executive, Keith Beaumont, commented:

> We are satisfied district councils will get a proper hearing at the LGA now, and there is a more coherent approach at a regional level. We had legitimate worries last year and it was right to wait and see what was

happening. We were not satisfied that the LGA would be properly organised. (*Local Government Chronicle*, 27 February 1998, p 3)

In Wales dissent was rather more serious, with the two biggest councils – Cardiff CC and Rhondda Cynon Taff CBC – both pulling out, complaining of inflated subscription charges and excessive bureaucracy. Cardiff leader Russell Goodway said that his council was facing severe budget restrictions and had decided that front-line services should come first. But when looking for a reason for Cardiff pulling out it is difficult to ignore personal differences between Goodway and WLGA leader, Harry Jones, of Newport CBC. In June 1997 the Local Government Minister, Hilary Armstrong, emphasised the value of the LGA to a local government audience:

> "Without your single association, local government simply would not have been able to put forward its effective and coherent message in the way it has. I firmly believe the creation of a single association to represent local government is essential if you are to have an effective voice in your dealings with government."

In a similar vein, the 1998 White Paper (DETR, 1998b, p 17) highlighted the LGA as being well placed to help local authorities carry through the modernisation process.

Despite teething troubles, the LGA seems to be here to stay and several senior local political leaders occupied key posts on the LGA's executive in 1998. However, while some local authority leaders devote considerable time and energy on LGA activities, many leaders regard association meetings as extremely time consuming and relatively low priority.

The reality is that activity at LGA level has little connection with the immediate leadership tasks of a local authority, as those who occupy key association positions readily acknowledge. At the margins, it may be important in relation to strategic direction, although the extent to which a single leader can hope to influence the LGA (or, even less, central government) to adopt a particular line is of course extremely limited. But there are sometimes strategic issues – local government reorganisation being a case in point – where the linked activities of groups of leaders may have a degree of effective lobbying power, and can thereby influence association policy in a way that might help achieve local objectives (eg unitary status). There may also be marginal gains in public image terms for an authority if its leader is known to be a powerful figure in the national world of local government. But in relation to the majority of association business, the contribution to local authority leadership tasks is at best indirect and long term.

The potential benefits to leaders are more likely to be in relation to their own political careers than to their local authorities. Of the various possibilities for extending a political career beyond leadership of a local authority, one is to become an MP; another is to play a high-profile role in the national world of local government. Thus, for those who, for whatever reason, have rejected (or have so far failed to achieve) the former option, a senior position within the LGA represents the pinnacle of a political career. To be the education or social services spokesperson of the LGA is a considerable achievement in political career terms. Even for those Association activists who fail to reach such positions of potential influence, the very feeling of being part of the national world of local government is often perceived as a boost to a political career.

Other leaders, however, see their political careers predominantly in *localist* terms, and either do not aspire to a significant role in the LGA (and hence do not regularly attend) or, having begun by attending Association meetings, quickly decide that it is not a good use of their time. Time commitment is of course an important consideration for leaders. Those leaders who are 'full-time' (or nearly so) and/or those leaders whose authorities are close to London are frequently more prepared to put in time at the LGA than those who are part-time and/or would incur long journey times to London.

In a highly politicised authority, there is certainly a danger that a leader who devotes large amounts of time to Association activities (particularly if he/she also has a full-time job) becomes vulnerable to changes in party group dynamics and relationships in the authority. In these circumstances, a loyal deputy who is not involved in the national world of local government is a considerable asset.

Party political networks

There are other senses in which the national world of local government may become a relevant consideration for local authority leaders. With the exception of independent leaders in independent-dominated authorities (of which there were 18 in Great Britain in 1999), leaders as party members and activists will be part of a wider party political network which extends all the way to Parliament. Local politics in certain circumstances becomes intertwined with national politics. There are three principal ways in which such interconnections become important: through the relationship between party group activities locally and the chances of electoral success in a general election; the use of links with senior national politicians to influence national decisions; and the selective use of local authority experience as a resource by central government. The second of these possibilities is potentially much greater for a party group of the same political complexion as the national government, but there are some opportunities for party groups of a different political complexion (see below). In each case the leader is likely to be directly involved.

The link between the activities of a party locally and the electoral prospects of the same party at a national election was well illustrated by the 1987 General Election results in London, where Labour candidates performed significantly worse than the national average in boroughs such as Haringey, Hackney, Islington, Brent and Lambeth which had been the subject of 'loony left' stories (and indeed campaigns in *The Sun*, the *Daily Mail* and the *Mail on Sunday*). Particularly in marginal seats, the potential influence of a council's perceived performance is taken extremely seriously. In York and Thurrock, for example, in the 1987-92 period Labour leaders were quite explicit about the fact that 'ensuring the return of a Labour MP' was one of their key objectives (in their local authority capacity). The most likely means of achieving this objective included customer care programmes, 'responsible' policies (particularly important in Labour-controlled authorities), low levels of local taxation and good public relations mechanisms to publicise all these achievements. In authorities covered by constituencies that are viewed as 'safe' seats for one or other of the parties, such considerations would normally be of less significance (except at by-elections during periods of political volatility).

Sometimes the initiative comes from the other direction. As we have seen, in Hertfordshire in 1987 the stance of the Conservative group on the county council in holding the chairs in a hung situation was regarded as unhelpful by local Conservative MPs, and their pressure was influential in the group resigning the chairs a month before the general election.

Even outside considerations of general election success, links with national parties may from time to time become important for the local authority leader. The Labour Party in particular provides guidelines for party group behaviour, the breaking of which would be regarded as serious breaches of party discipline. Thus, Labour leaders in the metropolitan districts and London boroughs were expected to pursue policies of non-cooperation in connection with the abolition of the GLC and MCCs until the 1985 Local Government Bill received royal assent. Only in the West Midlands was this expectation unfulfilled. The Labour Party also has guidelines concerning what Labour groups should and should not do on hung authorities, which in 1985 resulted in several deputations to Walworth Road (and lobbying of the Labour Party leader) to argue the case for their being allowed to vote for a minority Alliance administrations and hence end long periods of Tory domination in counties such as Wiltshire, Cambridgeshire and Devon. The problem here for the local party leader is typically a clash between the expectations of a national party and the local strategic priorities of the group. In 1993 the guidelines were changed in a way that permitted the sharing of chairs, largely as a result of local pressure. In practice, however, the grass-roots position is rarely one in which battle lines with the centre emerge.

As the main local–national link, the leader has the responsibility of either persuading the wider party to allow local discretion or persuading the party group to accept national guidelines. This potential problem is less significant for local Conservative or Liberal Democrat leaders, whose relationships with national parties are more consultative; their national parties may seek to persuade but they have few, if any, sanctions.

If MPs of all parties sometimes put pressure on local party groups to take action that they might not otherwise choose to take, they are also a potential source of support. Sympathetic backbench MPs of any party will normally be prepared to table questions in Parliament over matters of concern to a local authority party group (of the same party) where their constituency falls wholly or mainly within the local authority area. Backbench MPs of the party in power who have no ministerial ambitions may be prepared to take up constituency issues of this nature forcefully and publicly (rate capping and Rate Support Grant [RSG] settlements are examples) against the policy of the national party leader.

For those authorities with one or more cabinet ministers or other key influentials operating within their boundaries, there are other possibilities. The scope for protest speeches in Parliament against government policy is obviously much reduced, but the potential for informal influence on the detail of government policy is correspondingly increased. John Alston of Norfolk emphasised how such informal channels were used to modify the content of the Consultation paper on Local Government Reorganisation in 1991. This potential capacity for influence depends crucially, of course, on the distribution of cabinet ministers' constituencies.

This channel of influence may become two-way. The Conservative government, which between 1983 and 1997 introduced a wide range of legislation to which the majority of authorities were hostile or suspicious, needed sympathetic advisers from the world of local government to ensure that its legislative proposals were feasible and, ideally, compatible with party interests at the local level. In this capacity, high-profile radical Conservative leaders such as Shirley Porter (Westminster), Paul Beresford (Wandsworth), John Grudgeon and Tony Hart (Kent) and Eric Pickles (Bradford) proved useful information sources. In this process of exchange, there is always the opportunity to exert influence in the opposite direction. For more traditional Conservative leaders such as Peter Bowness (Croydon) and Colin Warbrick (Trafford), there were similar opportunities from time to time. In the runup to the abolition of the GLC and MCCs, for example, both these leaders and their colleagues were able to provide invaluable information about the practicalities of managing the transition.

Links with opposition leaders and shadow ministers provide fewer such opportunities, although in relation to bipartisan initiatives – for example, the launching of the Local Government Review in 1991 – the shadow minister concerned (in this case Jack Straw) may have a degree of influence, the exercise of which can itself be affected by such central–local political links. And of course, in formal debate over the details of a piece of legislation there are opportunities for MPs to express local interests, a process that will almost certainly reflect a briefing from the local party leadership concerned.

For most local authority leaders, most of the time, there will be little or no impact from the world of national politics in any of these ways. But occasionally the need to exert influence on, or respond to, pressures from national government does arise, and where this is the case it is almost invariably in relation to an issue of high local political salience. In so far as such issues involve differences of national/local party interest, they are likely to prove challenging tests of leadership ability.

Central–local party networks

There are various types of political network that may be of importance to local authority leaders and which certainly represent potential demands on their time. In the period immediately following 1974, county–district liaison machinery was initially expected to be one such network, but in most county areas it proved to be an unrewarding arena and soon fell into oblivion. Of much greater potential significance to the leadership task was the joint machinery set up in Greater London and the six metropolitan county areas in the runup to the abolition of the GLC and six MCCs in 1986. As soon as the 1985 Local Government Bill received royal assent, coordinating committees were established in each of the seven areas concerned to establish arrangements for the transfer of the county functions. The negotiation process was very important for the constituent districts, for two reasons. First, there was the issue of how many services were to be subject to joint arrangements rather than transferred directly to the districts. (All other things being equal, authorities preferred direct responsibility for as many services as possible, rather than joint arrangements.) Second, in so far as joint arrangements were to be established, either by central government insistence (fire, police, passenger transport, and in some areas waste disposal) or by local choice, there were advantages for metropolitan districts or London boroughs in becoming 'lead authorities' for such services. The lead authority would be responsible for all back-up services, such as finance, personnel and architectural design, and it was widely believed that lead authority status gave strategic leverage in relation to services such as passenger transport and highways. As a result, all the local authority leaders concerned gave these negotiations a very high priority.

Once abolition had been implemented and the joint bodies concerned assumed formal responsibility for the services that had not been transferred directly to the districts, the role played by leaders in these joint arrangements varied depending on their perceived political salience. In Greater Manchester and West Midlands, the coordinating committee survived as a metropolitan-wide forum which was taken seriously and attended regularly by all council leaders. Those who became chairs of such committees – for example, John Battye (Oldham) in Greater Manchester and Jim Cunningham (Coventry) in the West Midlands – were much more convinced of the importance of this role than they were about involvement in the Association of Metropolitan Authorities (AMA) and were prepared to make a significant time commitment to this activity. In addition, the Manchester Airport Board regularly attracted local authority leaders because of the strategic significance of the airport and its value as a source of revenue for the authorities concerned. Being chair of the Police Joint Board sometimes had attractions for party leaders, but as time went on Joint Board chair positions were more typically filled by councillors other than leaders, who found other demands on their time more pressing.

The choice faced by local authority leaders in relation to participation of this kind is to determine how central such participation is to the authority's strategic agenda. If the strategic relevance of such activities is limited, the logical response is to delegate the responsibility. The strategic relevance of such bodies may of course vary over time; for example, the role of county branches of the Association of District Councils (ADC) in deciding which structural options to pursue with the Local Government Commission could hardly have been more strategically central to the future of the individual districts concerned. In other circumstances, however, the agendas of such bodies may be much more mundane, in which case the primary reason for the leader's participation would be the maintenance of the body's status through the symbolism of the leader's continued attendance.

Networks of local economic and community interests

As *Modernising local government* emphasised:

> The days of the all-purpose authority that planned and delivered everything are gone. It is in partnership with others – public agencies, private companies, community groups and voluntary organisations – that local government's future lies. Local authorities deliver important services but their distinctive leadership role will be to weave and knit together the contribution of the various local stakeholders. (DETR, 1998a, p 7)

Tony Blair further developed this point:

> There are all sorts of players on the local pitch jostling for position where previously the council was the main game in town – TECs, Child Protection Committees, Health Authorities, NHS Trusts, Grant Maintained Schools, Further Education Colleges, Police Liaison Committees, Police Authorities, Fire Authorities, Single Regeneration Budget Partnerships, Probation Committees, Drug Action Teams, Magistrates Course Committees, Development Agencies, Joint Planning Committees and Joint Consultative Committees. (Blair, 1998, p 10)

The advent of local governance has brought with it far greater interaction with local economic and community interests that could have been envisaged 20 years ago. The extent to which these networks generate time demands on leaders depends on both the type of authority concerned and the political ideology of the majority group. An authority's interest in the local economy may be proactive or reactive; that is, it may be concerned to stimulate economic development (through the provision of appropriate infrastructure, etc) or to respond to external pressure to carry out such developments (eg out-of-town shopping centres, 'green field' development sites).

Although most local authorities nowadays have some commitment to the stimulation of local economic activity, there is a world of difference in the emphasis placed on this activity in Sheffield as opposed to Suffolk. In authorities encompassing urban areas, particularly those with relatively high unemployment levels, this type of activity has a high profile; in authorities encompassing more rural or suburban areas, it has a much lower one. It follows that the likelihood of the significant involvement of a leader in such activities is correspondingly greater in the former type of area than in the latter.

To take Barnsley as an example: in 1997 the town's controlling Labour group elected their youngest member, Steve Houghton (then only 38), as its leader. This produced radical change, as Valley (1998, p 24) notes. Key to this was the establishment of a Business Development Agency as a private company in partnership with the Chamber of Commerce and others. As Roger Nunns, chief executive of the Chamber, observed, Houghton "had a very hard job persuading the old guard on the council to accept it. Many of the die-hards would like to revert to the old ways of command and control". Houghton himself, however, was rather more sanguine: "We cede control but gain influence". For Barnsley's 'New Labour' leader, developing relationships with organisations and businesses outside the council was a fundamentally important leadership strategy.

It is in the urban areas that partnership schemes for town – or city – centre redevelopment are most likely to be sought. Whatever the authority, however, local political leaders need to have skills in the 'management of tension'. Painter cites the leader of one London borough:

> It is important for the local authority to be clear about its role ... being the advocate for the local community as elected representatives. But you also have to recognise the importance of working with the various agencies that exist ... it's striking a balance between being too assertive and too probing ... at the same time recognising the need to work with these people. (Painter, 1996, p 20)

Nevertheless, our research indicated that external networking with economic interests was not always a particularly significant role for most leaders. The importance of the activity was invariably recognised; indeed, successful developments of this nature were seen by some leaders as among their most significant achievements. But there was no indication, even in these circumstances, that the leader played much part in the detailed negotiations involved. That was likely to be left to officers and to other committee chairs with specific responsibilities for economic development or planning. When a large development investment was under discussion (eg Toyota in Derbyshire) the leader would certainly be involved when it was felt tactically or symbolically to be beneficial (David Bookbinder, Derbyshire). The same applied to Peter Soulsby in Leicester in 1997 in the context of securing £45.7 million for a space centre from the Millennium Commission. But otherwise involvement in external economic networks was not always a major commitment. Indeed, for many leaders it did not extend much beyond occasional 'good will' contacts with the local chambers of commerce or the managers of major locally-based companies. Today, however, an increasing number of local political leaders are developing a heightened profile through having a leading role on TECs, City Challenge companies and similar joint ventures.

In relation to community groups, the type of authority also makes a difference. There tends to be a wider range of active 'community groups' in urban areas than in rural areas, although developments perceived as threatening (for example a major waste disposal site) will invariably generate a critical organised response. However, in this connection political orientation is also important. Conservative groups (and leaders) do not generally see regular contact with community groups as a significant part of their job, which reflects the dominance of the concept of representative democracy (as opposed to participatory democracy) in their ideology. They will involve themselves in extremis, but not usually otherwise.

More traditional Labour leaders often have not dissimilar attitudes. However, 'New' Labour and Liberal Democrat leaders with a positive commitment to participatory democracy take a very different stance. Some of the leaders in our research chose to spend considerable amounts of time with community groups, or at meetings in local areas, because of the importance they personally attached to such activities. This importance may reflect the desire to disseminate an understanding of what the controlling party is trying to do or a commitment to build up and support networks of community groups. In either case, this type of activity can prove a significant time commitment for leaders, but one to which an increasing proportion of leaders with a particular view of participatory democracy are strongly committed (see Lowndes et al, 1998). The Blair government's emphasis on participatory democracy means that this leadership role is likely to be further developed:

It is necessary for authorities to be open and responsive. The Government wants to see the best authorities go even further and for their best practice to become the norm across local government. Increasingly, the degree to which an authority is engaged with its stakeholders may become a touchstone for the authority's general effectiveness. (DETR, 1998a, p 23)

Conclusion

This leadership task of representing the authority in the outside world has increased in significance in recent years. The fragmented structure of community governance means that increasingly local authorities have to work in partnership with other bodies. City Challenge and Single Regeneration Budgets (SRBs) are specific central government initiatives that have encouraged such partnerships.

It is not only in economic regeneration, however, but also in a range of other policy areas (environmental sustainability, community safety, community health) that inter-agency working has become a necessary condition for progress. Thus, although the starting point for the analysis of local political leadership remains the local authority itself and the dominant coalition within it, this external representation task is growing in relative importance and occupying more of the local authority leader's time. This task requires specific leadership skills – negotiation, networking, the search for common ground – which, although by no means absent in relation to other leadership tasks, are likely to assume greater importance in the late 1990s as local authorities increasingly 'share the turf' with a large number of other agencies.

A major problem is that 'external relations' activities can take a disproportionate amount of a leader's time. In large metropolitan authorities the possibilities for external activities of this nature are very wide-ranging. But an over-emphasis on external relations may have adverse consequences for other key tasks (organisational and party group cohesiveness, strategic and policy direction, task accomplishment). Leaders who recognise this dilemma ration their time accordingly or make explicit arrangements to delegate responsibility for some external activities among colleagues. Such leaders demonstrate an essential awareness of the need for task prioritisation.

Note

[1] Technically, to complete this list, the roles of 'service-specific' networks (eg community care) should be added. However, these are typically seen as the prerogative of the service specialists (at member and officer level) and hence do not normally involve leadership in the authority-wide sense.

SIX

Task accomplishment

Introduction

Why should political leaders want to become involved in detailed decisions concerned with policy implementation or changes in management structures or practices? The traditional distinctions between policy formulation and policy implementation and between policy and management (or administration) have become well established truisms in local government. Elected members make policy, set targets and monitor progress. Officers are (or should be) left free to implement policy and manage their organisational divisions without interference from politicians unless there is clear evidence of policy or managerial failure. We emphasised in Chapter Three the extent to which political leaders over the past 10 years had increasingly recognised the importance of strategic policy direction and had in various ways played an increasingly proactive part in setting it. What is the 'added value' for a leader of becoming involved in administrative and managerial detail?

Some illustrations from leaders whose careers and styles are discussed in more detail later provide an initial understanding of why they might want to do so. During the period after the death of Princess Diana, when floral tributes were being deposited by large numbers of people in public places, one of the authors attended a meeting in one of Leicester City Council's smaller public buildings, at which Peter Soulsby, the council leader, was present together with a number of senior council officers. On leaving the meeting, the leader noticed that around 20-30 floral tributes had been laid on the pavement immediately adjacent to the railings in front of the council building. He immediately initiated a discussion with the officers about whether the public should be provided with some kind of more formal and appropriate setting for their floral tributes – for example, some kind of raised platform in front of the building.

Shortly after Robert Parker became leader of Lincolnshire County Council in 1993 (heading a 'partnership' administration between Labour and the Liberal Democrats), he learned from a local newspaper that John

Major, the then Conservative prime minister, had been invited to the county to open a new school. When he challenged the chief executive the next day, it became clear that, although chief executive 'assumed' the leader had heard about it, he had not felt it necessary to inform him directly. Robert Parker subsequently insisted that the invitation be withdrawn. A few months later an important appointments procedure for a new chief executive was rendered abortive by the failure of another senior officer to keep the leader informed of the progress of negotiations with a key candidate.

The first example illustrates the way in which what appear to be 'implementation details' can become, in certain circumstances, appropriate topics for leadership action. When interviewed later about this incident, Peter Soulsby argued that, in the highly charged public climate following Princess Diana's death, it was important for the council to get the details right. To some extent, it was a matter of ensuring appropriate symbolic action. But the leader was clear that the situation required sensitive management and that his intervention was justified. Any high-profile issue in which the *way* the council responded could become a matter of media attention was, he argued, a reasonable concern of a council leader.

The Lincolnshire examples had similarities but also differences. The potential salience for a newly elected Labour/Liberal Democrat administration (whose electoral platform had included strong criticisms of the previous Conservative administration's education policies in the county) of an invitation to a Conservative prime minister to open a local school was not identified by the council's most senior officer. In the other example, the potential public embarrassment for the leadership of an aborted chief executive selection process was not recognised or, if recognised, was not acted upon. Both cases reflected a lack of officer sensitivity and helped persuade the Labour leader that major changes in structures and processes were needed to avoid such outcomes and also to strengthen the organisation's capacity to deliver the new administration's priorities (see Chapter Eight).

Another interview comment from Robert Parker provided further evidence of the importance of 'task accomplishment'. He argued that his group periodically expressed concern that implementation of the key manifesto priorities (education, social services, economic development, the environment) was not progressing satisfactorily and that they expected him as leader to take appropriate action. Politicians know they will be judged not by what appears in a statement of strategy or policy, but by what happens on the ground. The scope for the distortion of policy intentions through the implementation process is well documented (see, for example, Pressman and Wildavsky, 1977). Thus 'task accomplishment' is a legitimate concern, both for majority party groups (or coalitions) and for council leaders.

The quality of member–officer relationships

The major influence on the extent to which the legitimacy of this concern in principle leads to a need for action is the quality of the relationships between members and officers in the authority. Although the leadership task of strategic policy direction will almost always involve a good deal of interaction with officers, such interaction is typically confined to relatively senior levels (especially the chief executive) and has little potential in itself for member–officer conflict. Group and organisational cohesiveness and external relations, though they may be supported by officers, are normally member-dominated tasks. It is in relation to task accomplishment that member–officer relations have a major impact, not just at senior levels but throughout the organisation.

The two key concerns for members under this heading are the avoidance of political embarrassment in the way in which policy is implemented and the confidence that policy implementation is being undertaken enthusiastically and effectively by officers. At one extreme, where officer–member relations are stable and positive and there is a high degree of political sensitivity among officers, the level of trust that members have in officers to avoid political embarrassment and implement effectively can result in relatively little leadership energy being devoted to this task. Occasional progress-chasing may be all that is needed, although it only takes one major failure in either category to undermine such high levels of trust. At the other extreme, the perceived level of officer resistance to the priorities of the majority party – whether or not it is actually justified – and/or the fear of political embarrassment may make this leadership task the most time-consuming of all. One particular problem for members, in terms of time commitment, develops in situations where it is perceived that the only solution to the problems of task accomplishment is a major structural reorganisation, which may have both manifest aims (eg to develop a new structure to reflect our political priorities) and latent aims (eg to find a way of easing out the chief officers we can't work with).

Even in an authority where there is a high degree of mutual trust, there may from time to time be policy initiatives that have such a high potential for controversy and adverse publicity that a leader may feel the need to devote time to 'steering the policy through'. For example, when Leicester City Council set up a 'secondary schools review', because of a high level of surplus places, Peter Soulsby was well aware of potential implementation problems that would arise from the fact that several schools would be earmarked for closure and amalgamation during the process. As a result, he ensured that he became chair of the Education Committee for a period of six months when the review was identifying and making the key choices. This reflected not a lack of trust in officers, but a perceived need to be visibly responsible for dealing with the inevitable political flak. After six months he stood down from the chair, satisfied that the review process had reached a stage where his personal leadership had become unnecessary, although he still remained a member of the committee.

Among the leaders interviewed, there was a considerable variation of views about the importance of task accomplishment as a leadership task, reflecting the recent history and climate at the time of member–officer relations. An astute leader whose party takes power after a long period of control by a different party may reasonably anticipate problems of adjustment among professional officers, and will be on the lookout for evidence of resistance or delay.

In some cases resistance is quite explicit. Soon after Labour came to power in Ealing in 1986, Len Turner, the new leader, was told by the then chief executive that a number of changes that Turner wanted implemented 'couldn't be done'. Rob Parker, leader of the Labour–Liberal Democrat partnership administration in Lincolnshire in 1993, received a similar response from the sitting chief executive. Both chief executives took early retirement shortly afterwards. In Ealing, Len Turner soon realised that in the period before a new appointment could be made he had to become the de facto chief executive to ensure that his party's policies were taken forward, and did so, effectively on a full-time basis for about a year until a new chief executive was appointed.

To operate as chief executive, without of course assuming the formal responsibilities of the post, is an option for leaders who feel that at the time it is the only way to achieve 'task accomplishment'. There is a tradition of this practice in Leeds, where George Mudie and his leadership successors have endeavoured to retain a firm grip on a range of implementation and managerial issues (John, 1997). The current designation in Leeds of the most senior central officer as 'chief officer' rather than 'chief executive' reflects the dominance of this tradition.

Nottinghamshire County Council has long had a similar culture. Leaders and chairs have been expected to operate on a full-time basis and to become involved in the detail of policy implementation. Such practices may of course go well beyond any conception of what is politically justifiable (in the terms set out at the start of this chapter).

When the Liberal Democrats first won the London Borough of Sutton in 1986, Graham Tope found that some of the chief officers were more cooperative (in the sense of demonstrating an ability to work with the new political agenda) than others. His strategy was to concentrate on service improvements – particularly in education and social services – for the first term of office, and to wait until a second term before introducing a more radical package of measures, by which time several of this less cooperative chief officers had left of their own accord and been replaced by others more attuned to the Liberal Democrats' priorities (see Chapter Eight).

In some cases the problem is not so much officers who are used to serving another political party, but officers who are used to playing a dominant role in both policy formulation and implementation, relying heavily on their professional expertise. This was the problem facing David Bookbinder and his colleagues in Derbyshire in 1981. The previous Conservative administration (1977-81) had followed a period of Labour control, but in each case there had been a culture of 'officer dominance' which David Bookbinder was determined to change, using a range of different methods.

Other leaders interviewed, however, took over in situations where there was a long-term relationship of trust between members and officers. This was the perspective of Colin Warbrick (Trafford MBC) when he became leader for the second time in 1984, and Brian Clack in Coventry in 1991. But a long period of single party control does not in itself guarantee this level of mutual trust. As we saw in Chapter Two, a change of party leadership may represent the success of one party faction over another, with the successful faction having a different range of priorities, and a scepticism about the commitment of the chief officers not dissimilar to that experienced by a different incoming party. The non-reappointment of the sitting chief executive in Leicester in 1997, when the city gained unitary status, was not unconnected with the faction-related change of leadership that had taken place just before. John Harman in Kirklees commenced his leadership period with a conflicting set of member–officer loyalties reflecting internal party group divisions.

Task accomplishment and communication systems

One of the key requirements for effective leadership is the existence of a communication system that will keep the leader informed of progress and, equally importantly, of potential problems and opportunities in relation to each of the key leadership tasks. As we saw in Chapter Three, in respect of the maintenance of group cohesiveness, the most usual communication channel (or set of channels) for a leader is a group of trusted allies within the party group, on whom the leader will rely for a sense of how the party group as a whole (and, where relevant, different factions within it) is reacting to leadership initiatives. Deputy leaders are sometimes key confidantes in this respect. Quite apart from maintaining group cohesiveness, the more a leader can rely on such a network of key informants, the more secure his/her own position will be. Early warning will be received of potential rebellions or challenges which, assuming the leader has the skill to deal with such situations, can be defused. Any leader lacking such a network is intrinsically more vulnerable, especially in a turbulent or factionalised political environment. However, there exist alternative types of network. In some of the more rural authorities, and also in hung authorities, we came across leaders who saw the chief executive as a key source of information about current opinion within the leader's own party group, but also within other groups whose support was helping to maintain the leader in office (including loose alliances of Independents).

It will be the chief executive who typically acts as the main channel of information (or briefing mechanism) in relation to organisational cohesiveness. In close, mutually supportive leader–chief executive relationships, a similar role may be played by the chief executive in respect of task accomplishment, both in a progress-maintaining sense (keeping the leader informed of 'progress on the ground' in relation to high-profile political initiatives) and the sense of pre-emptive early warnings about impending obstacles and embarrassments. Indeed, it is this sense of 'sharing privileged information' that is the second of two processes around which effective leader–chief executive relationships operate. (The other, 'developing strategic direction', was discussed in Chapter Four.) Both chief executive and leader can in normal circumstances provide an exclusive and privileged source of information for the other. The chief executive can ensure that the leader hears about new problems, issues and opportunities before his/her colleagues do and can provide briefings on such items that are exclusive (in the first instance) to the leader. Particularly important for the leader in this connection are 'early warnings' about potential political embarrassments. This kind of early warning then gives the leader the option of sharing the information with colleagues at a time and in a way that he/she judges most appropriate. Similarly, the chief executive relies on the leader for information about the dynamics of the group, and in particular the likelihood (or otherwise) of the leader being able to persuade the group to accept tentative proposals emerging from leader–chief executive discussions. (In a hung situation such information needs to be supported by intelligence about the likely outcome of inter-party negotiations.)

It is difficult to overstress the potential importance of this communication channel. It can considerably strengthen the position of both leader and chief executive among their colleagues, although the way in which such power is exploited depends on their personal ambitions and the dynamics of the party group and management team, respectively. It is open to both leader and chief executive to supplement this information source with links to other chief officers or leading councillors, although this will be necessary only in a limited and selective way if the leader–chief executive relationship is working effectively. If there are problems – for example, if the leader perceives the chief executive to be ineffective – these supplementary links are more likely to be used, but in a clandestine rather than an open way.

These 'alternative channels' can take several different forms. A leader may rely for briefings of this nature on other chief officers with whom he/she has been accustomed to working in the past. There are a number of problems, however, with an alternative network of this nature. First, the information received by the leader will necessarily be selective and partial; the requisite 'comprehensive overview' is rarely ascertainable from a location other than the chief executive's office. Second, the potential disruptiveness to the effectiveness of the management team will be apparent. If, as is likely, it becomes apparent that some (but not others) of the management team have a 'special relationship' with the leader, then it is highly unlikely that the management team will be able to act as a cohesive force. In many ways, the best situation for a leader is a powerful chief executive who enjoys the full confidence of his/her management team, thus enabling the chief executive to brief the leader comprehensively about 'task accomplishment' issues on behalf of the whole team.

Other possible 'alternative channels' include a group of policy officers whose role may be defined as de facto advisors to the senior politicians (which may prove equally divisive to an authority's senior management, as evidenced by Leicester City Council's experience during Stewart Foster's leadership in 1995-97), or a group of middle managers. In one authority we studied, chief officers were aware how well briefed the leader was about implementation details and problems. There had been a number of occasions where the leader clearly had an awareness of departmental issues that went beyond the briefing that officers had given him (and which they had regarded as more than adequate). The information can only have come from operational managers further down the organisational hierarchy, and the favoured hypothesis was that it was coming from a group of Labour Party activists at such levels whom the leader knew through the local Labour Party network.

One leader we interviewed had over the years developed a quite conscious strategy for exploiting alternative informational sources. He had managed to make himself the centre of an information network involving not chief officers, but ambitious deputies and third-tier officers, who were prepared to provide him with 'advance notice' of crucial departmental issues before the particular committee chair knew of them. This leader operated in a shire county where the chief executive had a traditional legal background (and perspective), and where there was a tradition of autonomy on the part of linked departments and committees which the leader wanted to break down. Recognising that ambitious middle-ranking officers would see a direct line to an apparently stable leader as not unhelpful to their career prospects, the leader had been able to build a very effective 'alternative communication network' of this nature.

In the example discussed above, the leader's strategy reflected (inter alia) genuine doubts about the ability of some colleagues to deliver a political strategy, in so far as it affected the service areas for which they were responsible. It is not surprising that leaders should feel an across-the-board responsibility to ensure that a political programme is effectively carried out. In some circumstances – for example, a collegiate approach to leadership – it should be possible to trust colleagues to carry out their parts of the collective task, in the knowledge that any problems will be brought back into the collective arena. Some leaders distinguish between chairs they are close to and can trust, and chairs who are less trustworthy. However, in authorities with a tradition of strong links between chief officers and committee chairs and an expectation that services will be run in relatively autonomous fashion by such partnerships (in which the relationship may be dominated by either partner), a leader cannot necessarily rely on 'advance warning' of problems in implementing the programme or of potentially embarrassing issues. If leadership group relationships operate on the basis of trust, it may transpire that such trust is unjustifiable. If on the other hand the leader is in a dominant position in an officer-dominated information network, then he/she is less likely to be unpleasantly surprised.

Political careers and information networks

Thus far it has been assumed that the primary motive of a leader in challenging and changing customary patterns of information flow and decision-making procedures has been to implement a view held by the whole of the party group about how to achieve the party's programme; that is, that the leader has been acting 'on behalf of' the group in this respect. But to fail to consider other motives would be unrealistic in the light of earlier discussions of 'political careers' (see Chapter Two). In particular, our earlier discussion of the way a powerful leader can establish and use 'alternative' networks of information raises the issue of the scope that such alternative channels might provide for more personal objectives. Two possible objectives of this nature can be identified: a concern to strengthen personal power, and a defensive reaction to an unstable leadership situation.

For leaders whose motivation (however unconsciously) includes these objectives, the advantages of 'alternative channels' are considerable. They provide 'advance warning' of issues likely to be encountered in group (or issues that ought to emerge in group but might not if a powerful, relatively autonomous, chair is involved). They allow double checks on the information provided by normal channels (eg the chief executive), and they increase the indispensability of the leader to the group, in that only he/she receives a comprehensive range of strategic information (and often tactical information as well) covering the full range of council activities. The importance of a focal position in information networks was well recognised by many of the leaders interviewed. Indeed, it is not difficult to see how a combination of a focal position in relation to information sources, time availability and a powerful intellect can enhance a leader's dominance and apparent indispensability within the group.

A second reason for leaders to attempt to achieve this kind of dominance in informational terms is to protect themselves against challenges in a situation where the leadership position is unstable. In these circumstances, it is beneficial if the informational links extend into the party group as well as into the chief officer network (although chief officers are sometimes useful sources of information about the behaviour and intentions of potential rivals). However, the main potential payoff for leaders is that they can take advantage of a dominant position in informational networks to demonstrate leadership qualities within the group. Demonstration of the ability to anticipate problems or provide a perceptive evaluation of possible options that no one else is in a position to provide is a powerful boost to a leader's prestige in an unstable situation. An interesting contrast was observed among 'vulnerable' leaders between those who actively sought to manipulate information networks and the dynamics of group factionalism in this way, and those who were not prepared to play this kind of game, but relied instead on moral leadership or force of argument.

For whatever reason it is carried out – the interests of the party group or more personalised interests – the clandestine use and manipulation of 'alternative' information sources by a leader is always potentially disruptive of effective organisational performance and organisational cohesiveness. It poses real problems of 'divided loyalty' for the officers who are faced with it – divided loyalties between committee chair and leader in some cases, divided loyalties between chief executive and leader in others. Any attempt to circumvent or bypass the chief executive on a systematic basis undermines his/her position and credibility. It is therefore hardly surprising that authorities in which such practices occur lack organisational cohesiveness and often exhibit divided and mistrustful cultures. What may be effective and legitimate in responding to special circumstances on a one-off basis is unlikely to be justifiable when practised on a more systematic basis.

Changing management personnel and structures

One way in which leaders may feel the need to involve themselves in administrative detail is through the modification to organisational structures and the appointment of staff. The reasons why they should wish to do so are, in principle, understandable. We have shown how much a leader relies on a chief executive for various crucial forms of support, early warning, information and briefing. The same point holds for other members of a leadership team (eg a chair of finance) in relation to their 'opposite numbers' (eg a director of finance). If the relationship is not working effectively from the leader's point of view, for whatever reasons (eg personal incompatibilities, different conceptions of roles and responsibilities, inability of the chief executive to deliver on key tasks such as strategic direction within the officer structure), it is understandable that a termination of the chief executive's employment should be sought and a more effective replacement (in the leader's terms) found. It is also understandable that the leader and his/her colleagues would then expect to have a detailed involvement (going well beyond the setting out of selection criteria) in the appointment of the successor. The same argument applies in principle to the chair of finance/director of finance, the chair of social services/director of social services and so on (and also perhaps to the appointment of their deputies).

There may be politically legitimate reasons for undertaking a major structural reorganisation of the officer structure. The policy agenda of a recently elected majority group may well have structural implications (eg a prioritisation of community development, or decentralisation, or economic regeneration). A newly elected Conservative administration may feel that the organisational structure is top heavy (too many chief officers, too little delegation) or that the client–contractor split is not adequately reflected in the current structure. All these are in principle legitimate concerns.

These two areas of leadership involvement – individual staff appointments and organisational restructuring – can become interconnected. In local government, unlike the private sector, dispensing of the services of a chief officer is by no means easy. Their contracts will typically be 'permanent'. Fixed-term contracts are still the exception, and even here the date for consideration of renewal may not coincide with the wishes of the political leadership. Incentives can be (and generally have to be) offered. It is rare indeed to be able to demonstrate that a chief executive, or any other chief officer, has been incompetent, or has committed a breach of discipline that justifies dismissal. Although chief officers who realise that they are not wanted (for whatever reason) by the political administration are understandably reluctant to remain in post in such circumstances, they will typically want to negotiate the best possible financial deal and also to present their departure as a resignation (or 'mutual consent' outcome) rather than a de facto dismissal for perceived managerial or professional shortcomings. In the past decade many chief executives, directors of education and directors of social services have 'resigned' for reasons other than a successful application for another post. Very few have been subject to dismissal, at least in the terms of the press statement issued.

An administration eager for one or more chief officers to move elsewhere, but unwilling to pay the high price of initiating 'voluntary' resignations, may be tempted to set in motion a structural reorganisation with the hidden agenda of 'easing out' officers they feel they cannot work with. The intention here is to remove an existing post from the structure or to redefine it so that the current incumbent ceases to be a credible candidate. Such motivations were acknowledged by some of the leaders we interviewed as at least a partial justification for restructuring.

The problem is, of course, that reorganisations are costly and time-consuming processes. Although leaders and their colleagues will often have strong views about the merits or otherwise of different structures, they would rarely claim to be competent to undertake such reorganisations themselves. If the chief executive is trusted by the leadership and his/her role is not implicated by the manifest or hidden political agenda behind the reorganisation, then the job of advising on the restructuring may be given to him/her. If, however, it is the chief executive who is one of the targets, or if unease is felt about giving any officer the right to develop proposals that affect other officers, then it is usual to employ external consultants to advise on the new structure. That by no means implies a significantly reduced ability for leaders to affect the outcomes. Consultants are usually skilled at developing a politically acceptable solution on such occasions, and in so doing to add a stamp of external legitimacy to the new structure which it would lack had it come directly from the majority group. Because of the financial costs of such an exercise, and the fact that it inevitably delays the desired changes (the process from tender specification to the formal acceptance of a set of recommendations rarely takes less than a year), most examples of externally commissioned restructurings that we came across were either genuinely inspired by a set of political priorities, or triggered by a combination of such priorities and the desire to 'ease out' one or more individuals in key positions.

All these activities – finding ways of dispensing with unwanted chief officers, selecting suitable replacements, and setting up and managing restructuring by external consultants – can take up significant amounts of leadership time; nor are they without their risks. In particular, new appointments in which a leader has played a key role may damage the leader's reputation if they are perceived to have been less than successful. There is a good deal of political judgement required in these processes: how much pressure to put on a chief executive who is reluctant to move; how far to push a personal preference for a replacement candidate against a dominant view within the selection panel for a different candidate; and how to manage the relationship with consultants to achieve a balance between ensuring the desired outcome and accepting the legitimacy of external expertise which may point in a different direction, at least in part. A further problem is that such reorganisations are great consumers of organisational energy, and may divert the group from what appear in retrospect to have been more important tasks. Robert Parker, Labour leader of Lincolnshire between 1993 and 1997, acknowledged that the reorganisation he had advocated in 1993 was inspired by a desire to see the priorities of the partnership administration given a structural emphasis, but also by a concern to develop a rationale for generating more personal choice in the composition of the chief officer team. These outcomes were achieved, but they diverted energy away from work on a strategic direction for Lincolnshire, which was finally published in the last of the four years of the administration. It is much easier for leaders who inherit a senior management team that feel they can trust and work with, and that operates an effective early warning system. In these cases, task accomplishment becomes a minor, rather than a major, leadership role.

The limits of leadership involvement in task accomplishment

As we have seen, the blurring of the traditional policy–implementation distinction is by no means an irrational political standpoint. The relationship between these two stages in the policy process is symbiotic. Policies can indeed be distorted in the manner of their implementation, and in one sense policy is made as it is implemented – a broad policy statement applied to a range of different circumstances will inevitably throw up a number of 'anomalies' or 'test cases' which question the initial policy. (The operation of 'points systems' on housing waiting lists provides a good illustration.) Politicians understandably feel that they will be judged not by 'paper' policies, but by policies that are actually implemented and experienced on the ground. There are enough examples of the disastrous consequences of worthy policy intentions to demonstrate the 'policy gap' that can emerge in relation to housing redevelopment and rehabilitation schemes: see Davies (1972), Dennis (1972). Thus, in principle, the political claim of a legitimate interest in policy implementation can be upheld. The real issue is how that interest can be expressed in a way that safeguards the professional and managerial integrity of officers.

What should be regarded as a legitimate set of expectations regarding the facilitation of members' interests in policy implementation? First, there should be mechanisms for alerting members to implementation cases that challenge or raise important issues about a policy. The routine letting of council premises to outside organisations is an activity that is clearly sensible for members to delegate to officers; but members would have ample cause for complaint if a request by the British National Party (BNP) to rent a hall for a meeting were not referred back to them, even when this type of decision had been formally delegated to officers. If officers can be trusted to act in this way (which requires considerable political sensitivity), there is no need for delegation agreements to be revoked. Second, there should be mechanisms for allowing councillors to evaluate the way in which services are delivered – particularly services where the majority group is committed to a particular style of service delivery (eg positive discrimination, sensitivity to racial differences, building confidence in deprived groups). Third, there should be mechanisms to enable politicians to 'progress-chase' – that is, to monitor the speed at which particular types of decision are being carried out and if necessary to require their acceleration.

What is implied by all these expectations is a power of *selective intervention* based on a set of agreed principles. If that can be achieved, then a political commitment to 'task accomplishment' or 'getting things done' is compatible with an acceptable member–officer division of labour, and hence with organisational cohesiveness across the member–officer interface. If it cannot be achieved, then either members will waste a lot of time and energy on unnecessary detail, or member–officer relations will become conflictual and mistrustful, or both. Even if 'task accomplishment' is achieved from the members' perspective, it will be at the expense of other important political tasks, and certainly at the expense of organisational cohesiveness.

It should be emphasised that in many authorities the majority group leadership does not wish to devote much energy to this task. Conservative groups – particularly those of a more traditional orientation – are customarily uninterested in doing so. It is not viewed as a good use of their time, and is anyway deemed unnecessary (because officers can be trusted to do all of these tasks). The most that would be expected would be that officers would alert them to cases that were a potential political embarrassment, and the right to a bit of progress-chasing over 'pet schemes'. In Labour-controlled councils where there is a recent history of good member–officer relations, members often will not see any need to get involved in implementation detail beyond the opportunities for involvement invited by officers as part of normal practice. Thus, for many leaders interviewed, task accomplishment was rarely given a high priority per se although the agenda of items for action drawn up each week by the chief executive (at which there is usually also an input from the leader) would typically contain a quota of implementation or test case issues, as well as the 'reactive' type of strategic choices discussed in Chapter Four.

Conclusion

The challenge facing a leader in a situation in which a political commitment to hands-on management is perceived as threatening by chief officers (and hence as a potential threat to organisational cohesiveness) is whether he/she can manage the situation in such a way that the two key objectives involved – 'organisational cohesiveness' and 'task accomplishment' – are both safeguarded. This challenge involves a number of subtle and difficult judgements. To what extent is officer resistance 'unreasonable' (ie an unconsidered adherence to tradition)? If it is unreasonable, how plausible is it to remove and replace the officers concerned? How important is organisational cohesiveness on the officer side, if a cohesive majority group is happy that the new 'hands-on' style (however much it is disliked by officers) is actually succeeding in task accomplishment?

It was in relation to dilemmas of this nature, reflecting different aspects of 'task accomplishment', that several of the leaders in our research reported their most difficult problems and painful personal experiences of their period of tenure, particularly when the disputes about chief officer performances become personalised in nature (about which there is in these circumstances a high probability). While it is impossible to draw definitive conclusions about the relative effectiveness of different leadership tactics in this respect, some preliminary conclusions are possible. Leaders who gave existing chief officers the opportunity to demonstrate that they could serve the new administration were often pleased in retrospect that they had done so. Leaders who acknowledged that organisational cohesiveness was an important consideration not just within the majority group but across the officer–member divide, and who had developed patterns of communication and procedures that reflected this perception, usually felt that their actions had been justified. And leaders who dealt directly with problems of incumbent chief officers whose styles and priorities were ultimately viewed as incompatible with those of the new group, rather than indirectly (eg through setting in motion an organisational restructuring which would marginalise them) usually felt that their tactics had been vindicated. Some of the influential leaders interviewed (eg David Bookbinder) had experienced a succession of problems in this area which were felt to have hindered their administration's effectiveness. Others (eg John Harman) had faced similar problems but had overcome them (in the sense of generating a more unified organisational culture) more effectively. It is in this area that the personal judgements and skills of a leader may be most critical.

Part Two

Case studies of local political leadership

SEVEN

Political leadership in Leicester

Introduction: the Leicester context

As our conceptual framework (see Chapter One) emphasises, leadership behaviour is not displayed in a vacuum but rather is typically oriented towards a discrete number of key tasks. Previous chapters have discussed what we identified as the four key leadership tasks: maintaining cohesiveness; developing strategic and policy direction; representing the authority in the outside world; and ensuring programme implementation. This chapter attempts to put flesh on our conceptual framework by providing a case study of a full-time paid leader: Peter Soulsby, Labour leader of Leicester City Council from 1981 to 1999, apart from a break of 18 months in 1994/95. Essentially, this chapter is a snapshot of one party leader in one local authority during one relatively short period of time. As such, it has all the limitations associated with this methodology, but it nevertheless provides useful insights into the challenges and dilemmas facing local political leaders. Given the emphasis of the 1998 White Paper, *Modern local government: In touch with the people* (DETR, 1998b), upon executive models of leadership such insights provide useful inputs into the contemporary debate. The chapter is based on analysis of a wide range of documentary sources, including council papers, as well as interview material. It also incorporates extracts from the leader's diary.

Peter Soulsby qualified as a teacher and obtained a degree in English and Drama in Leicester in 1973. He subsequently taught in Leicestershire for over 20 years. It was while he was a student that his political career started. After having a sabbatical year as president of the Students' Union, he was elected on to Leicester City Council in 1973 at the time of local government reorganisation when the new district authority took over from the former county borough. Earlier in the same year he had unsuccessfully fought a Leicestershire County Council by-election before being offered, at fairly short notice, a safe city council seat.

From 1973 to 1976 Labour controlled the city, and during his second year in office, at the age of 25, Soulsby was appointed vice-chair of the planning committee following a reshuffle when Jim Marshall (then leader of the City Council) was elected as a Labour MP for the city. During the years 1976-79 in Leicester Labour was in opposition, and in 1978 Peter Soulsby was elected deputy leader of the Labour group, having secured a broad base of support within the party. Labour regained control of the City Council in 1979. By 1981, along with a number of other group members, Soulsby began to get very restless about the Labour group leader, Ken Middleton, who was also leader of the Labour group on Leicestershire County Council.

Perhaps not unnaturally, given the pending 1981 County Council elections, Ken Middleton was spending an increasing amount of time at County Hall and relatively little time in the city. With Labour control of the county a real possibility, there was a certain logic to Middleton's stance, but his downplaying of the city during this period led Peter Soulsby to challenge Middleton for the Labour group leadership in the city. Soulsby came within half a dozen votes of winning, and when Middleton left Leicester for another job in autumn 1981 he took over the party leadership uncontested. For much of the previous year Soulsby had exercised the leadership role in the city without having any formal leadership position. It was, nevertheless, difficult for him to attract support in his initial challenge to Middleton because of the pending County Council elections; some of his potential allies argued that it was unwise to stand against someone who was also Labour leader on the County Council.

Before the coup that toppled him (albeit temporarily) in April 1994, Soulsby had faced only one serious challenge to his leadership since becoming leader in 1981. This came in 1988 in the wake of the rate capping imposed by the Conservative government. Previous challenges at the Labour group's annual leadership elections (usually from the Left) had been insubstantial, but 1988 was different. The Labour group was deeply divided on the stance to be taken over capping. Essentially, capping led to a formalisation of existing informal factions, each of which consolidated around particular individuals in the group. For two or three years, there had been in effect four caucuses within the group, with only three or four members (including Soulsby) not belonging to any of the factions:

1) the 'left', numbering nine or ten (13 at their height), who regularly met in a local pub, with formal agendas, in advance of Labour group meetings;

2) the 'black' caucus (about eight members, including one white Muslim councillor), which again had formal pre-meetings;
3) the 'right', a group known by this name (although it gave itself no name), which was more informal than groups 1 and 2 with about eight members, largely from Leicester West constituency;
4) the 'non-aligned group' (NAG), as they called themselves, whose membership varied between six and eight.

As noted above, the membership of these caucuses consolidated after capping and made possible the challenges to Soulsby's leadership in 1988. In the event, the 'NAG' and the 'left' supported Graham Bett, Soulsby's opponent (Bett was deputy leader at the time), while the 'right' and 'black' caucuses supported Soulsby.

In the end, Soulsby survived the challenge by three votes. In many respects, the contest was about leadership style and came at a time when Soulsby was particularly vulnerable, not only from rate capping. He had personally become deeply involved in instigating a Service Appraisal Team in housing maintenance, responding to serious concerns about the quality of service provided. He had run into industrial relations difficulties with the unions. To quote Soulsby, "There was a feeling that my hands-on approach was not appreciated". People saw the specific issue as being symptomatic of something broader. During this episode Soulsby was very critical of the role of the local evening daily, the *Leicester Mercury*, which, he believed, excessively personalised the matter. He regarded himself as 'very seriously damaged' by a front page article with an accompanying picture and the caption 'A man with a mission', outlining how Soulsby was going to 'clean up' the City Council's housing maintenance section.

Reflecting on this period, Soulsby believes it shows how in the Leicester context it is important for a leader not to allow himself/herself to be seen as being someone 'above and beyond' other senior elected members. There was within the local culture a team approach to leadership rather than one that elevated a single individual too highly. Soulsby was perceived to have stepped too far beyond the team on an issue (direct labour/council housing) that was central to core values. In his determination to force change, he had been prepared to ignore other leading members, and this led to resentment in the Labour Party.

The second strand of our six-fold conceptual framework emphasised that the ability to exercise leadership behaviour is facilitated through the holding of a *formal* position and through the authority which that position bestows. The events in 1988 and, as we shall see, in 1994 (when Soulsby *was* ousted in a coup) are a timely reminder that formal office holders are vulnerable unless party colleagues (and especially senior members) are supportive. Leaders challenge in-built party norms and values at their peril. Party leaders owe their formal position to the support of colleagues; stepping too far out of line or alienating significant sections of the party is, therefore, potentially fatal. In terms of the Labour government's 1998 White Paper, the model of executive leadership suggested by Soulsby's experience is not that of an elected mayor but rather that of a Cabinet with a leader. Perhaps not surprisingly, this has emerged as the city's preference. To quote the City Council's chief executive, Rodney Green, "I would expect members to give consideration to options that are close to where they already are, and would be more likely to go for the cabinet" (*Local Government Chronicle*, 7 August 1998). In many respects, this would simply represent a formalisation of the status quo.

In April 1994 there was a further coup in the Labour group and Soulsby was replaced by Stewart Foster. A long period in office as leader inevitably builds up a group of disaffected people. Soulsby paid the price for a 13-year period in which elements within both the group and the broader party in Leicester became increasingly uneasy about his leadership, a scenario not unlike that of six years earlier. Essentially, he was ousted by an anti-Soulsby vote rather than by enthusiastic endorsement of his rival candidate, Stewart Foster. The *Independent's* interpretation of events was as follows:

> Mr Soulsby had made many enemies during his 13 years as leader. A caucus of left-wing councillors had not forgiven him after they had the whip removed for voting against introducing the poll tax. In 1993 Mr Soulsby had an acrimonious exchange of letters with Mr Vaz who became MP for Leicester East in 1987. In the spring of that year, Merlyn Vaz, the MP's mother and a leading city councillor, was ousted as a committee chairwoman. (*Independent*, 25 April 1995)

Alliances were forming against Soulsby; the Vaz dimension persisted. The *Independent* reported that Vaz wrote to Soulsby saying that his mother felt "personal bitterness and betrayal at the way in which she has been treated", and asked that a new pensioners' subcommittee be created with Mrs Vaz as its chair. Keith Vaz also asked for new roles for two councillors who had lost out in the Labour group elections. Vaz admitted, "You might think this letter is a bit of a cheek". Peter Soulsby rejected his requests.

The relationship between Vaz and Soulsby became increasingly antagonistic. The *Independent* reported that in September 1993 Soulsby wrote to Vaz accusing him of going to council officers behind councillors' backs and complaining of "constantly finding ourselves consulted by chief officers about how they are to deal with your frequent and critical letters about what are essentially political matters". A few weeks later Soulsby was defeated in the leadership election by Stewart Foster, a compromise candidate who gained the support of the still vengeful left and another group of councillors regarded as being close to Keith Vaz. The specific details are less important than the broader picture, namely recognising the vulnerability of a leader who has been in office for as long as 13 years. Maintaining group and party coherence amidst disparate ideological and community factions is a delicate task. Soulsby paid the price for standing firm against significant organised minorities, notably the eight Left-wing councillors who voted against the poll tax and from whom the Labour Party whip was taken.

Looking back at the Foster coup, Soulsby maintained that councillors from wards within Vaz's constituency (Leicester East) were strongly influenced to vote against Soulsby by the fact that their own reselection was imminent. There was also (after 13 years) a group of sitting councillors who felt that they had not been adequately rewarded by Soulsby – hence had become alienated. Before the leadership election Foster had offered specific jobs to individual councillors, so they knew exactly what they would get out of voting for him. In addition, the Labour group's annual meeting itself appeared to be highly organised by Vaz's allies, even down to who sat in which seats, so that the way people *actually* voted could be scrutinised. In the election, Soulsby argued three elements came into play: "the Vaz factor; opportunism on the part of some councillors; and the anti-Soulsby vote". Soulsby lost 21–20, and every vote at that meeting was lost by the same margin. For some years group coherence had been very difficult; now it had disappeared. The group was split down the middle, with Soulsby on the wrong side of the divide.

Stewart Foster's period in office was short-lived. In November 1995, he lost a vote of confidence in the Labour group following national newspaper revelations about his relationship with the head of the council's policy unit. Even before this, however, the fact that Foster was not a team player was losing him support. In the subsequent leadership election, 19 months after Foster became leader, Soulsby was re-elected as Labour group leader, defeating his rival candidate, Mary Draycott. With an air of understatement Soulsby observed: "There's no denying the group has had its difficulties recently. But we have come through hard times before as a united group and I am very confident we can manage it again". After regaining power Soulsby led a Labour group that, while still containing a number of disaffected individuals, presented a relatively united front on most policy issues. Maintaining group coherence became increasingly important for Soulsby, although in May 1996 there was a further challenge to his leadership position. Following the shadow elections for the new city unitary authority, he was challenged by Paul Sood, Soulsby's co-member in the city's Abbey Ward. But Sood polled only eight votes in the secret ballot compared with Soulsby's 32. There was one abstention.

In 1998 there were two rather than one Labour group meetings a month. In the old regime there were no papers presented other than those directly relating to forthcoming council meetings. There was no formal report from the leader (who also chaired the meeting). Some years ago a separate group chair was instituted, and the two group meetings per month are now preceded by meetings of the group executive. There is now a well established verbal report from the leader plus a written policy report. Soulsby then invites questions: this session can last from 15 to 45 minutes with Soulsby responding personally. He described this as a "very valuable occasion both for me to say things and for others to get things off their chest. It stops things festering". Questions sometimes can be very detailed – for example, specific local transport issues, the quality of signs outside city council offices – or more general, such as the progress of a major review of services.

Maintaining party coherence demands more than attention to the group; it requires regular dealings with the District Labour Party (or the Local Government Committee, as it is now called). Over the years this has been problematic. In the early 1980s it was particularly so because of the strong 'militant' influence. Soulsby was regularly accused of 'selling out' over the rate capping issue with a significant core, like Liverpool and Lambeth, wanting to go down the route of outright opposition. The Local Government Committee has fewer formal responsibilities than the former district party. It now has two major roles, one in connection with drawing up the local election manifesto and the other in drawing up a panel of local candidates. While in 1998 the relationship was much more collaborative than in the 'militant' era, the Local Government Committee officers, if not overtly hostile to Soulsby, were not particularly compliant. In October 1998 Soulsby commented: "I need to keep an eye on it. I need to go to every meeting, and do". There is a standing agenda item entitled 'Leader/Secretary's Report'; Soulsby always presents this (usually verbally) and the report is followed by questions. The Local Government Committee is particularly active in the period around elections. In order to maintain party coherence across the city, the leader cannot afford to ignore the Local Government Committee; he does so at his peril. By 1997, however, Soulsby was earning a substantial leader's 'allowance'.

The next section examines the moves towards establishing a 'salaried' political leader in the city, something that is likely to become the norm rather than the exception throughout England once the executive models of political leadership outlined in the 1998 White Paper are implemented.

Moving towards salaried leadership

In agreeing the detail of the scheme of members' allowances for 1996/97, Leicester city councillors determined that an independent panel of people be set up to consider and make recommendations to the City Council upon:

(a) a level of Special Responsibility Allowance appropriate for the position of leader of Leicester City Council; and
(b) a mechanism for gearing future increases in the leader's Special Responsibility Allowance (SRA) with the scheme of Member's Allowances adopted in August 1996. (LCC Public Protection and General Services Sub-Committee, 7 November 1996)

This Independent Panel comprised the vice chancellors of the two universities in the city, the chief executive of the Leicestershire Chamber of Commerce and Industry, the director of Voluntary Action Leicester, and the district secretary of the Union of Knitwear, Footwear and Apparel Trades.

In December 1995 Soulsby finally gave up his teaching career after struggling for many years to combine the leadership task with teaching. He formally became a full-time councillor but received barely £8,000 a year in allowances. The Independent Panel came up with a solution, accepted by the Council, namely a Special Responsibility Allowance of some £22,145. In addition, Soulsby then received £3,000 a year as a member of the Audit Commission. In his evidence to the Independent Panel, Soulsby cited the pay of an MP – more than £46,000 per year plus pension and severance pay – and that of a parliamentary under secretary

(£66,000 per year): "The Panel may be able to take a view of the direct responsibility of those in such jobs compared with the responsibilities and time commitment of a Council Leader in a major city" (Soulsby Evidence, 2 October 1996).

While the Independent Panel was persuaded of the need for a full-time leader with a realistic Special Responsibility Allowance, there remained a good deal of scepticism and some overt hostility from political opponents. In his evidence to the Panel, the leader of the Conservative group on the City Council, Roman Scuplak, registered his opposition:

> You asked what is the role of council leader. That is simple. It is the chairing of the Policy and Resources Committee. It is not getting involved in the day to day running of the Council. It is not attending countless working parties. It is not attending functions and meetings of outside bodies as representative of the Council. We have well paid employees to carry out these duties. Councillors set the policy guidelines; employees carry out that policy under the direction of departmental heads. All too often in recent years, the council leader and committee chairmen have usurped the roles of the chief executive and the directors. One sometimes wonders why we have directors! (Scuplak Evidence, 5 October 1996)

In his own evidence to the Independent Panel, Soulsby adopted a radically different tack, arguing that a full-time commitment demanded a sensible financial return. The next two sections focus on Soulsby's evidence to the panel.

The nature of the job

Soulsby emphasised that since 1974 the public expectation of councillors had changed considerably: "Few in 1974 could have dreamt that a leader might be expected to performance manage a chief executive or that the rise of interest groups and the contract culture would demand so much time and energy". He went on to argue that council leaders were required both to provide corporate consistency and coordination in the political decision-making process and to represent the Council and its community more generally. Reflecting the fifth strand of our conceptual framework, he maintained: "For a leader this involves handling the vital interface between the political decision making and the administration of the

Council – not just managing it, but designing it, shaping it and constantly modifying it to suit changing circumstances[11].

The first and third key leadership tasks were identified as maintaining political and organisational coherence, and representing the authority in the external world. These were given particular emphasis by Soulsby:

> It [leadership] also involves dealing effectively with government ministers and their senior civil servants, MPs, officers at all levels of the council's administration, the public – often in difficult situations, investors and partners from other sectors and, by no means always the easiest of tasks, their own backbench members with their aspirations. (Soulsby Evidence, 2 October 1996)

He also stressed the importance of developing strategic and policy direction in the world of local governance: "A successful leader also has to work with others to develop and to share with them a strategic vision of the future, not just of their council, but also of their community".

High-profile political leaders like Soulsby have to respond to the media on behalf of the Council most days. They are also required to carry out a range of civic functions alongside the lord mayor. Some tasks, those requiring a 'political' input, cannot easily be delegated to an officer. Similarly, Soulsby argues, the interpersonal skills required of a leader are of a high order. Particularly important are those needed for effective communication in writing, in public and through the media. He regards the skills required to chair meetings, analyse issues, build a consensus or set matters out clearly for a decision as being equally vital.

The range of work as defined by Soulsby is both very broad and very time consuming. The diary extracts presented in Table 7.1, submitted to the panel, provide some indication of the extent of the calls upon his time: "If I don't get in [work] at the weekend before Sunday afternoon, the security guards remark on it" (*Leicester Mercury*, 11 December 1996). There is a huge volume of post and telephone calls that pass through his office and he has to give at least some time not only to the potential investor or partner but also to some of the many complainants or lobbyists who want the leader's ear. The corporate tasks are endless, and in addition Soulsby has to deal with his own constituents; he holds a ward surgery every Saturday at 10.30am:

> "My surgery is invariably very busy and I often get people coming from other parts of the city. Their expectations of my ability, as leader,

to help them, are not always realistic. Inevitably as leader I get approached at meetings, in the street, by telephone at home and even at my front door by a incredible range of people with complaints, comments or lobbying – all with an expectation that I will at least give them a hearing. Even just pointing them in the right direction or ensuring that their concerns are dealt with by someone else takes a significant amount of time."

Given the pressures on his time, Soulsby has had to develop survival strategies, one of which comprises two lists, one of things he *will* do and one of tasks he *will not* do. He gives priority to the following: his family and chapel, elections/selections, regeneration, customer care, Policy and Resources, Environment City initiatives, *some* members/MPs, and 'going out', which means getting out of his office and seeing what is going on in the city rather than sitting in his office all day. The *will do* list, then, comprises mostly strategic activities plus some personal interests. Except when his own ward is involved, Soulsby's *will not do* list includes: individual complainants (he once used to reply to all complaints which arrived at the office with his name on the envelope), most officers, most agendas, minor plans, most voluntary groups, casual callers, many press calls. (He tries to guide these to the appropriate person.) Clearly, if the chief executive or the director of central services asked for an urgent meeting he would comply, but Soulsby finds the list extremely useful in helping him to determine priorities.

Table 7.1: Extract from Peter Soulsby's diary, 5-25 August 1996

	Monday 5 August	Tuesday 6 August	Wednesday 7 August	Thursday 8 August	Friday 9 August	Saturday 10 August	Sunday 11 August
8.00	Meeting a constituent	•		Meeting visiting	•		
8.30	•	•	Drs 8.50	US Congressman –	•		
9.00	•	Director of Resource	•	briefing re Leicester	•		
9.30	•	Veronica Moore	•			•	
10.00	•	Director of	Interview re	Chair Economic	Chair Economic	•	
10.30	•	Environment	Nolan Committee		Development	Surgery	
11.00	•	•	•	Chief Executive of	•		
11.30	Director of Resource	•	Press interview	City Challenge	•	Speech/photo/live broadcast	
12.00	Head of Property	Education Dept		Town Clerk		Perf. opening of	
12.30	Director of Housing	structures	Out over lunch	Policy Officer –	Briefing a PPC on	Youth Facility R. Mead	
13.00	•	•		prep. for Pol. Board, etc	council issues	Surgery	
13.30	Head of Policy Unit	•		Martin B			
14.00	Interview by J. Saliga	Chairing Major	Chairing Env. City	time off/meet friend	Chairing Policy	•	
14.30	of DMU	Schemes Working	Working Party		Board	•	
15.00	Chair of Housing	Party		Presentation on		•	
15.30	Chief executive		•	City Transportation			
16.00	Agenda meeting for		•	Study	'Stakeholders' with		
16.30	Policy & Resources	Chair Environment	Chair Housing	•	Chamber of Comm.		
17.00	Labour group exec.	Cllr Nasim	pre meeting, then		etc re partnership		
17.30	Education Committee	•	Social Services	Finance Sub-Cttee	& shared vision		
18.00	•	•	Committee	Labour Group	•		
18.30	Chair personnel	•	Presentation from		•		
19.00	•	•	library director on				•
19.30	•	•	new city service				•
20.00	•	•	•				•
20.30	•	•	•				•
21.00	•	•	•				•
21.30			•				•
22.00			•				

Note: • in office (preparation, correspondence, meeting colleagues, etc)

Table 7.1: continued

	Monday 12 August	Tuesday 13 August	Wednesday 14 August	Thursday 15 August	Friday 16 August	Saturday 17 August	Sunday 18 August
8.00		•	•				
8.30		•			Director of Arts	•	
9.00		Audit Commission	Meeting – Interim		and Leisure	•	
9.30			Evaluation of City		Interviews		
10.00		Future Strategy Panel	Challenge		(chairing		
10.30		until 3.00pm			until 2.00pm)	Surgery	
11.00							
11.30	Day off but in touch		•	•			
12.00	with office several		•	•			
12.30	times a day –	(in touch with	Chief Executive	•			
13.00		office at lunchtime)		•			
13.30	including:						
14.00	2 interviews with		Meeting with	•	•	•	
14.30	media on a mobile		Chairman and Chief		•	•	
15.00	phone from the		Executive of TEC	Chief Executive	Chairing City		
15.30	middle of a field!	•	•		Challenge Exec. Board	Castle Park	
16.00	and contact with	•	•	Cllr Gajjar	Social Services:	Festival	
16.30	Chairman, RWB	•		Federation of	Director's presentation		
17.00		Chairing Policy	Meeting with	Muslim Organisations			
17.30		and Resources	Leicester	County Council			
18.00		Committee	Promotions Ltd	Senior Members			
18.30			Directors	•			
19.00					Private dinner with		
19.30					Chairman of British		•
20.00		Deputy Leader		Dinner with	Waterways Board		•
20.30				candidates			•
21.00 •							•
21.30 •							•
22.00 •							

Note: • in office (preparation, correspondence, meeting colleagues, etc)

Table 7.1: continued

	Monday 19 August	Tuesday 20 August	Wednesday 21 August	Thursday 22 August	Friday 23 August	Saturday 24 August	Sunday 25 August
8.00							
8.30			With De Montfort	Director of Education			
9.00	David Pell re	Assistant town clerk	University and others	interviews	Chief Executive re		
9.30	Environment City	Principal, Southfields	discussion Arts	until 2.00pm	department structures		
10.00	Director of Edn Sh'li	College	Quarter, etc		•		
10.30	•				Chairing discussion	Surgery	
11.00	•	•			about disposal of a		
11.30	•	Veronica Moore			major asset		
12.00	•	•					
12.30	R. Bruccianni &	Charles Poole			With potential partners	•	
13.00	R. Lynch,	•			to discuss a multi-	•	
13.30	lunch	•			million pound project	•	
14.00	•	•	Assistant Chief Exec.		•		
14.30	•	•	Television Interview	Chairing City			
3.00	A policy officer	•		Challenge Board	Chair Economic Dev.		
15.30	Chairs, A&L + Leisure	Chief Executive	•		Chairing Policy Board		
16.00	Director, A&L		•				
16.30	Selection Panel	Labour group	•				
17.00	executive	executive	Chief Executive	Council meeting	•		
17.30	Audit Sub-committee		•		•		
18.00	(vice-chair)	Labour group	•		•		
18.30			•				
19.00	•			•			•
19.30	•		Dinner for	•			•
20.00	•		candidates	•			•
20.30	•			•			•
21.00	•	•					•
21.30	•	•					•
22.00	•						•

Note: • in office (preparation, correspondence, meeting colleagues, etc)

Specific leadership tasks

What specific enterprises has Peter Soulsby spearheaded as leader in recent years?

- *City Challenge* As leader of the Council, Soulsby chaired the City Challenge Steering Group which submitted a successful bid for £37.5 million of government money and which led directly to over £200 million of private sector investment. As a matter of deliberate policy – wishing to involve all partners fully – he arranged to hand over the chair of the company to a private sector representative once the bid was won. However, the partners re-elected Soulsby to the chair when his successor moved to work for one of the companies involved and when City Challenge entered a potentially fatal crisis caused by the abandonment by the County Council of the east–west link road.

- *Leicester Promotions Ltd* Soulsby was the founding chair of Leicester Promotions Ltd. In the face of some resistance, he carried it through the political processes, recruiting the board and the chief executive. To quote Soulsby, "The model we have adopted with this company is possibly unique and the tremendous success of the partnership is very widely admired".

- *Audit Commission* In 1994 Soulsby was appointed by the government as the then only serving council leader on the Audit Commission. Of direct relevance to the City Council, he has been a member of the Commission's study groups on Local Authority Capital Spending, the Planning of School Places and Environmental Stewardship. Of particular value to Leicester was his service on the Commission Study Group which examined the experience and lessons from the first tranche of unitary councils. Soulsby chaired the two national seminars that the Commission held for the leaders and chief executives of authorities involved in reorganisation. In 1998 he obtained an annual salary of £6,000 from this source.

- *'Environment City'* Soulsby remains centrally involved in ensuring Leicester's designation as 'Environment City' is retained. On behalf of the city he attended and spoke at the Rio Summit where he received the city's award. He regards 'Environment City' as of continuing importance and it continues to have a high profile.

- *British Waterways* In July 1998 Peter Soulsby was appointed to the board of British Waterways. Given his own interest in the subject – Soulsby's family owns a narrow-boat – he declared himself 'absolutely delighted' at this appointment, a part-time post, providing a salary of

£9,000 a year: "I'm looking forward to using my experience with British Waterways and learning from other towns and cities which have used waterways in their regeneration strategies". Environment Minister Angela Eagle emphasised that "Peter Soulsby has valuable experience of successful regeneration on initiatives and public/private partnerships" (*Leicester Mercury*, 17 July 1998).

In addition to the above, Soulsby is a former member of the Local Government Management Board; he also chaired the board of Leicester City Bus Ltd for a considerable period prior to privatisation. In 1994 he was appointed by the Local Government Association as one of 24 British 'alternate' members of the EU Committee of the Regions, which enabled him to have unparalleled access on behalf of the city to EU institutions. In addition there are numerous internal working parties, plus his work as group leader. For six months in 1997 he chaired the City's Education Committee following a particularly difficult time for what was a very high-profile policy area in the city at that time. In 1998/99 Soulsby chaired the Policy and Resources Committee, was chair of its Regeneration Sub-committee and vice-chair of its Finance Sub-committee. In addition, he remained a member of the city's Education Committee.

Given the multitude of pressures upon a leader, why should he spend time chairing committees other than Policy and Resources? Soulsby took over the Education Committee because he believed it was being insufficiently decisive in conducting its review of schools in the city. The committee was drifting into a lengthy three-stage review process, but Soulsby had been obliged to make a particular loyal and long-serving colleague chair of Education after unitary status: "There was no way I could not give it to her". Effectively the only way Soulsby could move her out was to take the post himself, but after six months as chair, having given the committee a more decisive steer, he handed over to Ross Willmott.

Becoming chair of Education for six months was a means to an end – that is, removing a chair whom it would have been politically impossible to replace directly. In becoming chair of the Regeneration Sub-committee, Soulsby took on a task that he saw as central to the city's future. It involved engaging with other partners, responding to government and maintaining the city's high profile. With both education and regeneration, Soulsby argued: "It was a question of choosing which issues are the heart of our corporate activity and hence need my attention for a period of time". His strategy is to step in to move issues forward and then step back at the appropriate time. It is a practical way of maintaining strategic and policy direction.

Soulsby emphasised the importance of a leader being available:

> "One of the most vital parts of the job of leader is being available. Problems and even crises in organisations as large and complex as the City Council rarely happen at convenient times or even one at a time. Whether it is a colleague who needs feedback on a sensitive issue, a damaging story in an early edition of the *[Leicester] Mercury* or a factory threatening to relocate to Bristol – a leader can rarely be unavailable if called on."

Soulsby regarded the local newspaper, the *Leicester Mercury*, with some scepticism, or even hostility, at the time of Graham Bett's attempted coup in 1988. Since then, however, he has developed a far closer relationship with the paper. He is invariably telephoned personally two or three times each day by the press and will even leave meetings to give quotes if the copy deadline is tight. Our diary extracts even show two media interviews from the middle of a field! Soulsby regards it as "very important to build up good working relations with the *Mercury*'s political correspondent". Reflecting on time spent responding to the press (October 1998), Soulsby maintained it was "well worth the time. It is absolutely invaluable. One of the few things I would stop everything for is to meet their deadlines. It is a very, very, high priority". A good working relationship with the *Leicester Mercury* is central to Soulsby's high-profile leadership style. He spares no effort cultivating it.

In his evidence to the Independent Panel, Soulsby noted that he effectively gave up his career prospects when he became leader. At that time (1981) he was 32 years old and head of a department in a secondary school. He could reasonably have expected to have continued to be promoted. Until he finally left teaching in December 1995 his substantive salary had remained unchanged, being then about £25,000 per year:

> However, my position as leader had long been effectively full-time. I was very fortunate that my employers were prepared to accept that I could nominally retain employment while effectively they only required me to work the equivalent of 80 days per year. There was, however, a proportional loss of pay for all but 20 of the days I missed! This meant a net loss of several thousand pounds per year for many years and of course a substantial accumulated loss of pension rights. Last year even

this nominal requirement of 80 days attendance became unsustainable, and I left employment on 31 December 1995 with no pension. (Soulsby Evidence, 2 October 1996)

Being a paid leader gave Soulsby a higher profile than hitherto – both for better and for worse. Complainants about the City Council frequently cited his salary en passant in their letters to page 6 of the *Leicester Mercury*. He became the public face of Leicester City Council. It needs to be remembered, however, that if he had the highest profile he also had most to lose. Defeat in an election means not only loss of office but also unemployment; the same applies to defeat at the annual leadership elections within the Labour group.

Research published in June 1998 showed that Leeds City Council's Brian Walker received £28,362 in 1997/98, making him the highest paid party leader in England and Wales. Walker estimated he worked more than 60 hours a week for the council, with evenings taken up with meetings or functions, "many of which I really don't want to go to, but the responsibility comes with the job. There's no way whatsoever, hand on heart, you can do the job I'm doing and still work" (*Local Government Chronicle*, 5 June 1998). The average leader's allowance in unitary authorities in 1997/98 was £9,228, compared with £13,291 in metropolitan districts and £3,471 in English district councils. The issue remains controversial. For example, the four counties that topped the 'allowances' list in 1996/97 – Essex, Staffordshire, Nottinghamshire and Hampshire – all reduced their leader's pay in 1997/98 with Essex axing entirely the £20,600 it had allocated. In 1998 Peter Soulsby, with his basic allowance and SRA totalling £27,603, plus £9,000 from British Waterways and £6,000 from the Audit Commission, remained one of the 'elite' paid political leaders among a sea of leaders who earned less than a junior clerk.

Crucially important for a leader, however well paid or not he/she might be, is 'getting the right officer team'. Soulsby emphasised "the difficulty of actually doing it". He put this in context by pointing out that as leader:

> "You are not in a position to have other than a slight influence on who is elected as councillors. In effect, the panel from which you draw chairs of committee is handed to you by the party machine. In addition, most leaders have very little opportunity to develop a team of chief officers."

The advent of unitary status, however, was a unique opportunity to put together a team, and he took it:

> "For every single director post I chaired the shortlisting group and chaired the interview panel. I was also actively involved in putting together the job descriptions. With some exceptions I was also actively involved in the appointment of assistant directors. Having chosen my team I can now leave a lot more to the officer core." (Interview, October 1998)

In the context of maintaining organisational cohesiveness and developing appropriate strategic and policy directions, Soulsby's central role in senior staff appointments has been pivotal. For any majority party leader, relations with the chief executive are crucial. Soulsby meets the chief executive twice each week for meetings ranging between 30 minutes and 2½ hours. One of these meetings is one to one; the other includes the deputy chief executive and the deputy leader. Such meetings help to eliminate 'surprises' and are regarded as crucial by both leader and chief executive. Soulsby also meets the chief executive every other Friday at the Policy Board (which comprises chief officers plus committee chairs – some 20 or more people in all). This meets for about two hours and has an important role in both developing strategy and ensuring programme implementation. The Policy Board also has quarterly away-days. Additionally, Soulsby speaks on the telephone to the chief executive two or three times a week. Soulsby sees the role of the leader in this context as welding "the core directors into a team so that they are *all* working together. One thing that is destabilising for the leader is chairs playing off departments one with another". Without positive working relationships, maintaining organisational cohesiveness becomes almost impossible.

Conclusion

In 1998 Peter Soulsby seemed relatively secure as party leader. He had withstood Sood's challenge in 1996 and was not challenged in the leadership elections in either 1997 or 1998. The disaffected comprised individuals rather than factions. This gave him some security, although the underlying tensions exhibited in the Foster challenge had not been swept away. His relative security meant that in both 1997 and 1998 he put forward quite explicitly a personal slate for all the leadership positions and this was accepted by the group. This required an understanding of who can deliver what and a significant amount of compromise in the context of what was a politically and culturally acceptable framework: "There is no tradition of a leader's slate but it is something I have increasingly brought into the culture". Such a slate is feasible while there are only a small number of dissidents in the group; it is naïve to see it as a permanent feature of local political leadership in Leicester. Opportunists are always ready to undermine a leader, and invariably, the longer a leader has been in office, the more dissidents there are.

Events in late 1998 emphasised the incipient factionalism, and hence the vulnerability of the Labour leader. On 13 November 1998 the *Local Government Chronicle* ran a story under the heading 'Selections Likely to Oust Long-Time Leicester Leader'. It stated that "Long-standing Leicester City Council leader Peter Soulsby is looking increasingly likely to be replaced after next May's city-wide elections". It based the story on a number of deselections at local ward level:

> Mr Soulsby and the Labour group's deputy leader, chair, secretary, chief whip and another whip have made a series of complaints against leading Leicester Labour Party members. Among the allegations is that of entryism by taxi drivers and their families, seeking to introduce more favourable tax licensing laws. (*Local Government Chronicle*, 13 November 1998)

This allegation evoked a response from John Thomas, a former city councillor, secretary of Leicester East Labour Party and himself a council candidate in May 1999. Thomas denied the allegations: "We can only assume Mr Soulsby wants to dispense with the members and choose the councillors himself".

Soulsby responded through the columns of the *Local Government Chronicle* (4 December 1998), pointing out that, of the existing 39 Labour members of the Council, only four had been defeated in selections – "an unusually small proportion". He also argued that the effect of these particular deselections on his own support "was probably neutral, insofar as you can predict these things in the shifting sands of council politics". This episode, however, is a reminder of the potentially transient nature of local political leadership. In this case the problem was resolved by the Midlands Labour Party, which insisted on the reinstatement of the deselected councillors. A contested leadership election within the Labour group following the May 1999 local elections looked increasingly likely.

The attempted coup in 1994 and the clear divisions exhibited within the Labour group in 1998/99 are salutary reminders that local political leadership, however secure it might appear at specific points in time, is always potentially vulnerable.

The Labour Government's 1998 White Paper, *Modern local government* (DETR, 1998b) emphasised (para 3.54): "It is clear that executive mayors, and some others in political executive positions or the scrutiny function in councils, may spend much if not all of their time on council business with a possible subsequent loss of earnings and pension rights. Where this is the case, the Government will make possible the payment of pensionable salaries", although precise levels would remain a matter for individual councils. With the advent of elected mayors and cabinet leaders, it is likely that paid council leaders will become the norm rather than the exception. Indeed in 1998 in Leicester, in addition to Soulsby earning a total of almost £43,000 from all sources, each senior chair of committee received a total basic allowance/SRA package of £8,446 a year. The 'cabinet with a leader' model from the White Paper is already, it seems, beginning to assume some form in Leicester. Executive leadership, however, requires the election of councillors of appropriate calibre; one of the challenges for local government in Leicester (and for cities of a similar size) is to attract such potential leaders so that the cabinet model can work effectively.

Postscript

Following the 6 May 1999 Leicester City Council elections, Sir Peter Soulsby (he had received a knighthood in the January 1999 Honours List) stood down as Labour group leader. The Labour Party lost nine seats in the elections and its majority slipped from 22 to four in its worst local government election results in Leicester for 24 years. The defeated councillors were disproportionately Soulsby supporters. It is likely that Soulsby did his arithmetic before the Group Annual Meeting on Saturday 8 May and knew exactly what the outcome of a leadership vote would be. He therefore stood aside, leaving the way clear for Ross Willmott to be returned unopposed. In an interview (*Leicester Mercury*, 10 May 1999), Soulsby commented: "I have been toying with the idea of standing down for a couple of weeks. Ross [Willmott] and I had a chance to talk at the election count and firmly came to a conclusion that the election was a good opportunity".

Saturday 8 May was not a good day for Soulsby who, after standing down as leader, then tried to get elected as chief whip but was defeated by one vote. He did, however, secure one of five open places on the group executive; he therefore remains in the wings but not centre-stage. The vulnerability of local political leaders remains clear; it is a transient rather than a permanent role. By standing down rather than forcing an election, he has arguably put himself in a good position to re-emerge in the future as a leadership contender. Indeed, Soulsby observed:

> "I won't talk to you about high points because I don't want you to write my political obituary. I am looking forward to playing whatever role the group and Ross feel is appropriate – but as he and I know, I'm particularly keen to take forward the physical regeneration of the city."

It might not yet be the end of Sir Peter Soulsby's career as a local political leader.

EIGHT

Case studies of leadership in action

Introduction

The previous chapter focused on the leadership perspective, style and experiences of Peter Soulsby, the long-time Labour leader of Leicester City Council. Although from the evidence of other interviews much of Soulsby's experience and perspective have parallels elsewhere, it is important not to over-generalise from one case study. Leicester has long been controlled by the Labour Party. Other councils are, or have been, controlled by other parties in recent years – principally Conservative and Liberal Democrat – where there are often different perceptions of the role of leader. Some councils are still dominated by independents, and leadership, if indeed it is formally recognised, has to operate without the support of more or less disciplined party groups. Many councils are hung (or balanced), and there the challenge of leadership is different again, requiring skills of inter-party and inter-personal negotiation which are much less important in situations of majority control. And even within Labour groups, there are important cultural differences with implications for leadership style and priorities. Peter Soulsby has long been accustomed to operating with a 'factionalised' group, whereas other Labour leaders have enjoyed a much higher degree of group unity.

In this chapter we examine the political careers and experiences of five other leaders chosen to reflect the kinds of variations and contexts discussed above. Robert Parker was Labour leader of Lincolnshire County Council between 1993 and 1997, when the council was 'hung' but Labour and the Liberal Democrats cooperated to form what was known as a 'partnership' administration. Richard Farnell was Labour leader of Rochdale MBC between 1986 and 1992, at a particularly eventful period in Rochdale's recent history; his experience contrasts with that of Peter Soulsby in that Farnell worked with a much less factionalised group. Eric Pickles was Conservative leader of Bradford MBC between 1988 and 1990, when it was regarded as a flagship Tory authority in terms of the prevailing ideology of the Thatcher government. Graham Tope (now Lord Tope) has been the Liberal Democrat leader of the London Borough of Sutton since 1986. And finally, Eddie Martin was leader of the relatively unpoliticised Rutland District Council (since 1997, Rutland Unitary Authority) between 1995 and 1998.

In each case we draw heavily on the perceptions and words of the leaders themselves and attempt to develop a coherent narrative of their experience. At the end of the chapter we draw out some comparisons between their experiences, attitudes and styles which illustrate some of the features of our analytical framework (see Chapters Two and Three).

Leadership in a hung authority

Robert Parker: Lincolnshire County Council 1993-97

Studying on an Open University course whetted Robert Parker's appetite for going into local politics. He had previously worked as a career civil servant for 20 years, latterly in the DHSS in the Rhodes Boyson era. While studying for a BA Applied Social Science degree in the early 1980s, he joined the Labour Party and on graduation became a social worker for Lincolnshire County Council. His interest in social work meant that becoming a county councillor was more attractive than becoming a district councillor. Robert stood for Lincolnshire County Council in 1989, having given up his social work job (which would have precluded him from standing for the county) and taken up a voluntary sector post in Scunthorpe.

Once elected, Robert immediately became shadow spokesperson on social services. He was elected Labour group leader in May 1991, following a dispute between some members of the Lincolnshire County and Lincoln City Labour groups over dual membership in the context of the Local Government Review. Robert decided to stand for the leadership because, on the one hand, more senior colleagues did not wish to stand and, on the other, he felt that it was time for a change. "Timing was of the essence", he said. He won a comfortable majority within the Labour group. Within two years of becoming a Labour councillor, he was leader of the Labour group.

In the run-up to the 1993 county council elections, it became apparent to Robert that there was a good chance of the council becoming hung, given the growing unpopularity of the Conservative government. He purchased the Leach–Stewart book *The politics of hung authorities* (Leach and Stewart, 1992) and initiated discussion in the Labour group about strategy and tactics, both in preparing for the election, and in what they would do if the council become hung. There was a specific policy of targeting winnable seats:

> "We decided to target particular seats and ended up winning in 25 out
> of our 36 target seats. There was of course pressure from Labour Party
> headquarters to stand in as many seats as possible but they didn't insist
> ... there was no pact with the Liberal Democrats about where to stand.
> It was very much a case of using our judgement and whether we had
> the right people to stand locally."

In addition, following the internal problems of 1991, all dual members had been precluded from standing. Robert worked with the county party to develop a much more serious manifesto than had previously been attempted. Then in May 1993, the night before the local elections, there was a round table discussion on local radio involving all the political leaders. Following this discussion, Robert went for a drink with the Liberal Democrat leader and they decided to meet again on the Friday immediately after the election if the result was that no one party had overall control.

The 1993 election resulted in the following distribution of seats in Lincolnshire: Labour 25, Liberal Democrats 15, Conservatives 32 and Independents 4. Thus, if Labour and the Liberal Democrats were prepared to work together, they would have an overall majority of four on the Council. With full support from the Labour group, Robert proposed a 'partnership administration' with the Liberal Democrat leader. Although the Liberal Democrats had been courted by the Tories as well, and there was some division in their ranks about alignment with the Labour Party, there was majority support for the 'partnership administration' which was duly announced to the media – subject to formal agreement of the party groups and national parties over the weekend.

Robert was confident that the Labour group would agree, but more doubtful about the views of the county Labour Party (where he knew there would be opposition from a number of key individuals) and the national Labour Party. He insisted on an 'open meeting' of the county party, where he managed to win majority support for the 'partnership' administration. With county party support, approval from Walworth Road was then sought. Headquarters agreed to 'shared chairs' but insisted that the party had to retain its identity.

Was the partnership ever under threat during the next four years?

"No, it held together well. The people of Lincolnshire had voted out the Tories so we had a duty to represent a centre/left perspective. The alternative was the Conservatives. We were preventing the adoption of Conservative policies."

The main problems faced by Robert were the intermittent scepticism of the county Labour Party and the need to sustain the trust of the party group.

"The problem I had (as did other leading Labour members) was all about parameters – knowing how far I could go with the Liberal Democrats without losing support from my own party. We would agree a position in group. The problem was how far I could amend that position following negotiations with the Liberal Democrats without coming back – how far was the group prepared to trust me?"

It was always about getting the balance right between principle and pragmatism.

That trust was sustained. The Labour group recognised the difficulties that Robert had with the Liberal Democrats, who lacked the sort of party discipline that Labour groups accept as second nature. The group was aware that Labour was in the driving-seat. The Liberal Democrats had not produced a substantial manifesto, and it was the ideas in the Labour manifesto that were driving the council's priorities.

Robert became chair of Policy Committee. Of the eight chairs, the agreed (proportional) split was five Labour: three Liberal Democrat. There was a similar split of vice-chairs. The Liberal Democrats chaired Highways, "which was good because this committee attracted a lot of criticism from the Tories because of budget cuts, and was not for us as high a priority area as education and social services".

In policy and expenditure terms, Parker argued that there were several achievements that would not have taken place under a Conservative administration:

"Education, social services, economic development and environment were the main priorities. We moved away from roads and highways.

We also introduced borrowing, which was never considered under the Conservatives. We had inherited significant balances which we could spend, and did, on 4 new nursery schools, 15 new nursery classes, £10 million allocated to a new university, and greatly increased social services spending. All these were agreed by the Liberal Democrats. Under the previous Tory administration the spending on social services had been 10% under the government guidelines."

Robert anticipated some problems with the more traditional chief officers who had served Tory administrations in Lincolnshire over a long period:

"One of the first things I did was to hold a chief officers' meeting where the message to officers was 'you are working for a different administration now'. We said that there would be no blood-letting so long as they recognised that there was a new political agenda, and so long as they did not attempt to undermine the new administration."

The reality was that the Labour/Liberal Democrat action plan was taken up with varying degrees of enthusiasm by different officers. In some cases, interpretation of policy was still based on 'old-fashioned thinking'. These problems soon led Robert to realise that a major organisational restructuring was required which would redesign the organisation to respond to the reordered priorities and at the same time would ensure that top staff were in post who were in tune with the new political agenda. KPMG was appointed to advise because "we wanted the benefits and legitimation of outside expertise. But it has to be said that they were given a tight brief to work to". The process of reorganisation in Lincolnshire, and of dealing with officers who lacked political sensitivity, has been discussed in more detail in Chapter Six.

Robert Parker emphasised the importance for a leader of having a chief executive with whom he could work effectively. He felt that Jill Barrow, the new chief executive, had been a successful appointment. It was an important troubleshooting role. There had been regular weekly meetings of the Labour and Liberal Democrat leader and the chief executive, but these had not always been particularly effective, and were inadequate vehicles for sustaining policy momentum. For this, Robert relied on regular informal discussions with the chief executive. Her task was also to work on maintaining a civilised relationship between Labour and Liberal Democrats and on seeking agreement and support on key proposals. The process of maintaining inter-party cohesion was a major time-consuming commitment for Robert. Although the process was helped by the skills of the new chief executive, he remembers this aspect of leading a hung authority as a particularly demanding and draining activity.

The regional world of local government was of some concern to Robert in his period as county council leader. The national Association of County Councils (ACC) was 'not a high priority', but the East Midlands Employers' Organisation, the East Midlands Local Government Association and the county Local Government Association (LGA) were, for the following reasons:

> "This was going to be the way of the future; regional government was ahead. The Labour Party would get marginalised in Lincolnshire if we stood alone ... we created a county LGA of politicians, of which I was the first chair. But I firmly believe that Lincolnshire stood to benefit from pushing itself in the East Midlands region."

Robert was keen to develop a coherent strategy for the county. In practice, it took a long time to do so. "It was three and a half years into our four year administration before we managed to get a strategy together, incorporating spending plans, reorganisation and mission statement. It was published in November 1996 and we lost control in May 1997. If we'd had majority party control we could have done it a lot quicker".

In 1997 the Conservatives regained power. Labour representation fell to 19 and that of the Liberal Democrats to 11. Robert Parker retained his position as Labour group leader, despite a difficult atmosphere in the first Labour group meeting after the election defeat. His main leadership tasks following electoral defeat were "to protect services and embarrass the Conservatives". His current political priorities (in 1999) are regional government (which he sees as facilitating the introduction of unitary authorities), and supporting the campaign to scrap grammar schools.

Labour leadership

Richard Farnell: Rochdale MBC 1986-92

Richard Farnell was first elected to Rochdale MBC in 1980, having been active for several years in his ward and constituency Labour parties He had also acted as a parliamentary agent in the 1979 General Election. Labour was in control at the time but between 1982 and 1986, although

Labour was the largest party, the Liberals and Conservatives formed an anti-Labour pact to keep Labour out of power. Richard was elected leader in 1985, at a time when Labour looked likely to regain power in 1986 (which they subsequently did). His election process was unusual. An 'electoral college' was used, with half the votes going to the party group and half to the district Labour Party (DLP), even though this approach was not endorsed by the national party at the time. Richard was seen as being located towards the right of the party and he knew that his more Left-wing opponent would gain a sizeable majority within the DLP. However, on the night of the election his opponent did not turn up and Richard gained a narrow majority. He was leader continuously from 1985 until 1992 when he lost his seat and the Labour Party lost control of the council.

Despite being associated with the Right wing of the party, Richard quickly gained the support of the left because of his preparedness to espouse radical policies. By far the most significant of these was the commitment to decentralisation, which became the dominant policy focus after 1987, and ultimately proved instrumental in the Labour group's loss of power.

Decentralisation was a key element in the 1986 manifesto, which had been drawn up by the DLP and which presented "a clear agenda which all the group had campaigned for, and which could be used to tell the chief officers what we wanted". The push for decentralisation had come from the left of the party. Richard decided to take over responsibility for it, to the exclusion of the left, because of "their refusal to compromise over details".

The particular version of decentralisation that was favoured in Rochdale involved the creation of 11 neighbourhood committees, to which were attached multi-service neighbourhood offices. It was the latter aspect of the scheme that engendered most resistance. The traditional departmental structure of Rochdale was to be dismantled in favour of an area-based structure. Not surprisingly, there was a good deal of officer resistance to this fundamental change, and "chairs increasingly came under pressure". This was despite the setting up, early in Richard's period of leadership, of a 'chairs panel' which was specifically designed to 'maintain a unified group' (see below).

The chief executive was not seen as particularly helpful in the process of driving through the unpopular (with officers) policy of decentralisation. The leadership group's response was to "freeze him out of the management processes by working directly with lower-tier officers". There were some chief officers who were supportive and could be worked with, but otherwise it was mostly middle-tier officers who worked directly with chairs in drafting reports for the Labour manifesto, developing policy and playing a major role in the development of the decentralisation initiative. Richard recognises that this was very much a 'hands-on' style of political management, necessitated, he argues, by the circumstances.

Although 'decentralisation' was actually implemented, the new committees and neighbourhood offices were set up only a few weeks before the 1992 local elections, at which Labour lost control of the council:

> "The opposition got their act together and presented decentralisation
> as a wasteful exercise costing millions of pounds. They presented an
> image of the Labour administration as incompetent and wasteful. The
> decentralised structures had not been in place long enough for the
> public to know better."

In retrospect, Richard felt that the formal meetings (at party level) that had been set up to meet representatives of the unions within the authority to discuss plans for decentralisation and restructuring, with the aim of avoiding problems and keeping them informed of developments, had slowed down the process, and led to its late implementation, although this was "by no means all the unions' fault".

Richard introduced and acted as chair of the *Chairs' Panel*, which enabled senior councillors to get together regularly, with a couple of senior officers as advisers, to develop strategy and enable the group to act collectively, without being sidetracked by chief officers. However, this was too large a body to work as a leadership team. Key issues were debated, and the budget was usually set there, but "real decisions were made informally elsewhere". Its prime function was "to preserve political unity within the group". For example, all budget papers would come to the Chairs' Panel, where it would be agreed where cuts should fall and whose expenditure should be increased. The chairs would then take this package to the group, where Richard would thus have a large block already formally committed to his policies. He would, however, work behind the scenes prior to the chairs' meeting to develop support for his policies from key members and officers.

Richard Farnell developed a good rapport with the DLP which was relatively strong but not as strong as it thought:

"The DLP liked to think that its resolutions were binding on the group, but it was play-acting on my part to make them think that this was the case ... if resolutions did get through that weren't to my liking, I would sit on them, or interpret them in my own way, or even amend them through the group."

In fact, the DLP sometimes proved very helpful in terms of the leader's own priorities. Once he had decided to make decentralisation the key policy initiative, it was useful to remind chairs who had begun to question the policy that it had the support of (and had indeed originated from) the DLP.

Richard Farnell was a full-time leader, whose sole source of income came from the leader's allowance and other council payments. He 'led from the front', which, he claims, was appreciated by most members, although he recognises he may have been too autocratic, with members sometimes complaining 'that decisions had been made for them'. His leadership style was very informal. He would identify people whose support he thought he could rely on, and persuade them to provide assistance in getting policies through. His network of influence embraced group members, council officers (including middle-tier officers) and district party members. Indeed, he was adept at exploiting his privileged position within such networks, and his full-time commitment to the job. Ultimately, however, he was brought down by the perceived failure of his flagship policy of decentralisation, a perception induced, he would argue, by poor presentation and officer resistance, and by running out of time, so that the policy was not given a chance to prove itself before the crucial (1992) election.

Conservative leadership

Eric Pickles: Bradford City Council 1988-90

There can be few examples of local political administrations that made such a powerful impact, in relation both to policy change and media interest, as did the Conservative Party in Bradford in an 18-month period between 1988 and 1990. In October 1988, Bradford Conservatives won their second by-election victory since the summer recess, a result that meant that they held exactly half the council seats. The mayor at the time fortuitously happened to be a Conservative, which meant that, if all the Conservatives were present and voted together and the mayor exercised his casting vote, the group would have an effective majority. The Conservatives immediately took advantage of this position and held power on this basis until May 1990 (1989 was a non-election year), when Labour regained a majority position. During this relatively brief period of power, the Conservatives, led by Eric Pickles, enjoyed a reputation as a radical Tory authority equalled only by Wandsworth and Westminster – and indeed in the May 1990 election were widely regarded (together with these two London boroughs) as one of the three key 'flagship' Tory authorities.

Eric Pickles joined the Young Conservatives in 1968, "the day the Russian tanks rolled into Prague", and gradually rose within this organisation to become its national chair by 1980. The previous year he had been elected to Bradford City Council 'by accident' ("I turned up late to a branch meeting and was told I'd been selected"). When the Conservatives gained power in 1982, he became chair of Social Services for two years and then from 1984 until 1986 chair of Education, during which time Bradford was hung, but with the Conservatives still the dominant party. During this period he developed a particular interest in social services, particularly community care, which he has retained ever since. But in retrospect, this period represented "a waste of four years in my life". He felt that he was "merely helping to run a municipal socialist council more efficiently than the Labour Party" and operating "as though I were an officer", an experience he was determined not to replicate in 1988-90.

After the Conservatives lost power in 1986, Eric Pickles reviewed his political career and had almost decided to seek a parliamentary candidacy and (if successful) to resign from the council, when in 1987 the current leader of the Bradford Conservative group, Ronnie Fawley, suddenly and unexpectedly announced his resignation. Although Eric Pickles did not particularly want to be leader at the time, he allowed his name to be put forward and was duly elected, causing him to postpone his parliamentary ambitions for the time being.

His main priority as opposition leader was to "get our policies together". To this end, he assembled a group of members representing a cross-section of the group in terms of age, sex and political viewpoint. This 'policy group' began what was in effect a manifesto planning process, meeting regularly to discuss policy issues and working extremely effectively as a unit. As a result, six months later "we had a philosophical position on most issues and a 40-page manifesto, which was indexed". Members were expected to take it with them to committee meetings (where "it could be used as a crib") and to use it to challenge the arguments of the Labour administration.

This level of commitment to policy development was unprecedented for the Bradford Conservative group. Eric Pickles was the catalyst in the process, but his initiative clearly struck a responsive chord among his colleagues and built up group members' confidence during a period of increasingly effective opposition ('we ran rings round Labour'). The commitment also paid off when the Conservatives gained power in 1988 with a 'knife-edge' majority:

> "The manifesto held us together when we were in control. We never lost a vote and no one ever rebelled because *they owned the policy*. That's what was unique."

Once the Conservatives gained power, the same organisational skills were used in pushing the Conservatives' programme through the Council as had been used in opposition. Pickles observed:

> "I'd purchased a piece of computer software called Brainstorm. I realised I had a number of decisions to make. So I sat in front of the computer and developed a critical path analysis using Brainstorm. At the first council meeting 120 decisions were made, linked to a number of key decisions. Everything was covered. It looked like a classic Marxist/Leninist take-over."

It is hardly surprising, given this experience, that Eric Pickles should identify the key leadership qualities of his period of office as 'organisational ability' and 'the commitment to see something through'. He also had a strong commitment to getting the best out of his group – for example, through encouragement, praise, matching talents to opportunities, training programmes and 'never taking the group by surprise'. Having experienced problems of officer resistance (and the effectiveness of officers in delaying and diluting potential initiatives) in the 1983–86 period, Eric Pickles quickly head-hunted and appointed a chief executive he felt he could work with (Richard Penn from Knowsley), following a mutual agreement to bring forward the date of retirement of the incumbent chief executive by one year. He also gently engineered the departure of two other chief officers whose approach was, he felt, incompatible with the philosophy of the Conservative group.

The policy standpoint of Eric Pickles and the Conservative group was premised on the enabling authority ('as set out in the Audit Commission paper'): not to provide services directly unless it was the most efficient way of doing so; to use the city's considerable economic powers to bring about beneficial projects for local communities; and to devolve power to customers. His aim was to 'fuse together political structure, management structure and policy' in such a way that the policy momentum of the Conservative group could be sustained. To this end, there was a streamlining of the decision-making system and a clarification of member and officer roles:

> "I wanted to get member–officer relations back to the way it should be. We'd got to a stage in the previous administration where officers determined the policy direction and members decided the detail. We went back to first principles, and produced a mission statement which attempted to summarise and refine the 40-page manifesto. We gave it to the top officers and said look at it and give us your views. Then we set up meetings between the top officers and the group, out of which came a series of business plans and performance indicators. Committees became more policy-orientated."

Eric Pickles' main regret is his failure to implement quickly enough the policy for disposal of Elderly Person's Homes (EPHs) to the private sector, coupled with an indignation about the way in which Labour closed down the EPHs as soon as they regained power when "we were trying to keep them open".

In May 1990 the Conservatives lost power in Bradford, having achieved an unprecedented level of radical change over an 18-month period. What made this achievement possible was the thoroughness of the preparation for power, the organisation of the group to get things done once they had gained power, and the way the group held together in a conflictual and precarious period of control. In all these respects Eric Pickles played a leading role, although his style was very different from the traditional rather authoritarian Conservative model. He was not a full-time leader – his involvement in running a small business concerned with training in industrial relations continued throughout his period of leadership. In May 1991, 12 years after first becoming a councillor, he resigned from the Council, and in April 1992 he was elected to Parliament as Conservative member for Brentwood.

Liberal Democratic leadership

Graham Tope: London Borough of Sutton 1986 – present

There were several leaders we interviewed who, after distinguished careers in local government, went on to become MPs (eg Eric Pickles [Bradford] and Jim Cunningham [Coventry] in 1992 and Alan Whitehead [Southampton] in 1997). Graham Tope's political career represents a reversal of this familiar sequence. After a relatively short career at Westminster (1972–74) his political aspirations switched unequivocally to the local government level.

After joining the Young Liberals in the mid–1960s, and subsequently rising through the ranks of that organisation, in 1972 Graham Tope was elected as the prospective Liberal parliamentary candidate for Sutton and Cheam (where he had lived and been politically active for several years). When the sitting Conservative MP for Sutton and Cheam was appointed Governor of Bermuda a by-election became necessary, and, in one of the most spectacular by-election results of the 1960s and 1970s, Graham Tope won the seat for the Liberals at the age of 29. However, after only 15 months as an MP he lost the seat to the Conservatives in the first 1974 General Election, and shortly afterwards, in May 1974, stood as a candidate for the London Borough of Sutton. He was elected together with five party colleagues in an otherwise Conservative-dominated council, and was subsequently elected as Liberal group leader, a position he has held unchallenged ever since. He unsuccessfully contested the second general election of 1974, but his political sights were by now set locally rather than nationally, and he has not contested a national election since.

Although the Liberals did badly at the local elections of 1978 (when they retained only two seats) and 1982 (when the Liberal/SDP representation increased to three), the base of active support and party membership that had been built up during the high-profile 1972–74 period survived. In 1982 there were 20 seats, in which Liberal/SDP candidates came within 150 votes of winning. Five by-elections were won between 1982 and 1985, and there was a real sense of momentum by the time of 1986 local elections, at which the Alliance won exactly half the seats. A postponed election in a Conservative ward ensured that the Alliance was able to form the administration, and, after 12 years as leader of a small opposition group, Graham Tope became one of the only three Alliance leaders of London boroughs in 1986.

The Liberal Democrats (as they had then become) increased their majority in Sutton in 1990 and in 1994 and 1998 won overwhelming majorities. Thus, over a period of 10 years, a dominant Conservative political culture was replaced by a dominant Liberal Democrat culture. (At the 1997 General Election, both Sutton's parliamentary seats were won by Liberal Democrats.)

In 1994, Graham Tope was elevated to the peerage, and became a frontbench Liberal Democrat local government spokesperson in the House of Lords. He is still leader of Sutton, although the time demands of his new role has meant that he has increasingly shared some of his leadership tasks in Sutton with other colleagues. In this sketch, we concentrate on the 1986-94 period.

Of the Liberal Democrat group that gained power in Sutton in 1986, only two (including Graham Tope) had been there for more than four years; five had been returned at by-elections between 1982 and 1986, and the remaining 21 were new to the council. In these circumstances Graham was very much looked to for a strong lead. The group was inexperienced, the new chairs were inexperienced, and, although he would have preferred more of a team approach (which he subsequently helped to develop), Graham acknowledged that during the 1986-90 period his leadership role was necessarily more 'from the front' than a Liberal Democrat leader's role would normally be. That was a reflection of the borough's political history.

Even though the Council was technically hung between 1986 and 1990, it was run as if it were majority-controlled. Labour did not invariably support the Liberal Democrats, and the casting vote of the (Liberal Democrat) mayor or committee chair was often needed. However, Graham acknowledges the effect of the political arithmetic on group cohesion and discipline:

> "Everyone knew that one vote against the group line could result in a defeat at council. The group was on a 'high' following the election win, and we all got on well together. All this helped to generate a positive attitude towards collectivity."

Other Liberal Democrat leaders have experienced much more difficulty in generating this kind of group cohesion, and have also experienced a much greater circumscription of the leadership role.

During the 1986-90 period the strategy was very much a *service-oriented* one. The pervious Conservative administration had attempted to keep spending as low as possible and the Liberal Democrats' main concern, once elected, was to improve delivery in those services where provision was seen as inadequate. Education and social services, in particular, experienced major increases in expenditure. The main task was seen as redressing 12 years of underfunding. The most difficult decision that faced Graham Tope and his colleagues during this first period of office was the future of grammar schools in Sutton:

> "We came in committed to comprehensive education and the scrapping of grammar schools. It had been a priority in our manifesto. After the 1987 general election we had to decide what to do. The Secretary of State was not going to agree to scrap grammar schools. There was a lot of internal debate – in fact, dealing with this issue really matured the group. The majority view, which I supported, was that we should stop the policy. The chair of Education felt very strongly that we shouldn't. But we all agreed to abide by the majority view and present a united front at council."

After the 1990 election there was a very different political culture. The Liberal Democrats had a comfortable majority, and there were now over 20 councillors who had experienced at least a full four-year term. It was now possible to develop an approach that was based more on teamwork. Graham saw his main task as switching emphasis from 'improving service' to strategic direction, vision and organisational change: "Some councillors were more at ease with this change than others, who wanted to continue the service emphasis, particularly at a time of cuts".

Graham set up a 'weekend away' for leading councillors (an innovation in itself for Sutton) facilitated by an external adviser (as it happens, one of the authors of this book). At this session a commitment to a strategic approach was built among the leadership group and was subsequently accepted, more or less enthusiastically, by the rest of the group.

The leader also recognised that this was the right time for major organisational changes. During the 1986-90 period there had been some feeling among chief officers that "things will return to normal in 1990" (ie that the Liberal Democrats would lose power). Once re-elected, "we wanted to reorganise the council structure to be more geared to what we wanted to do". The chief executive left for a similar post in another London borough, which provided the opportunity to appoint someone who "could deliver the kind of changes we wanted". Patricia Hughes, a solicitor working with the London Borough of Islington, was appointed in November 1990.

During the 1990-96 period Sutton became something of a pioneer in a number of fields. It developed and gained public support for a corporate strategy and mission statement. It developed an imaginative and innovatory environmental strategy, with an emphasis on conservation and green issues. It pioneered a number of imaginative public participation initiatives.

During the period under discussion, and indeed since, Graham Tope's position as leader has never been seriously threatened or challenged. He was the obvious leader following the 1986 election, and his open consultative style and emphasis on team-building (particularly after the 1990 election) was appreciated by other group members. He was well liked personally, and, while his experience and growing status on the national Liberal Democrat scene gave him a de facto authority within the group, which came to look to him for a proactive lead more than would normally be the case in Liberal Democrat groups, he has never pushed that authority beyond the level of the acceptable. There has been a congruence between leadership style and political culture.

Leadership in a non-politicised council

Eddie Martin: Rutland Council 1995-98

Leadership in politicised authorities is a well understood concept. Only in politically fragmented hung authorities is the term eschewed (typically for political reasons). But what of leadership in authorities dominated by independents? Does the term have any meaning – formally or informally – in this context? How can an aspiring leader achieve his/her ambitions in an authority that does not even recognise the concept of political leadership? How can he/she hope to lead the council when there is no formal party recognition within the authority? And what of authorities where members are elected under a political label but then eschew that label in favour of some notion of independence?

One such authority was Rutland District Council (RDC), which in April 1997 became an all-purpose unitary authority as a result of the Local Government Review. RDC could justifiably claim to be the smallest unit of local government in Britain in terms of both elected members and directly employed staff. Since its inception in 1974, it has operated with 20 elected members. For a brief period between 1993 and 1995 the workforce dropped to as few as 59. Organisationally, RDC was a very small district council. All employees were housed in the main Council offices, a building that used to be the Earl of Gainsborough's hunting lodge. Since it has become a unitary authority, its workforce has of course expanded significantly but council membership has remained at 20.

The tradition within RDC, both pre- and post-Widdicombe, had been to operate without party political groups. While councillors may have stood for election on party political tickets, once elected they eschewed party discipline. During the last three or four years of RDC's existence, however, the case for the identification of a 'political leader' of the Council came to be increasingly recognised. The decision to create the position of leader within RDC, however, was a contested and uneven process. The shift from the old system involved a series of minor changes before the position of leader was fully legitimised. The process by which this was achieved is looked at in more detail below.

Instrumental in the process leading to the formal recognition of the leadership position, and, as it transpired, the first holder of that position, was Councillor Eddie Martin. Prior to becoming leader of the Council, Martin had occupied a number of other posts in his career at RDC, including chair of Housing and Health, and vice-chair of the Council. To fully understand how RDC operated in general and Martin's style of leadership in particular, it is important to discuss the political and organisational context within which Martin worked.

Rutland's 27,000 population is dispersed widely around the district. The two main centres of population, Oakham and Uppingham, both contain public schools, which form the largest employer in Rutland. Councillor Martin was a teacher at the school in Oakham. While Martin's occupation may appear irrelevant, it actually provided him with the opportunity to exploit his considerable political talents to the full. The location of the school in relation to the Council offices was of critical importance. Martin used the proximity of the two organisations to full effect. Judicious use of time allowed him daily access to the Council offices. Availability, however, was not the only factor he used to become the first leader in Rutland. Martin had been a member of RDC for the previous 11 years. Initially a member of the Conservative Party, he stood for the Council as an independent eschewing what he calls "political party dictates" *(Rutland Times*, 25 April 1996). Martin's sense of position is apparent from his recollection of past events. As he observed:

> "I have tended to be, since being in this authority, a leading member, whatever that may mean, for the last ten years. The first task that they asked me to take on was to chair the new and fairly innovative

> Competitive Tendering Working Group.... As a consequence of which
> we then proceeded inexorably down the competitive tendering route,
> whether it was VCT, which it was in our case, or CCT, which it was in
> other cases."

It was not a tradition that new members were appointed to such high-profile posts. Rather, it reflected the number of candidates and the number of new members. When Martin was first elected member turnover was, in his own words, "relatively low". As a result, it was necessary "to prove one's mettle in the debating chamber".

Events conspired to Martin's advantage. In 1993 the chair of the Council, Colin Forsyth, resigned owing to professional commitments. The vacant position was filled by the vice-chair with Martin becoming vice-chair himself. This coincided with the Local Government Commission's review of English shire local government. Rutland District Council had taken a policy decision to externalise services while attempting to gain unitary status (see Wilson, 1996). The ensuing workload for the relatively few elected members was immense. Martin's commitment to what he perceived to be the cause of Rutland's 'independence' from Leicestershire meant that he was in effect doing two full jobs: teacher and politician.

Of equal importance to Martin's role was the prevailing belief among the elected members of RDC that it was an independent council, when technically it was a balanced authority. No group has ever exercised its right, post-Widdicombe, to inform the chief executive that it wishes to be recognised as a political group. As a result, the members of RDC all believe that they enter the council chamber as independents regardless of the political affiliation they took at their election. One outcome of the absence of political groups has been the lack of political group leaders. As a result, the combination of the roles of civic head and political head of the authority have resided in the chair of the Council.

Most of the contentious changes in Rutland's recent past were driven through by a strong chair in conjunction with a powerful chief executive. The chair could deliver a compliant group of councillors providing he had brought the high-profile members on board. The chief executive led the officer core and ensured that the decisions were carried through. During the most turbulent period in RDC's recent history, such a combination existed in Colin Forsyth, chair, and Keith Emslie, chief executive. In 1995 Keith Emslie resigned as chief executive and was replaced by a temporary appointment, Allen Dobson. Dobson stayed in post until the appointment of a permanent chief executive immediately prior to gaining unitary status.

Dobson, previously chief executive of Wear Valley DC, brought a wealth of experience in dealing with politicians in a political setting. His early experiences at RDC convinced him that the politicisation of elected members need not necessarily constrain the role of chief executive. Dobson was concerned at the lack of 'steer' from the politicians and the propensity for every Council meeting to become a talking shop. The reality of the situation was that decisions were made by a small group of influential members. While the exact number of influential members varied, one previous chief executive indicated that there were probably five members you had to get 'on side'. Martin was one of these.

Dobson suggested to the members that they became a political group *pace* Widdicombe and elect a 'leader' separately from the role of chair. Such was the antipathy towards the title 'leader', that the members formed a group but decided to use the title 'coordinator' instead. Martin was duly elected coordinator. Initially he was supportive of the use of such a title. He stated that the traditions within RDC were such that the members would never acquiesce to acknowledging a political leader. What Martin was actually recognising, however, was the limits of his power. Other members of the group of five previously identified would have quickly challenged his use of the title 'leader', and Martin was aware of this.

Martin used his time as coordinator to reinforce his power base. His deputy was a member of the Liberal Democrats who was to stand in the 1997 General Election as candidate for Melton and Rutland. Another potential rival for the role of coordinator was installed as chair of the Council. The remaining two members of the group of five had both narrowly retained their seats in the elections of 1995. Given that shadow elections were to be held in 1996 for the new Rutland District County Council, their concerns were on issues closer to home. As it transpired, one declined to stand for election in 1996 while the other was defeated. Martin filled the ensuing power vacuum within the council. It was noticeable that the title 'coordinator' was replaced by the more usual title of 'leader' soon after the shadow elections.

What was also apparent after the shadow elections was the election of a notionally more politicised membership which included Labour councillors. The newly elected Labour members indicated to Martin that they wanted to form a political group of their own. Martin's response was to inform the Labour members that they were fully entitled to claim their right, but that the other members would 'swamp them'. The Rutland way was not to politicise business on party political lines but to work for the benefit of the authority as a whole. This was one of Martin's key tactics. His longevity and political acumen had placed him at the head of a relatively inexperienced group of elected members. The consecutive elections of 1995 and 1996 resulted in a total of 13 new members being elected. Reflecting on the six new members elected in 1996, Martin observed:

> This is all to the good, but the six new members are going to have to be licked into shape pretty rapidly. I am sure they all realise the challenges they face. As everyone knows, though, I am evangelical about keeping party politics out of local politics and I just hope that the new members who do come to us with announced party affiliations realise that the job in hand must not be prejudiced by preconceived and doctrinaire attitudes. (*Rutland Times*, 9 October 1996)

The 1996 elections had seen party politics intrude further into Rutland politics, notably with the election for the first time of two Labour councillors. In addition, the new unitary authority required a completely new management structure that included a new chief executive. Martin was instrumental in appointing the new officer team.

With the benefit of hindsight, it can be argued that Martin possessed a sense of the possible and the political acumen to realise what he could achieve at a given point in time. The ability and willingness to work long hours both in paid employment and in Council activity is another major factor. Of equal importance, however, was the opportunity provided by the physical location of his workplace in conjunction to the Council offices. Added to both the above factors was Martin's 'luck' that the replacement of so many longstanding members and the appointment of a new management team occurred simultaneously and undoubtedly strengthened his position. The need for visible leadership, which was generated by the Local Government Review battles, was also important.

Paradoxically, in 1998, when his position was most secure, Martin did not stand for re-election as leader. Indeed, because of work pressures, he resigned from the council in that year.

Conclusion: common themes

The five case studies discussed in this chapter, taken in conjunction with the extended case study of Sir Peter Soulsby's leadership in Leicester City

Council in the preceding chapter, stimulate a number of interesting comparisons and contrasts. In this concluding section we first draw out a number of common themes and discuss them in a way that tries to make sense of these similarities and differences. The material in the two chapters is then reinterpreted in terms of the four leadership tasks discussed in Chapters Three to Six.

The definition of an effective leadership role is more problematical in authorities that lack majority control, but it is possible

When Peter Soulsby, Graham Tope, Eric Pickles and Richard Farnell became leaders of their local authorities, there was a reasonably clear set of expectations about what 'leadership' involved (least so for Graham Tope, given the lack of experience within his group in 1986). These expectations left a good deal of scope for the individual to interpret and modify current practice and ultimately to partially redefine the leadership role in his own terms. All four leaders in one way or another took advantage of this scope. For Eddie Martin and Robert Parker, however, there was little by way of precedents. The idea of a partnership administration was new to Lincolnshire, and Robert learned the job in the practice of it. The idea of council leadership itself was new to Rutland, which had for a long time managed without the position and the concept; Eddie Martin had to persuade his colleagues (with the help of an influential chief executive) that a leadership position was necessary, and then used his skills and charisma to develop the role in the atypical context of quasi-independent politics that operated in the district.

In Lincolnshire, Robert Parker soon learned that 'leadership' required an ability to negotiate with the leader of the party with whom Labour was in partnership, a process that often proved frustrating and indecisive. Such inter-party discussions were of very limited concern to those leaders whose parties enjoyed a majority. Similarly, the 'balancing act' that Parker had to operate between retaining the confidence and trust of his own group and being able to negotiate effectively with the Liberal Democrats was not an issue for the other leaders. The sustained support that Robert received from his group facilitated his ability to provide effective leadership of the council. Leaders in other hung authorities often have a much more difficult task, either because of the lack of any form of partnership with another party, or because of a lower level of group trust than that enjoyed by Robert Parker.

The scope for proactive leadership is greatest following an electoral victory involving a change of control and where there is an enthusiastic and shared commitment to a distinctive programme

In the euphoria following a good electoral result, particularly where it involves winning power after a significant period in opposition, there is often a strong predisposition to support a leader in his/her perception of priorities for action. The status of a leader is enhanced by electoral success. Richard Farnell, Eric Pickles and Graham Tope all experienced and took advantage of this kind of celebratory euphoria. In Robert Parker's case the gains Labour made, and the fact that the Conservatives no longer had a majority in Lincolnshire, was seen understandably as a de facto victory. In each case, the leader found himself working with an inexperienced group comprising many new councillors, which enhanced the tendency to follow the leader. This effect was most pronounced in the case of Graham Tope and Robert Parker; least so for Richard Farnell, whose scope for manoeuvre was also limited by a relatively strong and active district party.

In each case, too, the existence of a coherent and innovative programme of action helped retain the coherence of the group and provide a basis for the exercise of leadership. The best prepared group in this respect was probably the Conservatives in Bradford in 1988 under Eric Pickles. But in each of the other three cases the parties came to power with clear priorities – increased expenditure on education and social services in Sutton; a more extended set of service priorities in Lincolnshire; and (more problematically) the commitment to decentralisation in Rochdale.

In each case the leaders proved adept at building on this initial base of trust and enthusiasm, sometimes initiating a change of direction over which differences of view existed within the group (eg Graham Tope in Sutton in 1990). The one exception to this pattern has been Peter Soulsby, who has never enjoyed the security that his counterparts have to a greater or lesser extent enjoyed. Peter has had to exercise leadership in the context of a factionalised and divided group ever since his accession to power in 1981, although the disruptive effect of the factionalism has varied over the 17-year period.

A leadership role can normally be developed in a way that transcends formal definitions, depending on the individual skills of the leader and the political context

The case studies demonstrate a number of ways in which leadership roles can be developed by leaders themselves in a way that moves beyond 'normal expectations'. Graham Tope developed a much more high-profile leadership role than is usual in Liberal Democrat groups through a combination of political circumstances and personal credibility. Robert Parker enjoyed more personal authority and scope than is typical in Labour groups because of the recognition by the group of the problems of inter-party relations. Richard Farnell strengthened his position through an ability to work the political network which went well beyond that of any of his colleagues.

Whatever the limitation of their formal authority, the leaders in the case studies were all able to strengthen their positions (and, in particular, the predisposition of group members to follow) by their own personal qualities. Eric Pickles and Robert Parker in particular had personal visions for their authorities which generated enthusiasm and commitment among their colleagues. Peter Soulsby has long been recognised as an effective advocate for Leicester in the world of external relationships. All were articulate, effective in debate, and able to deal publicly with opposition criticism. These skills carry weight. A leader's position is strengthened by his/her ability to give the opposition a hard time – or to speak out effectively for the authority. And the power to argue articulately, particularly when combined with the 'special knowledge' that leaders have access to via the relationship with chief executive, strengthens a leader's ability to convince his/her colleagues, in debate, that leadership preferences should be supported.

It should not be assumed that all leaders have these kinds of qualities. We have concentrated in these case studies on leaders who were able to exploit their positions positively. Other examples were encountered where these qualities of articulateness, networking ability and public presence were less apparent.

Task emphasis is to some extent a reflection of the perceptions of the leader, which may not always be shared by the group

Our final conclusion reinforces the key point made sporadically throughout Chapters Three to Six, namely that, although the four key leadership tasks identified are all important, their *relative* importance varies in response to both the particular circumstances facing the authority and the personal/political predispositions of the leader.

Maintaining the cohesiveness of the dominant group (or governing coalition), for example, has been a much greater challenge for some of the case study leaders than for others. In very different circumstances, it has been a major problem for Peter Soulsby (because of the factionalism within the Labour group) and for Eddie Martin (because of the lack of an identifiable self-defined group within the council). For Richard Farnell there were problems of group cohesiveness which developed as the implications of the decentralisation initiative became clearer, and which were accentuated in the last year or two of Labour's period of control. On the other hand, Graham Tope and Eric Pickles were able to rely on group cohesiveness, for the reasons discussed above, and thus could devote their energies to other priorities. In the particular circumstances of a hung Lincolnshire, Robert Parker had to make many judgements about the extent to which group cohesiveness could be sustained, but benefited from a much more understanding and supportive group than many leaders of hung authorities.

All the case study leaders were concerned with establishing a strategic direction, but the way in which they interpreted this task varied considerably. For Robert Parker, Peter Soulsby and Graham Tope, strategies that were concerned with the enhancement of particular services were replaced with moves towards a corporate strategy which transcended service considerations. In each case the challenge of persuading groups to follow the latter course was much greater than was involved in the former. For Eddie Martin, the de facto strategy was initially to build an enabling authority (a priority shared by Eric Pickles in Bradford) and later to gain unitary status for Rutland. In Rochdale the strategic agenda was dominated by the decentralisation issue. Thus, all the leaders were aware of the importance of developing a clear strategic direction; but what they meant by it differed.

External relations have been much more of a priority for some leaders than others, and, again, the interpretation of priorities within this context has varied. None of the leaders (unlike several of their counterparts) has devoted much energy to the world of the local government associations, Richard Farnell being the most active in this respect. For Graham Tope the priority was relationships with local groups, although he also gradually came to be more involved in national Liberal Democrat politics. Peter Soulsby has long given priority to furthering the interests of Leicester in external arenas, particularly the range of partnerships in which the city has become involved. He has also necessarily spent a good deal of time with the local media, especially the *Leicester Mercury*. The local media have also been an important consideration for Richard Farnell, much less so for the other leaders.

Finally, there is the question of the extent to which the leaders have felt it necessary to devote valuable time to ensuring that the officer structure is delivering on political priorities. In each case, what was crucial was the perception (and early experience) of the leader and his/her colleagues of the ability and readiness of the officer structure to respond effectively to the new administration's priorities. For Eric Pickles, Graham Tope and Robert Parker, there were some initial doubts about this capacity. In Bradford the problem was overcome by two factors: the appointment soon after the Conservatives came to power of a chief executive with whom Eric Pickles and the rest of the group felt they could work, and the exceptional level of preparation and organisation of the Conservative group when it came to power, which enabled it to push its priorities through an, initially at least, partially resistant officer structure. In Sutton the problem was not seen by the leader as a priority until the Liberal Democrats' second term of office in 1990, after which a change in chief executive paved the way for an organisational restructuring. Robert Parker used a firm of management consultants to engineer change in structure and personnel that would fit better with the new administration's priorities. Richard Farnell and his colleagues in Rochdale made few initial changes but felt the need, as the decentralisation initiative gathered momentum, for an increasingly 'hands-on' approach to the implementation of this policy. In Leicester there is a long tradition of 'hands-on' political involvement and a high casualty rate among chief officers. In each case, the importance of a congruence between political culture and priorities and organisational culture was recognised by the leadership. Once it had been established, political energy could be concentrated on other objectives.

What is apparent from this process of comparing and contrasting the experiences and priorities of six leaders is that, although their specific local agendas have, as one might expect, varied, there has been a good deal of common ground in the *type* of problems they have faced and the choices they have had to make. Details may differ, but it is possible to identify common elements in the role, tasks and skills of local political leadership.

Part Three

The transformation of local political leadership

NINE

The emergence of a mayoral agenda in Britain

Mayors and the New Labour agenda

In its 1997 general election manifesto the Labour Party pledged to restore democratic city-wide government to London, with a mayor and an assembly, both directly elected. As John Prescott wrote in his Foreword to the subsequent Green Paper, *New leadership for London*:"The Government believes that this is essential to preserve and enhance London's competitiveness, to tackle London's problems and to speak up for Londoners and their interests" (Prescott, 1997). The DETR Consultative Paper, *Modernising local government*, developed this theme more generally:

> The Government is very attracted to the model of a strong executive directly elected mayor. Such a mayor would be a highly visible figure. He or she would have been elected by the people rather than the council or party and would, therefore, focus attention outwards in the direction of the people rather than inwards towards fellow councillors. The mayor would be a strong political and community leader with whom the electorate could identify. (DETR, 1998a, p 31)

In its 1998 White Paper, *Modern local government: In touch with the people* (DETR, 1998b), the Labour government argued that local authorities are uniquely placed to provide vision and leadership to their local communities but lamented the fact that at present "there is little clear political leadership". The White Paper continued:

> People often do not know who is really taking the decisions. They do not know who to praise, who to blame or who to contact with their problems. People identify most readily with an individual, yet there is rarely any identifiable figure leading the local community. This is no

> basis for modern, effective and responsive local government. (DETR,
> 1998b, p 25)

The government's solution to this perceived problem is, as we have seen,
strong executive leadership, preferably an elected mayor. Yet much of the
supporting material for elected mayors is drawn from very different political
systems and political cultures. This chapter contains a section on
comparative perspectives which warns against policy transfer or
institutional transfer from one country to another without a thorough
knowledge and understanding of the constituent systems.

1990-98: The development of a mayoral agenda

The Labour government's interest in directly elected mayors needs to be
set in context. The decade opened with the arrival of a new prime
minister, John Major, and a new Secretary of State for the Environment,
Michael Heseltine. At the Department of the Environment (DoE),
Heseltine immediately launched a wide-ranging review of the local
government system, one element of which included an examination of
internal political management. It was in this context that elected mayors
first began to be seriously discussed as a possible model for local political
leadership. In July 1991 Heseltine produced his Consultation Paper, *The
internal management of local authorities in England* (DoE, 1991), which put
forward a range of alternative management models, most of which involved
replacing the committee system (which Heseltine regarded as inefficient)
with some form of either a separately appointed or an elected executive,
thus splitting the executive and representational roles of the council.

The Consultation Paper did not put forward all the logical possibilities
for further consideration. For example, it bypassed the French model of
nominated or indirectly elected mayors, thereby appearing to presume
that any individual political executive should be elected directly and
separately from the council. This reflected Heseltine's much publicised
personal enthusiasm for elected mayors.

The Conservative government's next move was to set up a joint working
party of DoE nominees and representatives of the local authority
associations, which in July 1993 produced a report entitled *Community
leadership and representation: Unlocking the potential* (DoE, 1993). One of
the recommendations was that councils should consider the merits of
more radical and experimental forms of internal management. Four
models were identified by the working party:

1) *The single party executive committee* The council would delegate to a single party policy committee certain powers of strategy and policy formulation, the council itself retaining control over, for example, the annual budget and planning decisions.

2) *The lead member system* The council would delegate powers to named lead members rather than to a collective political executive. The lead member – for example, the chair of the Education Committee – would be free to take decisions in a way that would currently be illegal, but would be accountable to the whole council.

3) *The cabinet system* This would extend the principle of delegation to a single party policy committee whose membership has both individual and collective executive powers. Decisions taken by this executive would be decisions of the council, and individual members would have delegated areas of responsibility. The full council would retain certain powers – such as setting the budget – and the right to overturn at least some decisions taken by the executive or lead members.

4) *The political executive as a separate legal entity* In this scenario there would be a separate – perhaps separately elected – political executive with its own legal powers, which would take control of the decision-making process on behalf of the council. The full council would become very largely a scrutinising and reviewing body.

Interestingly, the one option that did not receive much attention from the joint working party was the one that had most attracted Michael Heseltine personally: directly elected mayors. The issue was, however, kept on the agenda by the independent Commission for Local Democracy (CLD), which in its 1995 report, *Taking charge: The rebirth of local democracy*, put elected mayors centre-stage with its first recommendation:

> Local authorities should consist of a directly elected Council and a
> directly elected Leader/Mayor. Both Council and Leader/Mayor should
> be voted in for a term of three years but the elected Leader may only
> serve two full terms in office. (CLD, 1995, p 54)

The CLD believed that a directly elected mayor was an important means of enhancing local democracy by providing a focus of power which would be "highly visible and thus highly accountable" (CLD, 1995, para 4.15); but at the same time it recommended a number of direct and indirect means of limiting the power of such executives, thus reducing the extent to which direct accountability would be achieved (see Pratchett and Wilson, 1996, Chapter 12).

Jones and Stewart (1995) reflected the scepticism of many traditionalists within local government, arguing that the report's section on directly elected mayors was simplistic:

> It is as if the Commission regards it as a piece of magic which will automatically increase turn-out and build a vibrant local democracy. But the magic does not seem to work in the US. In 1991 in Phoenix – an authority with a city manager and directly elected mayor – only 17% of the electorate voted, and that is of the electorate who bothered to register as voters. (Jones and Stewart, 1995, p 8)

In November 1997, well before the Labour government's White Paper appeared, Lord Hunt introduced his Local Government (Experimental Arrangements) Bill into the Lords which aimed to give councils the freedom to experiment with new management structures, from elected mayors to cabinet-style executives. The Blair government provided support for the Bill, which also aimed to pave the way for new backbench scrutiny committees. "The important thing", Lord Hunt emphasised, "will be for individual councils to develop reforms which are suitable for their own authority and the people who live there". No universally applicable blueprint was prescribed by Hunt, but Stoker (1998, pp 8-9) identified four possible models:

- *Model 1* largely formalises existing informal practices in some local authorities by recognising the role of leading members in the working of the authority. The creation of a single party executive or a lead member system are examples of potential reforms under this model. Examples of this system are found in Sweden.
- *Model 2* involves establishing a separate executive of political leader and cabinet by appointment from the body of councillors. This model operates in both France and Spain.
- *Model 3* involves the establishment of a separate political executive by direct election, the model that has been chosen for the new Greater London Authority. Under this arrangement, the mayor could appoint a cabinet which might or might not be drawn from members of the separately elected assembly. Examples of this model can be found in Germany, Italy and parts of the United States of America.

- *Model 4* sees formal executive authority being vested in the chief executive (as chief local manager) but the establishment of a high-profile policy leader and ceremonial figure by the direct election of a mayor (as in parts of the United States of America and New Zealand).

The Labour Party's 1997 election manifesto had included a commitment to "encourage democratic innovations in local government, including pilots of the idea of elected mayors with executive powers in cities", reflecting widespread concern about local political leadership. The new government's White Paper, *Modern local government: In touch with the people* (DETR, 1998b), emphasised the need for strong executive leadership. The White Paper proposed three possible models of political management, each of which separates the executive role from the backbench role. These are summarised in Table 9.1 and are discussed more fully in Chapter Ten. The government made it clear where its preference lay:

> The benefits of these new structures are greater the more the executive role is separated and the more direct the link between the executive and the community it serves. The Government is, therefore, attracted to the model of a strong directly elected executive mayor. However, such a figure may not be the right form of political leadership for every council. (DETR, 1998b, p 31)

Table 9.1: New models of political management

Option	Description
1	**Directly elected mayor with a cabinet** The mayor will be directly elected by the whole electorate and will appoint the cabinet from among the councillors.
2	**Cabinet with a leader** The leader will be elected by the council, and the cabinet will be made up of councillors either appointed by the leader or elected by the council.
3	**Directly elected mayor with a council manager** The mayor will be directly elected by local people, with a full-time manager appointed by the council to whom both strategic policy and day-to-day decision making will be delegated.

Source: DETR (1998b)

The advent of new forms of executive leadership, and particularly directly elected mayors, represents a radical break with the past, with much of the inspiration coming from Europe and North America.

Comparative perspectives

Advocates of elected mayors invariably argue that such executives function well in other countries. Opponents argue equally strongly that we need to beware of uncritically adopting practices from elsewhere. All political systems have their own values, cultures and legal contexts; what works well in one country is not necessarily appropriate elsewhere.

The most frequently cited example of a directly elected local leader is that of the mayor in the *United States*. The positive attributes of this system invariably focus on leadership capacity. To quote Stoker and Wolman:

> Especially in the management of relations with other government agencies, external interests and local citizens the mayor could provide a key focal point and driving force for a more dynamic and influential local government. (Stoker and Wolman, 1992, p 264)

Against this, the potential narrowing of representation by the concentration of power in the mayor and a small group of about a dozen councillors is frequently cited. In a similar vein questions are asked about whether, outside London, sufficient people would come forward with the necessary skills to fulfil a mayor's role successfully. Powerful directly elected mayors are common in US cities, but governance in the USA is very different from that in the UK. Perhaps scrutiny of experience in Europe is more useful since, as Stoker notes, countries such as Germany and Italy, both of which have recently moved towards directly elected local political leaders, "have local welfare systems and a form of party politics that are in many respects close to the British case" (Stoker, 1996, p 21).

In *Germany* the move towards directly elected executives needs to be seen as part of the process of democratisation within the country, part of a broader move towards greater political participation. It also has the virtue of providing "a more direct influence for voters over its government leadership without going through the filter of the party groups" (Stoker, 1996, p 21). There are a number of different mayoral systems within Germany, but by 1999 much of German local government had some form of directly elected mayor.

The German experience has thrown up a number of questions. Should the assembly and the mayor (*burgermeister*) be elected at the same time? Is the cost of the system too great? What is the appropriate term of office? What about the role of backbenchers? Issues such as these are addressed in the 1998 White Paper (DETR, 1998b) and are discussed later in the book.

Turning to *Italy*, legislation in 1993 introduced directly elected mayors. Corruption had been a major problem in Italian local government; and this, along with the move away from proportional representation systems towards majoritarian systems, is the stark backdrop against which the emergence of separately elected mayors took place. The two electoral rounds ensure that the winning candidate has the support of the majority of voters. Mayors have emerged as powerful figures, but they are restricted to two four-year terms of office. The profile of mayors has been increased with the introduction of direct elections, and greater political stability seems to have resulted from the change.

In Italy the mayor nominates the board (*Giunta*), composed of 'assessors' (who cannot be elected councillors), which oversees the major policy areas such as education and environment. Mayors also have the power to sack the assessors. Stoker sums up the Italian position thus:

> The administration of the system is effectively in the hands of the mayor, the chief executive and the assessors. They meet together in a management team. The business of the assembly is conducted through a mixture of commissions and standing committees. Each council has the right to decide how to conduct its affairs, so systems vary considerably. (Stoker, 1996, p 28)

While useful lessons can be drawn from the USA and Europe, it is important not to copy uncritically from such experience. Too often policy 'solutions' drawn from other countries are based on a partial understanding of the operation of political systems and of the conditions that contribute to their success or failure. As Page has observed: "Valid lessons from cross-national experience can only be drawn on the basis of the systematic application of knowledge about how policies and institutions work" (Page, 1998, p 1). As Page emphasises, lesson drawing requires systematic evaluation of a number of factors:

- whether the different jurisdictions from which lessons are sought are the best or even appropriate ones;

- whether the institutions or policies compared are truly successful models to be emulated (or failures to be avoided);
- whether the conditions that make for their success are present in the different legal, political, social, economic and cultural contexts in which their application is contemplated.

Clearly, a proper understanding of the operation of elected mayors in any country necessitates a thorough understanding of the constitutional, political and legal structure of that country. The transferability of policies or institutions from any other political system to Britain must take account of such differences or else they may be of very limited usefulness. To quote Page:

> To draw valid and useful lessons requires more than a casual invocation of experiences of other countries as, for example, has been demonstrated by attempts to import economic planning from France or Japanese styles of management into the United Kingdom. (Page, 1998, p 1)

Nevertheless, much of the debate about elected mayors still focuses on comparisons with other countries, notably the United States. Judge et al (1995, p 12) emphasise that there are certain fundamental contextual differences between Britain and the USA that counsel caution. Five such differences are identified:

1) Differences in governmental structure result in greater emphasis on spatial politics in the USA and on party politics in Britain. The USA federal structure means that urban governments are in effect creatures of state governments. Party conflict and partisanship are central to the unitary British system. The weaker party politics of the USA creates greater scope for a local politics.
2) The more direct role of central government in Britain (and greater local autonomy in the USA) provides less scope for British local government to engage in activity of its own choosing.
3) A much more fragmented local structure in the USA encourages economic competition among localities. The US system is incredibly complex. There are some 80,000 local government agencies in the USA, about 200 times more than there are elected local authorities in Britain.
4) There is a lack of a focused local executive in Britain compared with the USA, where the elected mayor, or in some instances the city manager, has a prominent role in urban politics.

5) A local fiscal system in Britain substantially reduces incentives for local governments to compete against each other's tax base

As Judge et al emphasise, "cross-national research requires conceptual and theoretical rigour if comparison is to advance beyond description into the realm of explanation" (1995, p 12). Nevertheless, Hambleton reminds us, that good ideas do not need a passport to cross international frontiers:

> If the approaches of different local authorities in different countries can
> be juxtaposed in a reasonably organised way, it is possible to stimulate
> new insights which are grounded in experience. (Hambleton, 1996, p 2)

It must be repeatedly emphasised, however, that uncritical policy transfer or an uninformed adoption of institutional arrangements that work well elsewhere is likely to be a recipe for disaster. Stoker and Travers, in a comparison of New York and London, recognise that the exercise is fraught with difficulties, but maintain that in the absence of alternative bases for critical judgement, cross-national learning has much to offer:

> The idea that the uniqueness of each country totally blocks the prospects
> for such learning needs to be challenged. This issue is a matter for
> investigation rather than sweeping generalisation. (1998, p 26)

Enhancing local democracy

Advocates of directly elected mayors have drawn much ammunition from the depressed state of British local government in the 1990s (see Doyle, 1996). There is little interest in its activities. Turnout in elections is low – only 29% in the 1998 local elections, with five local authorities having turnouts of less than 20%. Indeed, in a by-election for a ward on Tamworth Borough Council in December 1998, only 6% of the electorate turned out to vote. Turnout in the 1999 local elections in England was 32% and in some urban authorities such as Wigan, below 20%. The 'first past the post' voting system means that a large number of local authorities are now 'one-party states' with no effective opposition. As we have seen, in such contexts allegations of corruption in places such as Renfrew, Doncaster, Glasgow and Westminster have hit the headlines.

Allegations of corruption are not, therefore, only the prerogative of cities with elected mayors. There is no reason why, with sensible safeguards, corruption should be any more likely with an elected mayor system than within the 'one party states' that characterised British elected local government in the 1990s. At present, as the 1998 White Paper observed, it is not unusual for significant decisions in a local authority to be "taken behind closed doors by political groups or even a small group of key people within the majority group. Consequently, many councillors, even those in the majority group, have little influence over council decisions" (DETR, 1998b, p 25). Elitism is not restricted to cities with elected mayors.

Elected mayors can provide a good chance of significantly increasing electoral turnout by giving local government a higher profile; such an increase would help to undermine the widespread criticism about local government's accountability. Similarly, the civic leadership role of local authorities would be enhanced through the visibility and legitimacy of the mayor's position. Interestingly, though, a national survey of nearly 3,000 people by Strathclyde and Glasgow Universities in 1995, carried out as part of the ESRC Local Governance Programme, found that, while over 70% of the public supported the introduction of elected mayors, only 16% of councillors liked the idea. Many councillors were fearful that they would be marginalised if directly elected mayors emerged. Not surprisingly, they feared the emergence of elitist decision making and a marked diminution of their own spheres of responsibility.

Advocates of elected mayors do not accept this line of argument. On the contrary, they maintain that a directly elected executive would in many ways strengthen the role of ordinary councillors. Hodge et al (1997, p 26) outline a number of factors that, they suggest, would increase the attractiveness of standing for council membership:

- explicit recognition that, except for the leadership, it was part-time non-executive role and hence compatible with other full-time employment;
- more realistic levels of remuneration than hitherto;
- substantial reduction of time-consuming 'committee business' which dominates councillor activity;
- opportunity to specialise in a particular area of interest;
- decreasing domination of party politics in local government (given the increased likelihood of no overall control under the proportional voting system advocated by the authors).

In a similar vein, Hambleton argues that if there was a separation of the executive and the assembly "it would have the effect of providing greater clarity which is the prerequisite for better accountability" (Hambleton, 1998, p 8). He believes that the assemblies would be able to serve as voices for their local communities and would be particularly important as policy scrutineers. He outlines four ways in which the local councillor could be empowered by a separation of the executive and the assembly:

1) *devolved decision making:* many decisions that are important for local areas but lack strategic significance can be devolved to local decision-making arenas, thereby empowering councillors;

2) *developing the scrutiny role:* councillors can serve on a range of scrutiny committees or panels;

3) *community catalysts:* councillors can develop a stronger leadership role in their local communities;

4) *policy development:* freed from the burden of service committees, councillors will be liberated to put more effort into working groups concerned with developing new policy initiatives.

Linked with this, there could be greater participatory democracy via neighbourhood forums, focus groups, local scrutiny panels, citizens' juries and the like (see Lowndes et al, 1998). Local democracy would thereby be enhanced as representative democracy was supplemented by participatory democracy. There could also be further development of technological facilities such as internet websites, assisted computer access via terminals and even video conferencing. As Hodge et al observe:

> We would expect the scrutiny role to be divided up so assembly members could pursue their specific interests. It would be likely, for example, that a small group of members would have a particular interest in artistic and cultural activities in the area. They could play a lead role in monitoring, scrutinising, and suggesting improvements in this policy area. (Hodge et al, 1997, p 27)

This would take place alongside their present representative role; they would still defend the interests of the ward they represent – their grievance-chasing role would in no way be diminished. An elected mayor would certainly not have the time (given his/her policy formulation, external representation and advocacy roles) to deal with individual casework, although Beecham, for many years leader of Newcastle upon Tyne City Council, argued that "the most effective leaders, in the long term, are those whose concerns are rooted in the problems of their own constituents and who maintain regular contact with them" (Beecham, 1996, p 43).

The 1998 White Paper maintained that the separation of the executive role "will give all councillors a new enhanced and more rewarding role" (DETR, 1998b, p 33). Councils will be required to establish scrutiny committees of backbench councillors who will have an explicit duty to review and question the decisions and performance of the executive. "They would also review the policies and direction of the council, proposing changes and submitting policy proposals to the executive". Besides their grievance-chasing role, the White Paper outlines other responsibilities:

- reviewing and questioning decisions taken by the executive;
- advising the executive on decisions and policy on local issues;
- reviewing policy, formulating policy proposals and submitting proposals to the executive;
- considering the budget proposed by the executive, proposing amendments and voting on the final budget; and
- taking responsibility, either with or without members of the executive for those quasi-judicial functions, such as planning, licensing and appeals, which it would not normally be appropriate to delegate to an individual member of the executive (DETR, 1998b, p 34).

The government envisages, despite fears to the contrary from some quarters, that the new role of backbenchers will be 'high profile, involving real and direct responsibilities for the well-being of their community'. It also argues that this will be a more challenging and rewarding role than backbenchers have hitherto enjoyed. Backbench councillors will need to remain vigilant to ensure that the focus on 'executive leadership' does not leave them marginalised.

Critics of the elected mayor scenario argue that, if the mayor was from a different party to the party controlling the assembly, effective government would be impossible. Conflict and policy stagnation would result. But even under the present system there are frequently strong factions within the majority group that can provide conflict and division. As we saw earlier, in November 1995 two majority group leaders – Stewart Foster in Leicester and Valerie Wise in Preston – were overthrown on the same day, following votes of no confidence by their respective Labour groups. Similarly, in May 1999 Theresa Stewart was ousted as leader of the ruling Labour group on Birmingham City Council by Albert Bore. Theresa Stewart had led the council for almost six years but lost the decisive leadership election in the party group by 40 votes to 36. It is possible to devise strategies to handle the mayor–assembly division, but if a single transferable vote system is ultimately adopted for the elections of mayor and assembly (who are elected at the same time) such a discrepancy becomes very unlikely anyway. What becomes most likely is a mayor working with a hung assembly; such hung councils are relatively familiar in British local government. Following the 1999 local government elections, for example, 149 authorities (34.1%) had no overall control.

Towards executive leadership

At the 1998 Labour Party Local Government Conference John Prescott, Secretary of State for the Environment, Transport and the Regions (DETR), argued that there was a need to look at 'sharpening up the distinction between the executive and representative roles of local councillors'. This was a theme further developed in a discussion paper, *Modernising local government*, published by the DETR in February 1998. The theme of local experimentation was also emphasised. In the event, however, the 1998 White Paper was rather more prescriptive. Councils will be able to choose which of the three executive models outlined in Table 9.1 they prefer, and they have an obligation to present the government with operational proposals based on one of these models. While the government will allow councils to "set their own timetable for adopting one of the models," it also proposed a reserve power "to tackle cases of abuse or inertia" (DETR, 1998a, p 32). In a nutshell, recalcitrant councils will not be tolerated. Executive leadership at local level is set to emerge once the provisions of the 1998 White Paper are on the statute book – a process begun with the introduction of the draft Local Government (Organisation and Standards) Bill in March 1999. This Bill requires all local authorities to make proposals for political management structures based on one of the three models outlined in Table 9.1. It also allows the secretary of state to add further models at a later date.

Advocates of directly elected mayors see them as part of the regeneration of local democracy. As Hodge et al argue:

> It's not the only way forward. Neither is it a complete response to the problems we face in revitalising local government. However, as part of a package of reforms it is one exciting option which offers great potential for delivering local democratic renewal. (Hodge et al, 1997, p 1)

Nevertheless, controversy is never far away from the elected mayor concept. Speaking at a workshop in June 1997, Labour MP Margaret Hodge cited the 'low calibre' of many elected members as a reason for introducing elected mayors; but John Fletcher, Labour leader of Coventry City Council, was not impressed: "what I object to is Margaret Hodge muscling in on this debate in order to give a 25 minute piece of propaganda in favour of elected mayors". Fletcher argued that Coventry was keen to cooperate with the government on Welfare to Work, regeneration of cities and best value services, but in his view elected mayors were irrelevant to these (*Local Government Chronicle*, 27 June 1997, p 1). The debate about forms of executive leadership remains divisive.

Stoker, nailing his colours firmly to the elected mayor mast, outlined three consequential changes:

> First it would create a leader with some independence. The legitimacy of direct election would create a figure more confident in their ability to speak and act for the public than under the current system. Second a directly elected leader will create a well-known and accountable figure. The assembly would also have an enhanced profile as supporters and opponents of the leader's actions use it to make their case. Finally, the elected mayor or leader would provide a steering capacity within and beyond the locality. A French mayor or German bürgermeister are notable players in their political systems. We need similar 'big-hitters' in our local politics. (Stoker, 1998, pp 11-12)

The Hunt Bill was 'talked out' by the Conservatives in the House of Commons, but the July 1998 White Paper and the March 1999 draft Local Government (Organisation and Standards) Bill took on board and developed its major themes. The draft Bill was included as part of a DETR Consultation Paper, *Local leadership, local choice* (DETR, 1999) which gave local authorities and other interested parties two months to comment on the government's proposals. As John Prescott wrote in his Foreword to the discussion paper:

> We want councils to ask their local communities about how they want to be governed. We want to see lively local debate and discussion. Some councils have already begun to consult their local people on these issues. Those that have not should start now ... we will be introducing, when Parliamentary time allows, legislation so that new forms of local governance, including directly elected mayors, can be adopted. (DETR, 1999)

While the adoption of directly elected mayors remains controversial, such mayors are likely to emerge in a number of urban authorities beginning with London, where the newly elected mayor and Assembly will formally take up their powers on 3 July 2000. Indeed, Andrew Adonis predicted that within 10 years most of Britain's major cities will have elected mayors. The mayoralties will be more sought after than membership of the House of Commons, and they may come to wield greater power than all but a handful of Westminster politicians (*Observer*, 14 December 1997).

The advent of such 'big hitters' would undoubtedly raise the profile of local authorities, but critics continue to argue that this could be at the expense of democratic values and grass-roots needs. However, as we demonstrate in the final chapter, the overwhelming preference at present among British local authorities is for the cabinet-plus-leader model, rather than a mayoral option.

TEN

The future of local political leadership

Introduction

As we have demonstrated, the nature of political management in local authorities and local political culture will both be profoundly affected by the changes proposed in the 1998 White Paper and the draft Local Government (Organisation and Standards) Bill, March 1999. The draft Bill was included as part of a DETR Consultation Paper, *Local leadership, local choice* (DETR, 1999), which allowed a two-month period of consultation with interested parties. Effectively, the draft Bill contains plans to compel virtually all councils to scrap their existing structures. Unless the public backs the no-change option in a referendum, all councils will be obliged to establish one of three models: a directly elected mayor with a cabinet, a cabinet with a leader, or a directly elected mayor with a council manager. Every council would have to consult its community about how it is to be governed. A range of options will need to be offered: councils will not be allowed "simply to choose which is most convenient for it".

The draft Local Government (Organisation and Standards) Bill states that if a council wants a directly elected mayor, or if 5% of the electorate petition for a referendum on one, then the council will have to hold a binding referendum. Mayors would be elected by the supplementary vote system which allows a second preference. Councils will be allowed to keep the existing system only if a referendum rejects alternatives. If one is not held, the government will "require that council to hold a referendum on a question determined by the secretary of state".

Cabinets would usually be formed by a ruling party or coalition. The mayor or leader would generally establish the cabinet, and would be able to change its structure and membership at any time. The cabinet is limited to 10 members or 15% of the council, whichever is smaller.

The draft Bill proposes that mayors would have the power to delay a decision of a committee or full council, and ask the full council to reconsider the issue. Scrutiny committees of backbenchers, open to the public, will have the right to question executive members and make decisions independently of the executive's wishes. Alongside all this, each council will be required to have a standards committee with at least one non-councillor on it to oversee ethical issues. In a similar vein, a new independent body, the Standards Board, will investigate alleged breaches of the councillor's code of conduct and will have the power to disqualify a councillor for up to five years.

A number of local authorities were, however, moving towards some form of executive leadership (in so far as the rigidity of the existing legislation allowed) before the draft Bill was published in March 1999. Notable among these were Trafford MBC, Sefton MBC, Cheshire CC, North Tyneside MBC, Barnsley MBC, Breckland DC, Lewisham LBC, Barnet LBC, Southwark LBC, Kent CC, Birmingham City Council, Watford BC, Kirklees MBC, Hammersmith and Fulham LBC and Cumbria CC. By 2002, it is likely that the local political landscape of Britain will have been transformed.

If political management structures and political culture are certain to be profoundly changed, so too will be the nature of local political leadership. The dominant theme of the government's proposed changes is the separation of the executive role from the representative (or assembly) role. Three options of executive–representative splits from which local authorities can choose were set out in the 1998 White Paper and are outlined in Table 9.1. Councils will be expected to adopt one of these three models, produce a version of it that suits local circumstances, and set out a timetable for change.

Each of the three options will arguably strengthen the leadership role in local authorities. But they will do so in very different ways. The two 'elected mayor' options will personalise political leadership and provide democratic legitimacy for an individual leader, in a way that goes well beyond current practice. However, in the case of the *council manager–elected mayor* option, the political leadership role is defined in relatively weak terms. The mayor's role is seen as predominantly one of influence, guidance and leadership rather than direct decision making. Indeed, it can be plausibly argued that in this model the de facto (non-political) leader is the council manager. At the very least, leadership will be exercised through some kind of division of responsibilities between this pairing.

The *elected mayor–cabinet* option, however, creates a visible and extremely powerful political leadership role, strengthened through the legitimacy provided by direct election, and with a range of powers of both policy initiation and executive action. Although some form of collective leadership involving the cabinet would no doubt be an important element of the arrangements adopted, the personalisation and potential impact of political leadership is strongest under this option and provides a basis for legitimate authority which leaders elected under the current system could not even aspire to.

The *cabinet-plus-leader* model involves a different kind of balance between individual and collective leadership. The leader in this case will lack the legitimacy provided by direct election. There will be a much greater expectation of shared/collective responsibility, linked to an allocation of individual portfolios and responsibilities for cabinet members, not dissimilar to what happens in central government. Within this option, a considerable range of practices and operating assumptions are likely to be adopted. Much more will depend on the political culture of the majority party and the personal dynamics of the cabinet. At one extreme, the leader could operate very much along the lines of a directly elected mayor; at the other, leadership roles could be fragmented among the leadership group or operated on a predominantly collective basis.

So political leadership will certainly change. But before we can develop more specific arguments about how it will change, it is important to re-examine the crucial relationship between political leadership and political culture. Throughout this book, we have argued that the scope for political leadership reflects the political culture of the party or parties involved. The relationship is not a deterministic one because local political culture is itself amenable to influence by political leaders. But at any one point in time, *what* a leader is permitted to do and *how* he/she can operate will be constrained by the norms and expectations of the local political culture (both within parties and within the authority as a whole). One of the reasons why this is so is that local authorities are not currently required to identify 'leaders' (although the majority of them do so). Leadership of local authority level is voluntaristic, not a legal requirement.

One of the most direct effects of the legislation following the 1998 White Paper will be to formalise the leadership position. In each of the three options, it will be necessary to identify a leader. In two cases the leader will gain his/her position through popular election, which is in itself a highly significant change in the context of local leadership. The authority and legitimacy that stem from direct election go beyond what can be claimed by a leader of the successful party in a general election. In the third option, the leader is elected from within the authority. In each case the key question to consider is the extent to which the party group can continue to exercise the kind of authority it has traditionally exercised in all three major parties. The new set of formal arrangements will impinge upon existing political cultures, including the role of party groups, resulting in a set of negotiations through which a new perception – more or less shared – of the leadership role will emerge. The likely results of those negotiations for each of the three models, and within each of the major parties, will be examined in the remainder of this chapter. In this context, it will be helpful to return to the four key leadership roles, discussed in Chapters Three to Six, to draw out the way in which the three variants proposed in the 1998 White Paper are likely to affect the interpretation of, and balance between, these four leadership roles. Table 10.1 provides a summary of the major issues.

Table 10.1: Leadership roles and new political management models

	Party/group cohesiveness	Strategic direction	Partnership/ external networking	Making things happen
Directly elected mayor with a council manager	Of limited relevance to elected mayor; role passes to party leaders in the assembly	A matter of negotiation between council manager and elected mayor	A – possibly the – dominant role for the elected mayor	Possibly only indirectly via council manager
Directly elected mayor with a cabinet	Of limited relevance to elected mayor; role passes to chair of council with cabinet members experiencing role conflict	Elected mayor has dominant role	Certain to be a key role for elected mayor	Greatly enhanced leadership involvement and capacity
Cabinet with a leader	Likely to remain a major concern of cabinet collectively and leader individually	More of a collective responsibility with scope for key leadership role	Likely to be a key role for the leader but with more collective involvement	Greatly enhanced leadership capacity but role likely to be shared within cabinet

Directly elected mayor with a council manager

The directly elected mayor–council manager option is unlikely to appeal to politicised local authorities of any description. This model reduces the formal power of the key politician (the directly elected mayor) to that of adviser to a non-elected permanent officer, in whom executive authority is vested (subject to policies, budgets and major decisions being approved by the assembly). No political party in an authority in which party politics dominates is likely to find such a switch of power acceptable.

There are, however, two sets of circumstances in which the elected mayor–council manager option may prove acceptable (or the least undesirable of the three options). The first and most likely situation is an authority in which politics, in the party sense, is a relatively low-key affair, with Independents holding a significant proportion of the seats, and group discipline in those party groups that do exist being much looser than in a party politicised local authority.

In these circumstances, the idea of 'forming a cabinet' is likely to be seen as an anathema, both in principle and practice, going against the grain of political culture. As the only model that does not require a cabinet is the council manager–elected mayor, it will have an appeal, simply through a process of elimination. The appeal will be strengthened if there exists a 'natural leader', known and trusted by the majority of council members, who is felt to be likely to win a mayoral election. In relation to the council manager element, in many relatively unpoliticised shire districts, the chief executive is already a potent force in relation to policy formulation, and in some cases more of a de facto leader (in the proactive sense) than either chair of the council or leader of the largest group. While the formalisation of an informal set of practices is not without its problems, it may prove more acceptable in a relatively unpoliticised local authority than the other options.

In this option, it is possible that a leader (the directly elected mayor) could exert a great deal more effective power than the formal definition of the position implies. If the leader already enjoys (or can develop) a network of consultation and support with a critical mass of council members, then he/she will have a powerful potential sanction in attempts to 'influence' the council manager. It is the council manager who will actually prepare policy statements and budget recommendations for the assembly. But if the elected mayor has enough influential allies in the assembly, then the council manager may find it a struggle to generate majority support for recommendations that the elected mayor does not support (and where, in extremis, the elected mayor's network has been activated to block such proposals). Similarly, assuming, as is likely, that there is scope for executive decisions that raise policy issues to be referred to the assembly (even though they are formally the responsibility of the council manager), there is scope for the elected mayor to ensure that the necessary 'referral' process takes place if he/she is unhappy about a particular executive decision. Thus, if the elected mayor enjoys a 'supportive network' of this kind, he/she can play a strategic direction role at least equal to that of the council manager, and enjoy a selective veto power over executive decisions ('ensuring effective implementation'). Without such a network, the elected mayor's role-set is likely to be dominated by the task of external representation and involvement in partnerships.

The second (arguably less likely) situation in which a directly elected mayor–council manager may be preferred is that of a hung authority in which no two parties show any predisposition to work together in a joint administration, and where, as a result, there is the problem of 'forming a cabinet' that can operate effectively. In particular, there would be considerable scope for disagreement within the cabinet to spill over into the assembly, with an aggrieved minority of cabinet members seeking to overturn in assembly a cabinet recommendation that they did not support. In these circumstances, there may just be an acknowledgement that an elected mayor–council manager model would at least facilitate the flow of council business. The elected mayor and council manager would know that they had to informally negotiate an adequate level of support within the assembly for all major recommendations. The elected mayor's role would greatly depend on his/her ability to influence sufficient members of a divided assembly in support of his/her preferences. Alternatively, such a leader could be rendered effectively powerless, with the external representation role the dominant (and possibly only) area in which leadership could be exercised.

Directly elected mayor with a cabinet

The directly elected mayor-plus-cabinet option may ironically prove even less appealing to local authorities than the elected mayor-plus-council manager option. An LGA survey, published in early 1999, showed that only 2% of councils were opting for a directly elected mayor. (Lewisham LBC and Watford BC appeared particularly keen to move quickly in this direction.)

This represents the most fundamental change in the range of options available, in that it combines the novelty of direct election with the allocation of considerable power to the successful contestant. Unlike his counterpart in the council manager option, the elected mayor in this case has the authority to propose policy and budgetary measures to the assembly and the powers of direct executive action. Unlike the situation in the cabinet-plus-leader model, the elected mayor is not dependent on the assembly for the accession to leadership, and can choose his own cabinet, rather than being obliged to work with a cabinet that has not been personally chosen.

The transfer of power on this scale to a single individual, whatever range of checks and balances are introduced, is alien to the culture and practice of all three major parties, particularly the Liberal Democrats. Equally worrying to all three parties is the way in which an elected mayor would become detached from the party group. In the cabinet-with-leader model, discussed in more detail in the next section, leaders know they owe their position to the group and know that the group can, if it so decides, replace them. Thus, whatever the formal right of the leader and cabinet colleagues to take independent executive action, they are highly likely to acknowledge their dependency upon the goodwill and support of the group and to consult with the group over a wider range of issues (especially executive actions) than is necessary to ensure the passing of cabinet proposals through the assembly. The elected mayor who selects his/her own cabinet, however, is not beholden in this way to the group, since authority stems not from internal election by the council, but from direct election by the people. Cabinet members who are not prepared to work to the directly elected mayor's agenda can be dismissed and replaced with those who are. While it is highly likely a cabinet (and leader) who are internally elected will have to regularly take account of the views of the party group, an elected mayor need not do so except on occasions where there is a need to steer a proposal through the assembly.

The fear of diminution of the power of the group is widely perceived as the single most threatening aspect of the 1998 White Paper's proposals. Thus, all other things being equal, the option that is seen as most threatening will be rejected and the option seen as least threatening will be favoured. On this premise, directly elected mayors are not likely to be opted for by many authorities. The few exceptions are likely to be those Labour authorities that wish publicly to demonstrate their 'New Labour' credentials, who will know that the elected mayor is the party's (and the prime minister's) preferred form of political executive, or perhaps one or two Conservative authorities who are excited by the possibility of having a formal base for a strong leader (a concept that has a long tradition at local government level within the Conservative Party).

Another possibility is that there may be a 'snowball effect' in the large cities. If Bradford opts for an elected mayor, Leeds may feel pressured to follow suit (equally Manchester/Liverpool, Birmingham/Coventry, etc). In the London area, for example, David Wilson, chair of Lewisham LBC's Democracy and Government Select Committee, observed (October 1998): "There is a real feeling that Lewisham needs an elected mayor as a countervailing force to the Mayor of London". It is also possible that, if there are very few volunteers for elected mayors when the range of preferences becomes apparent, the government may become more prescriptive. It could, for example, introduce a requirement that certain types of authority (especially perhaps unitary authorities and London boroughs) must hold referenda on elected mayors. The evidence of an ICM poll of 1,013 people in five major English cities in May 1999, which found that 64% of respondents would welcome the opportunity to directly elect a mayor, suggests that such a move on the government's part could have a significant impact. Enthusiasm was greatest in Birmingham and Sheffield, where 68% responded 'yes' when asked: 'Do you support the idea of having a directly elected mayor?'

In May 1999 the influential New Local Government Network argued that ministers should impose directly elected mayors on major urban areas without first holding referendums. In its response to the draft Local Government (Organisation and Standards) Bill, the Network said that opinion polls consistently showed that about two thirds of voters supported elected mayors, but most councils were opting for cabinet structures. It called on the government to override municipal opposition and impose elected mayors on at least 11 English cities outside London: "To simply legislate for elected mayors would be consistent with every major local government reorganisation during the 1960s, 70s, 80s and 90s", it argued; if ministers backed away from imposing change, referendums on elected mayors should be made compulsory. Another alternative would be to cut the number of voters required to sign a petition demanding a referendum from the 5% suggested in the draft Bill to 1%. The Local Government Association, responding to these proposals, said that imposing elected mayors would be undemocratic (see *Local Government Chronicle*, 21 May 1999). The debate continues, not without some acrimony.

An elected mayor, for the reasons discussed above, would have little interest in maintaining 'group cohesiveness' – typically one of the most important leadership roles in current circumstances. He/she would of course need to work behind the scenes to ensure that major proposals (eg the community plan, the budget) secured approval in the assembly. However, it is likely that one of the criteria for selecting cabinet colleagues would be their ability to generate support within the group network. It is anyway by no means certain that the customary adversarial culture of inter-group politics would continue to operate in the new assemblies. Thus, it is not clear what the 'group cohesiveness' (or authority-wide cohesiveness) role would involve in the new situation. What does seem likely is that elected mayors would have so much to occupy them, with the three other leadership roles, that there would be at the very least a strong incentive to delegate whatever needed to be done in respect of cohesiveness to cabinet colleagues.

The other reason why an elected mayor could not wholly disregard party colleagues in the assembly is that their support would be needed to gain party endorsement of his/her mayoral candidacy at the next election, assuming there was a wish to stand for re-election. Thus, the likelihood is that the local party network (including the group) will be used to test out responses to controversial proposals, build up or sustain constituencies of support, justify departures from the party manifesto and explain difficult executive decisions. This tendency is likely to be strongest in the Liberal Democrat Party, which sets the greatest store by a negotiated consensus. The pressure to operate in this way in the Labour Party would be most pronounced in authorities where there was a strong relatively independent local party in existence.

In relation to the other three major leadership roles, the enhanced authority of the directly elected mayor is clear. The issue becomes the extent to which the mayor wishes to share such responsibilities with his/her selected cabinet, either through the adoption of the doctrine of collective responsibility, or through the dividing up of responsibilities on the basis of individual portfolios. For a large local authority, the corporate strategy will provide a likely source of ideas about who does what. The development of corporate strategy (and its various offshoots), the identification of, and action in relation to, executive decisions with strategic implications, and the involvement in external relations that are of strategic significance would provide a logical basis for the concentration of the elected mayor's energies.

Cabinet with a leader

The option of a cabinet with a leader is likely to be the choice of the vast majority of local authorities in England. A major survey of local authority chief executives in early 1999 showed that well over 90% believed their members could go for a cabinet because it fitted most closely to existing structures (see Leach et al, 1999). Despite challenging the current political culture in several ways – most fundamentally in its embodiment of a formal executive–representative split – it is the option that in overall terms is seen as most compatible with current assumptions and practices. As we have shown, informal cabinets have long existed in the vast majority of politicised councils, the exception being hung authorities where nothing resembling a coalition exists. The position of leader, selected by party group and subject to annual re-election procedures, is also a well established feature of local government. Given that, in a majority-controlled authority, the majority group would continue to have the power to elect, re-elect or not re-elect the leader and cabinet colleagues, it is highly likely that they would expect the role of the group as ultimate source of authority (and veto) for the proposed actions of the leader and the cabinet to continue. In such circumstances, apart from the changes in the formal structure, it is conceivable that the way things are done at present could survive more or less intact. The leader and cabinet members would no doubt wish to exercise their newly acquired executive authority more independently of the group. However, given their vulnerability to re-election by the group, they may not have a lot of choice.

There would of course be differences. Currently, in addition to the regular meetings of the whole group, 'sub-groups' of each party in a politicised local authority meet before each committee to decide how they are going to vote on all major items. (The scope of items subject to group discipline varies between parties and authorities.) With the disappearance of committees – or at least of the traditional decision-making service committees – that facility would be lost. Group meetings to discuss major issues, including the content of policy statements that the cabinet intended to put before the assembly, could and no doubt would continue. But the way in which executive decisions – previously the responsibility of committees, but now the responsibility of the cabinet (or individual members thereof) – could be subject to group scrutiny would necessarily change. There are two possibilities, depending on the extent to which the group wished to retain its current powers.

First, the cabinet could publish a list of intended decisions, on a regular basis, and then allow a period of a few days before these decisions were implemented, during which time it would be possible for any group member (or a minimum number of members) to identify an item or items that they wished to form the subject of a group discussion before being implemented. The item would then be referred to the group's next full meeting. The second option would be for regular meetings to take place between the cabinet member responsible for, say, social services, and a sub-group of party members from the assembly with a particular interest in that topic. The cabinet member would consult with this sub-group about preferred executive decisions, in much the same way that a committee chair currently does with party colleagues on that committee. Any sources of major disagreement would be referred to a full group meeting before action was taken.

Both these measures, but particularly the second, are out of line with the spirit and purpose of a 'separation of powers'. If executive authority is given to a cabinet or individual members within it, but the use of that authority remains subject to the approval of the party group (at least on a selective basis), then in effect the division of powers has been fudged or incorporated within traditional expectations of the operation of the leadership–party group relationship. Powers to refer contentious items is a likely element of the array of scrutiny powers that an assembly would have in the allocation of checks and balances in a cabinet system. But this is very different from an informal power of referral to the group; and the existence of the latter, for majority party members at least, would often be a preferred substitute for the former. Indeed, a quid pro quo, which no doubt cabinet members would wish to extract from any system of group involvement in executive decisions, would be an assumption of group support in the assembly (as operates at present in council meetings). If such an expectation were fulfilled, that too would challenge the logic of the cabinet–assembly split, which assumes an independence from group discipline (with certain exceptions) on the part of assembly members. In particular, the 'scrutiny' role of the assembly could, in a one-party-dominated council, become a charade if assembly members from the dominant party were not prepared to publicly challenge on a post hoc basis the actions of their cabinet colleagues.

It is the cabinet-plus-leader model that offers the widest scope for the interpretation of the leadership role. At one extreme, it could involve relatively little change in role. An existing informal cabinet would become formalised, but the way it operated, and in particular in the extent of effective power of the party group, would change little. Sub-groups of majority party assembly members would continue to discuss with executive colleagues the range of executive decisions facing them. The full group would pick up the big issues that transcended individual services, including the policy statements that the executive would formally present to the assembly. The group would in these circumstances continue to support the cabinet at assembly meetings, as currently happens. The scrutiny role would be operated half-heartedly, if at all. Of course, opposition members would take this role seriously, but in the many authorities that are currently dominated by a single political party, the capacity of the opposition to play this role would inevitably be limited, as it is at present. Indeed, in such authorities the replacement of service committees by executive responsibilities would remove one of the few safeguards in relation to public debate and scrutiny.

At the other extreme, if there was a relaxation of group discipline (which, especially in the Labour Party, would have to be sanctioned or initiated at national party level) and majority party group members were persuaded of the potential value of the new scrutiny, representative, and local advocacy roles that the government hopes to see operated by assembly members, then it is conceivable that the cabinet would actually be allowed to behave as a genuine executive. In this case it would move closer to the elected-mayor-plus-cabinet model, though without the added ingredient of 'legitimacy through direct election' for its leader. There would thus be a less firm basis for individual leadership on the part of the cabinet leader, although no doubt a strong charismatic leader could, as now, enhance the scope of what fell under their personal jurisdiction. Such a cabinet would certainly wish to continue to consult, negotiate with and try to persuade their party colleagues in the assembly to support the measures they proposed to introduce; but that process would be equally necessary in an elected-mayor-plus-cabinet system (see Wilson, 1999).

There is also the question of how a hung authority that opted for a cabinet-plus-leader model would be likely to interpret the model. If there was a potential coalition, the effect of a cabinet would be to formalise it, probably through an allocation of posts and portfolios in proportion to the relative strengths in the assembly of the cooperating parties. The private setting of cabinet discussions would be a source of strength to the coalition, as it is already informally in this type of hung authority. No single party group can require its leaders to make or change a particular decision, because there is no guarantee that such a decision will generate the necessary support in the cabinet (or at present the council). There is a good deal of scope here for interpretation by the leadership to party groups as to what is or is not possible. This would strengthen the ability of the cabinet to exercise its executive responsibilities, although the cabinet is always vulnerable to dissolution if one of the cooperating parties becomes too disaffected.

In a hung authority, where the sharing of cabinet posts is not premised on any programmatic cooperation between any two parties, the task of leadership becomes an extremely difficult one (as it is in this type of hung authority at present). Support would have to be generated first within the cabinet itself for a particular measure (eg the budget; a service plan) and then within the assembly. The extent to which this latter task would fall to the cabinet leader, or could be devolved to trusted colleagues, would depend on the inter- and intra-group dynamics. Certainly the leader is in a weaker position in this situation than a directly elected mayor would be.

The scope for choice *within* all the three models is well illustrated in a publication on the practical implications of the new forms of political executive (LGA/LGMB Democracy Network, 1998). Unless the government becomes more prescriptive in its approach, especially in relation to the division of responsibilities between executive and assembly, there is much a local authority can do to limit or enhance the power of the executive, whichever of the three models is chosen. The report demonstrates that the cabinet (or executive) would be strengthened if, for example, policy is tightly defined and the definition of operational and executive action left open; if policy requiring council approval is restricted; where all powers are given to the cabinet except those specifically retained by the council; where cabinet members have extensive virement powers; and where the cabinet has veto powers over council decisions that cannot be overruled. On the other hand, the cabinet's role would be significantly weakened if the reverse of all the conditions prevailed: that is, if policy is defined to encompass a wide range of procedural and operational matters; where all policy has to be approved by the council; where the powers of the cabinet are specified and all other powers reserved for the council; where cabinet virement powers are tightly restricted; and where there are no cabinet veto powers.

So far we have discussed the extent to which political leadership may (or may not) become detached from traditions of group cohesiveness in each of the three models of political leadership on offer. But there is a further important question of how opposition parties would see their role in the new arrangements. If it became clear that the sense of group discipline continued to underpin the activities of the majority party, there is little doubt that there would be an 'equivalent reaction' from opposition parties. They would see it as their job to challenge, embarrass and in due course depose the party in power. To these ends, it is very likely they would continue to behave, as they do now, in a highly disciplined and organised fashion. The council meetings and the meetings of scrutiny committees would be used 'politically', that is, to present, as far as possible, an unfavourable picture of the ruling elite. In these circumstances, leadership of an opposition group would continue to highlight 'group cohesiveness' and 'effective opposition' as the key leadership roles. But what if the party (or coalition) that constituted the executive did decide to behave in the spirit of the 1998 White Paper, and to relax group discipline so that assembly members of the same party were free to pursue their representative roles (which may often imply criticism of the executive's actions) and scrutiny roles (which would certainly involve criticism, in the absence of a group whip). Would the opposition parties follow suit, that is, relax group discipline, and permit an individualistic approach to representation and scrutiny, as the White Paper appears to require? That response seems to be doubtful. The political incentive of effective opposition (and ultimate political success) would be likely to be a stronger incentive than that of facilitating the more detached scrutiny and representative roles of individuals, at least in the first stage of implementation. There would then be a danger of the majority party, which had chosen to relax group discipline, then having to reconsider its position, in the light of the 'united front' of opposition it was receiving from other groups, and probably choosing to re-impose group discipline. We return to this dilemma in the conclusion to this chapter.

General trends and party differences

The leadership role will differ, depending upon which of the three options is selected. But it will also differ in relation to the political culture of the authority. Thus, the cabinet-plus-leader model in particular is open to a wide variety of interpretations, and the way it operates will reflect a process of intra-group (and sometimes inter-group) negotiation. But there will also be common features, whatever the model chosen or the political context. In this section we first discuss the common features and then highlight the major differences.

First, there is no doubt that all the different options require and imply a strengthening of the leader's external relations role. This role, as we saw in Chapter Three, has increased considerably in significance since the fragmentation of local governance, developed under successive Conservative governments, in the 1980s. Many existing leaders already spend a good deal of their time meeting with representatives of other agencies – local and national – to tackle issues of common concern (or to attempt to bring resources into the area), as the experience of Sir Peter Soulsby illustrated (see Chapter Seven). In many cases, local authority leaders are well equipped for this, or are able to develop the requisite skills. But in other cases there is a mismatch. Leaders who have been elected for reasons other than external networking capacity – most typically an ability to manage a set of disparate factions within the party group – may struggle with a role that requires different skills. Similarly, long established leaders who regret the passing of the 'self-sufficient authority' (ie direct provision of all services that the authority is required to provide) may allow their resentment at losing powers to other bodies to show in meetings with such agencies.

The importance of the external relations role is emphasised at various points in the 1998 White Paper: "Successful councils' priorities are to lead their local communities. They organise and support partnerships to develop a vision for their locality, and to contribute to achieving it" (DETR, 1998b, para 1.1). 'Partnership', 'community leadership' and 'stakeholders' are terms that appear at regular intervals. Two of the roles proposed for the executive are to "represent the authority and its community's interests to the outside world" and to "build coalitions and work in partnership with all sectors of the community, and bodies from outside the community" (para 3.39). The outward looking role of local authorities, supported by the idea of the community plan and the proposed new duty to "promote economic, social and environmental well-being" (para 8.8), is a key feature of the 1998 White Paper; a separation out of the executive is intended to strengthen it. Candidates for elected mayor positions are likely to recognise this emphasis and to set out their stalls accordingly. Leaders of cabinets may continue to reflect other intra-party priorities which have little to do with skills in community leadership.

Second, the importance of strategic direction and the setting of a policy framework for the authority receives an equally strong boost in the White Paper. We argued in Chapter Four that, although strategic choices have always faced local authorities, the extent to which such choices have been anticipated, interrelated and justified in a written strategy has varied from authority to authority. Some authorities have paid little attention to the idea of corporate strategy, preferring to muddle through on an ad hoc basis. Thus, although in principle the leadership task of strategic direction exists, little may be made of it in explicit terms. During the 1990s, there was a surge of interest in corporate strategy, with increasing numbers of authorities producing visions or mission statements or strategic plans for their area, of considerable variability in quality (Leach and Collinge, 1998). The White Paper emphasises the importance the government attaches to such corporate strategies or visions. All authorities will be required to produce community plans and to develop a concern for the social, economic and environmental well-being of their areas. The task of initiating the community plan and whatever other corporate strategy documents are felt to be desirable falls predominantly to the executive (although there is some scope for the involvement of assembly members). This leadership role is also enhanced by the *Modernising local government* consultative paper, although there is scope within the two cabinet models as to whether this role is exercised individually (by elected mayor or cabinet leader) or more collectively. In the council manager–elected mayor model the leadership role may come to be dominated by the council manager. In cabinet models where the power of the party group is retained to its maximum extent, the domination of the executive may become diluted.

In principle, the fourth leadership task of 'making things happen' (or delivering the majority party or coalition vision) is also immeasurably strengthened by the provisions of the 1998 White Paper. The clear-cut allocation of executive powers to an individual politician (the elected mayor) or a collectivity (the cabinet) is one its key elements, based on a profound dissatisfaction with the opaque nature of decision making in conventional committees. If elected mayors or cabinet members are taking executive actions directly, rather than having to steer them through the committee structure, then one would expect this change to greatly facilitate the power to ensure that policies and priorities are implemented effectively. However, as discussed earlier in this chapter, the direct involvement of the group in executive decision making (as currently exercised through committees) is likely to be fiercely contested. Given the scope for informal arrangements to sustain the group's influence, the extent to which this leadership task will be strengthened in reality is an open question.

Finally, all three of the models proposed in the 1998 White Paper in principle reduce the significance of the leadership task of maintaining group–council cohesiveness, or perhaps even transfer it elsewhere. The important challenge for an executive is no longer group cohesiveness per se, because in principle the executive is now a separate entity from both the group and the assembly. This task is replaced by the challenge of ensuring that the executive's proposals are approved by the assembly. Clearly, one way of achieving this is to work informally with the group to persuade them that they should support such proposals. But if majority support can be achieved in other ways, then that is equally acceptable to the executive. The task of maintaining group cohesiveness may be paramount for the chief whip, or even the chair of the council. It is not in itself any longer a primary concern of the elected mayor or a cabinet with leader (beyond a knowledge of their need for group support to gain re-election).

The logic of the executive–assembly split thus implies a broadly uniform pattern of change in leadership roles. External relations, strategic direction and 'making things happen' are all likely to be strengthened, while 'ensuring group cohesiveness' becomes replaced by 'building a constituency of support in the assembly for the decisions that need its approval'. The reality of political culture, however, implies that this logic is likely to be distorted, depending on the nature of political control and the recent political history of the local authority.

The attitude to individual leadership has long varied between the three major parties. There is a long tradition of strong Conservative leaders at local level; Dame Shirley Porter (Westminster), David Wilshire (Wansdyke) and Eric Pickles (Bradford) provide some recent examples. There is a tradition of collective leadership in the Liberal Democrat Party, playing down the role of the leader per se and emphasising the importance of reaching group consensus through discussion. Liberal Democrats are often sceptical of the elected mayor model. Referring to the Mori poll in October 1998, which showed 66% of respondents favouring a directly elected mayor, Flo Clucas, Liberal Democrat deputy leader of Liverpool City Council, observed:

> "If people realised what is being referred to, and have learned of the problems of places like Chicago and Nice, I believe they would be very wary of such untrammelled power. In Liverpool we have all had direct experience of one or two people having overwhelming control of what goes on in the council. The idea of local democracy is to represent all views, not give ultimate power to one individual."

This is, however, not to say that formidable leaders cannot emerge from this culture, for example, Graham (now Lord) Tope in Sutton and Linda Short in Congleton.

The Labour Party is in an intermediate position. There is a formal emphasis on the authority of the group as final arbiter; yet, as we have seen, the emergence of strong leaders within this apparently democratic culture is by no means uncommon, for example, David Bookbinder (Derbyshire), Sir Peter Soulsby (Leicester), Alan Whitehead (Southampton).

To the extent that these traditions survive, the acceptance of a real executive–assembly separation (whether or not it involves an elected mayor) seems most likely in the Conservative Party and least likely in the Liberal Democrats. So long as the Conservative group concerned is not factionally divided, and so long as backbenchers (ie Conservatives in the assembly but not in the cabinet) are consulted on a regular basis about matters that concern them, it is certainly plausible that they would concede executive authority to the leader/mayor/cabinet and not insist on resurrecting group authority in the new circumstances. On the other hand, Liberal Democrat groups are highly likely to try to set up informal machinery that maximises consultation with the party group and tries to avoid executive action that lacks the support of a majority of the group. A series of topic-based deliberative committees would seem the most likely way of achieving these ends. In addition, the allocation of powers between executive and assembly would be likely to be balanced towards the assembly.

The attitude of Labour groups is less easy to predict. On balance, the tradition of group authority is likely to lead to informal ways of retaining group influence, and to a division of powers biased towards the assembly (as with the Liberal Democrats), unless the politics of the authority are such that there are perceived benefits in limiting the power of the assembly (eg a particularly effective opposition). On the other hand, it is a Labour government that is insisting so strongly on the benefits of a genuine executive–assembly split, and which is most likely (of the three parties) to change the standing orders of governing party groups in order to facilitate the operation of this split (eg changes in the circumstances in which executive members are bound by the whip). There have already been examples of Labour-controlled authorities eager to assume the mantle of leaders in good practice (as defined by the Labour government).

Thus, although the dominant response is likely to be to play down or dilute the executive–assembly split, there seems certain to be a number of exceptions which may well spread if there develops a sense of momentum towards a new orthodoxy. Table 10.2 sets out a summary of the most likely responses by the different political parties to the choices presented by the 1998 White Paper.

Table 10.2: Dominant party attitudes to the 1998 White Paper options

	Labour	Conservative	Liberal Democrat
Directly elected mayor plus cabinet	Limited degree of support confined to 'New Labour' leaders/ authorities who wish to be seen as 'pacesetters' in modernisation agenda	Attractions for 'dry' Conservative administrations who see parallels with private sector practices and/or groups who support need for 'strong' leadership	Little appeal, because of incompatibility with participatory group ethos
Cabinet plus leader	By far the most popular option for traditional Labour leaders/authorities because of opportunity to retain links between executive and party group	Likely to be the most popular option, because of concerns of group members about over-concentration of power if elected mayor	The 'least worst' of the 3 options, which Liberal Democrats would try to remodel to retain maximum degree of group authority
Directly elected mayor plus council manager	Unlikely to be supported in any circumstances by Labour groups	May have some support in rural areas where existing leader has been dominant figure	Unlikely to generate much, if any, support

Conclusion

As we have seen, the draft Local Government (Organisation and Standards) Bill was published in March 1999. Legislation was promised 'as soon as time allows'. Given that the Bill did not go through Parliament in the 1998/99 session, some local politicians thereby concluded that elected "mayors were on the sick list of local government reform" (see *Local Government Chronicle*, 20 November 1998). This was fiercely denied by Hilary Armstrong, Minister for Local Government, who argued that the draft Bill was "the right way to bring in the legislation needed to complete one of the most radical reforms of local government in this country":

> It is the right way to proceed because this government recognises the enormity of the task facing local government. We want to ensure change is deeply embedded in the political culture of local government, and

that is why we want to lead a national debate about the future shape of councils' political management. That's not the action of a government relegating mayors to a supposed sick list, but the action of a government making sure they are secured at the centre of the debate about the future of local government. (Armstrong, 1998, p 13)

There remains a crucially important choice facing local authorities in the way they interpret the Labour government's 'democratic renewal' agenda, a choice that will have direct repercussions on the nature of local political leadership. Colin Copus (1999) has identified two possible scenarios:

- *Worst case scenario* In a council with a political culture of secrecy and intense group loyalty, the adoption of an elected mayor or, more likely, a leader and a cabinet could see the council operate as though nothing had happened. The power of the party group would be retained through discipline and expectations of loyalty, but secrecy would be increased through executive decision making. Only symbolic public scrutiny would occur by majority party backbenchers, who had previously decided upon issues in private group meetings. Moreover, existing one-party states would remain intact, with the problems of democratic accountability in such circumstances intensified. Executive councillors would attempt to use group discipline procedures to ensure that backbenchers supported the executive in public. Non-executive members in the majority group would be able to bind the executive to support, in public, group decisions. Both these processes reflect current practice. Councils with powerful new political executives would in these circumstances be further distanced from the community they represent, and the health of local democracy further damaged – perhaps terminally.

- *Best case scenario* Councils and parties would embrace a new political culture and a new approach to conducting council affairs. Backbenchers would be freed by the group to play a genuine scrutiny and representative role, even in one-party states. Public and open deliberation of local issues would return to the council chamber, which would also regain its importance as a real decision-making body. Council chambers would become the place where local democracy is exercised by councillors unfettered by current patterns of group discipline. Party groups would still meet to decide local policy responses to the major issues impacting upon the council and the area that it governs. Councillors would support such outcomes not as a result of disciplinary procedures, but because they reflect choices based on a shared political outlook among party colleagues. Local democracy would become more fluid, and the outcome of council meetings more difficult to predict. Ultimately the health of local democracy would be enhanced and the community would come to view the council as a genuine representative body, reflecting its concerns and priorities, and not the dictates of the group meeting.

Depending on which scenario develops, so the roles and tasks of leadership will vary. In the worst case scenario, there is little overall change in the role-set of leaders. Group cohesiveness remains a crucial element, coexisting with the more intensive role demands of external relations, strategic direction and policy implementation which the community leadership approach implies. The fact that the executive or cabinet is likely to comprise full-time councillors will at least strengthen the collective leadership capacity to fulfil these role demands. A degree of division of labour is highly likely.

In the second, more optimistic, scenario, group cohesiveness becomes a less significant element in the leadership role-set, and changes in emphasis from control (through group discipline) to persuasion. Group cohesiveness, though still crucial at election time, becomes a less important condition for getting policies through the assembly, assuming that other (minority) party groups are prepared to adopt the same relaxed approach to group discipline. The leadership is then freed up to concentrate its energies on the remaining three leadership roles, and to do so in a way that is much less constrained by the current necessity to achieve group backing for a wide range of decisions. In this scenario, the very nature of local politics would change, becoming less adversarial and ideological. The current widely accepted but implicit 'reality' that 90% of the decisions an authority makes are not a source of inter-party difference of view would become explicit. The balance between party policy and local discretion would change in favour of the latter.

While existing council leaders cannot determine the direction of change, they can provide a strong influence upon it. In situations of uncertainty, party groups of all persuasions tend to look to the leadership for advice and guidance. If enough council leaders embrace the vision that underpins the 'best case' scenario, and are prepared to use their positions to persuade group members to modify the habits of a political lifetime, we may yet see the transformation of local politics in Britain and the democratic renewal that the 1998 White Paper sought to achieve.

Bibliography

Abdela, L. (1989) *Women with X appeal: Women politicians in Britain today*, London: Optima.

Armstrong, H. (1998) 'Reform: from sick list to rude health', *Local Government Chronicle*, 27 November, p 13.

Audit Commission (1989) *More equal than others: The chief executive in local government*, London: HMSO.

Bachrach, P. and Baratz, M.S (1962) 'Two faces of power', *American Political Science Review*, vol 56, no 4, pp 942-52.

Barber, J. (1977) *The presidential character: Predicting performance in the White House*, New Jersey, NJ: Englewood Cliffs.

Barron, J., Crawley, G. and Wood, T. (1991) *Councillors in crisis*, Basingstoke: Macmillan.

Beecham, Sir J. (1996) 'Leadership in local government', *Public Policy and Administration*, vol 11, no 3, pp 43-6.

Blair, Rt Hon T. (1998) *Leading the way*, London: Institute of Policy Practice and Research.

Burns, J. (1978) *Leadership*, New York, NY: Harper and Row.

Carvel, J. (1984) *Citizen Ken*, London: Hogarth.

CLD (Commission for Local Democracy) (1995) *Taking charge: The rebirth of local democracy*, London: Municipal Journal Books.

Copus, C. (1999) 'The party group: a barrier to democratic renewal', *Local Government Studies*, vol 25, no 3, pp 76-97.

Davies, J. (1972) *The Evangelistic bureaucrat*, London: Tavistock.

Dear, E. (1996) 'Leadership and local democracy', *Local Government Policy Making*, vol 23, no 1, pp 3-5.

Dennis, N. (1972) *Public participation and planners' blight*, London: Faber.

DETR (Department of the Environment, Transport and the Regions (1998a) *Modernising local government: Local democracy and community leadership*, London: DETR.

DETR (1998b) *Modern local government: In touch with the people*, London: The Stationery Office.

DETR (1999) *Local leadership, local choice*, Cm 4298, London: The Stationery Office.

DoE (Department of the Environment) (1991) *The internal management of local authorities in England*, London: HMSO.

DoE (1993) *Community leadership and representation: Unlocking the potential*, Report of the Working Party on the Internal Management of Local Authorities in England, London: HMSO.

Doyle, P. (1996) 'Mayors or nightmares?', *Public Policy and Administration*, vol 11, no 3, pp 47-50.

Dunleavy, P., Dowding, K. and Margetts, H. (1995) 'Regime politics in London local government', Paper presented to ESRC Local Governance Programme Conference, Exeter, September.

Elcock, H. (1996) 'Leadership in local government: the search for a core executive and its consequences', *Public Policy and Administration*, vol 11, no 3, pp 29-42.

Elcock, H. (1998) 'Council leaders in the "New Britain": looking back and looking forward', *Public Money and Management*, vol 18, no 3, pp 15-21.

Filkin, G. (1990) 'Putting political objectives into practice', *Local Government Policy Making*, vol 17, no 1, pp 43-7.

Forrester, K., Lansley, S. and Pauley, R. (1985) *Beyond our Ken*, London: Fourth Estate.

Game, C. (1979) 'Review essay: on local political leadership', *Policy & Politics*, vol 7, no 4, pp 395-408.

Game, C. and Leach, S. (1995) *The role of political parties in local democracy*, CLD Research Report No 11, London: CLD.

Green, D. (1981) *Power and party in an English city*, London: Allen and Unwin.

Gyford, J., Leach, S. and Game, C. (1989) *The changing politics of local government*, London: Unwin Hyman.

Hall, D. (1996) 'The national Labour Party and local government: Walsall and its implications', *Local Government Studies*, vol 22, no 4, pp 146-52.

Hall, D. and Leach, S. (2000) 'The changing nature of local Labour politics', in G. Stoker (ed) *The new politics of British local governance*, London: Macmillan, pp 150-65.

Hambleton, R. (1996) *Leadership in local government*, Occasional Paper No 1, Bristol: Faculty of the Built Environment, University of the West of England.

Hambleton, R. (1998) 'Strengthening political leadership in UK local government', *Public Money and Management*, vol 18, no 1, January–March, pp 41-51.

Harding, A. (2000) 'Regime formation in Manchester and Edinburgh', in G. Stoker (ed) *The new politics of British local governance*, Basingstoke: Macmillan, pp 54-71.

Hatton, D. (1988) *Inside Left: The story so far*, London: Bloomsbury Press.

Hodge, M. Leach, S. and Stoker, G. (1997) *More than the flower show: Elected mayors and democracy*, Discussion Paper No 32, London: Fabian Society.

Holliday, I. (1991) 'The conditions of local change: Kent County Council since reorganisation', *Public Administration*, vol 69, no 4, pp 441-57.

John, P. (1997) 'Political leadership in the new urban governance: Britain and France compared', Paper presented to the International Seminar on 'Governing Cities', Brussels, September.

Jones, G.W. and Norton, A. (eds) (1978) *Political leadership in local authorities*, Birmingham: INLOGOV.

Jones, G.W. and Stewart, J. (1995) 'Directly elected nightmayor', *Local Government Chronicle*, 7 July, pp 8-9.

Judge, D., Stoker, G. and Wolman, H. (eds) (1995) *Theories of urban politics*, London: Sage Publications.

Kotter, J.P. and Lawrence, P.R. (1974) *Mayors in action: Five approaches to urban governance*, New York, NY: John Wiley.

Leach, S. and Collinge, C. (1998) *Strategic planning and management in local government*, London: Pitman.

Leach, S. and Pratchett, L. (1996) *The management of balanced authorities*, Luton: LGMB.

Leach, S. and Stewart, J. (1990) *Political leadership in local government*, Luton: LGMB.

Leach, S. and Stewart, J. (1992) *The politics of hung authorities*, London: Macmillan.

Leach, S., Stewart, J. and Walsh, K. (1994) *The changing organisation and management of local government*, Basingstoke: Macmillan.

Leach, S., Davis, M. Game, C. and Skelcher, C. (1992) *After abolition*, Birmingham: INLOGOV.

Leach, S., Pratchett, L., Stoker, G. and Wingfield, M. (1999) *Political management arrangements in local government: The position at the beginning of 1999*, London: LGMB.

LGA (Local Government Association)/LGMB (Local Government Management Board) Democracy Network (1998) *New forms of political executive in local government*, London: LGA/LGMB.

LGMB (1994) *Fitness for purpose*, Luton: LGMB.

LGMB (1998) *First national census of councillors*, London: LGMB.

Livingstone, K. (1987) *If voting changed anything, they'd abolish it*, London: Collins.

Lowndes, V., Pratchett, L., Stoker, G., Leach, S., Wilson, D. and Wingfield, M. (1998) *Enhancing public participation in local government: A research report* London: DETR.

Madgwick, P. (1978) 'Councillor H.H. Roberts, Cardiganshire and Dyfed: a modern leader in rural Wales', in G.W. Jones and A. Norton (eds) *Political leadership in local authorities*, Birmingham: INLOGOV, pp 51-69.

Marinetto, M. (1997) 'The political dynamics of Camden: 1964-94', *Local Government Studies*, vol 23, no 2, Summer, pp 26-41.

Norton, A. (1991) *The role of the chief executive in British local government*, Birmingham: INLOGOV.

Page, E.C. (1998) 'Future governance: lessons from comparative public policy', Draft proposal to ESRC, University of Hull

Painter, C. (1996) 'Local authorities and non-elected agencies: the dilemmas of multi-dimensional relationships', *Local Government Policy Making*, vol 23, no 2, pp 18-25.

Painter, C. and Isaac-Henry, K. (1999) 'Managing local public services', in S. Horton and D. Farnham (eds) *Public management in Britain*, Basingstoke: Macmillan, pp 162-79.

Parkinson, M. (1985) *Liverpool on the brink*, Bristol: Policy Journals.

Pratchett, L. and Wilson, D. (eds) (1996) *Local democracy and local government*, London: Macmillan.

Prescott, J. (1997) 'Foreword', in *New leadership for London*, Green Paper, London: HMSO.

Pressman, J. and Wildavsky, A. (1977) *Implementation*, Berkeley, CA: University of California Press.

Saunders, P. (1980) *Urban politics: A sociological perspective*, Harmondsworth: Penguin.

Seabrook, J. (1984) *The idea of neighbourhood*, London: Pluto.

Selznick, P. (1957) *Leadership in administration*, New York, NY: Harper and Row.

Stewart, J. (1983) *Local government: The conditions of local choice*, London: Allen and Unwin.

Stewart, J. (1988) *Understanding the management of local government*, Harlow: Longman.

Stoker, G. (1991) *The politics of local government*, London: Macmillan.

Stoker, G. (1996) *The reform of the institutions of local representative democracy: Is there a role for the mayor–council model?*, London: CLD.

Stoker, G. (1998) 'Local political leadership: preparing for the 21st century', Mimeo, Strathclyde: Strathclyde University.

Stoker, G. and Travers, T. (1998) *The government of New York City: Lessons for London?*, London: Association of London Government.

Stoker, G. and Wolman, H. (1992) 'Drawing lessons from US experience: an elected mayor for British local government', *Public Administration*, vol 72, no 2, pp 241-67.

Stone, C. (1995) 'Political leadership in urban politics', in D. Judge, G. Stoker and H. Wolman (eds) *Theories of urban politics*, London: Sage Publications, pp 96-116.

Valley, P. (1998) 'Taking on the die-hard flat caps', *Independent*, 7 March, p 24.

Wainwright, H. (1987) *Labour: A tale of two parties*, London: Hogarth Press.

Weale, A. (1999) *Democracy*, London: Macmillan.

Weber, M. (1978 edn) *Economy and society*, Berkeley, CA: University of California Press.

Willis, J. (1990) 'David Bookbinder: behind the mythology', *Local Government Chronicle*, 12 January, pp 24-5.

Wilson, D. (1996) 'The Local Government Commission: examining the consultative process', *Public Administration*, vol 74, no 2, pp 199-219.

Wilson, D. (1998) 'From local government to local governance: re-casting British local democracy', *Democratization*, vol 5, no 1, pp 90-115.

Wilson, D. (1999) 'Exploring the limits of public participation in local government', *Parliamentary Affairs*, vol 52, no 2, pp 246-59.

Wilson, D. and Game, C. (1998) *Local government in the United Kingdom*, Basingstoke: Macmillan.

Index